From Moses to Muhammad

© 2011 by Jean-Pierre Isbouts
This book was previously published in non-illustrated versions as follows:

Apó ton Mousé ston Moámet
Athens: Skeanida Press, 2007
ISBN 978-960-410-464-2

Od Mojzesza Do Mahometa
Warsaw: Bertelsmann Media sp./Swiat Ksiazki, 2009
ISBN 978-83-247-0077-6

From Moses to Muhammad:
The Extraordinary Shared History of Judaism, Christianity and Islam
(First Edition, 2010):
ISBN 978-1-4500-1750-3

FROM MOSES TO MUHAMMAD
The Shared History of Judaism, Christianity and Islam
Second (Illustrated) Edition (2011):
ISBN 10: 1460919041 • ISBN 13: 9781460919040

Published in the United States by Pantheon Press, an imprint of
Pantheon Studios, Inc. Santa Monica, CA 90403
www.pantheonTV.com

Library of Congress Cataloging-in-Publication Data

Isbouts, Jean-Pierre
From Moses to Muhammad: The Shared Origins of Judaism,
Christianity and Islam/Jean-Pierre Isbouts
1. Comparative Religion/Biblical history – non-fiction.

For more information about other works by the author,
please visit www.jpisbouts.org

FROM MOSES TO MUHAMMAD:
The Shared Origins
of Judaism, Christianity and Islam

Illustrated Edition

Pantheon Press
Santa Monica, CA

For Cathie

Unless otherwise noted, all illustrations in this book are by the author.

TABLE OF CONTENTS

Preface   Page 7

Introduction   Page 10

Chapter 1: The Story of Creation   Page 31

Chapter 2: Adam and Eve in Paradise   Page 38

Chapter 3: Cain and Abel   Page 50

Chapter 4: A Chieftain named Abraham   Page 56

Chapter 5: Ishmael and Isaac   Page 82

Chapter 6: Joseph in Egypt   Page 96

Chapter 7: Musa in the Desert   Page 112

Chapter 8: Moses and the Exodus   Page 124

Chapter 9: Rise & Fall of Ancient Israel   Page 138

Chapter 10: From Alexander to Herod   Page 168

Chapter 11: A Child in Nazareth   Page 189

Chapter 12: A Rabbi named Jesus   Page 210

Chapter 13: Passover Events of 30 CE   Page 220

Chapter 14: The Rise of Christianity   Page 233

Chapter 15: A Prophet in Mecca   Page 273

Chapter 16: A Unified Arabia   Page 302

Chapter 17: Rise of the Islamic Empire   Page 312

Chapter 18: Golden Age of Three Faiths   Page 333

Epilogue   Page 344

Select Bibliography   Page 348

Notes   Page 356

Other Books by the Author   Page 364

Preface

Mount Rum in Wadi Rum, southern Jordan, a region of many cultures since prehistoric times

This is a book for all those who approach the history of the three great faiths with an open heart and mind. It is written for those who, given the astonishing rise of fundamentalism in all three faith communities (and particularly Islam), would like to know more about the history of these traditions, and particularly the wellspring of their origins. In doing so, I hope to demonstrate that these three cultures have far more in common than today's news headlines would have us believe.

As an archaeologist and historian, I am not so much interested in theological issues as in the cultural fabric, the geographical setting and the literary context in which these faiths originated. What fascinates me is the moment when the narratives from either the Bible or the Qur'an overlap with archaeological and anthropological findings; when we have an actual intersection between scriptural narrative and forensic evidence. This is what will drive much of our story: how the foundational narratives of the three great faith traditions have their roots in the experiences of men and women who lived in the Middle East some 2,000 to 4,000 years ago.

For example, we will find that the earliest stories in Genesis bear the imprint of Mesopotamian culture (and particularly Babylonia), which was followed by a clear shift to Egyptian influences as the cult of *El*, the God of Genesis, moves to the Lower Kingdom on the Nile. Similarly, the Deuteronomistic history (the biblical narrative from Joshua through the fall of Jerusalem to Neo-Babylonia) bears all the hallmarks of the language, religious culture and artistic motifs of Syria-Canaan, just as the world of the gospels is clearly determined by Greco-Roman civilization. The same is true for early Islam, which found expression in the primary concerns and aspirations of 7th century Arab culture, even as Muhammad and his successors labored to excise pagan idolatry and literature.

A few notes on the use of terminology. Since this book is explicitly non-denominational in nature, written for a broad audience, I will use the new dating form of *B.C.E.* ('Before the Common Era') instead of the traditional *BC* ('Before Christ'), and likewise use *C.E.* (Common Era) rather than *AD* (*Anno Domini* or 'Year of the Lord') to identify dates.

As we enter the phase of the New Testament, I will likewise distinguish between the figures of Jesus and 'the Christ', a name that is based on the Greek translation of Messiah or 'Anointed One' (*Christos*). We will use the name 'Jesus' as we try to reconstruct the footsteps of the historical figure, who lived in Palestine between approximately 4 B.C.E. and 30 C.E. With 'Christ', we will refer to the religious figure as venerated in the emerging Christian theology from the early 50's onwards.

Throughout this book, I will follow the example of modern Muslim and non-Muslim authors by translating the Islamic name of biblical figures in the Qur'an to one that is familiar to a Western audience. Hence, *Allah* is translated as 'God'; *Ibrahim* is

Abraham, *Musa* is Moses and *Isa* is Jesus. The sole purpose of this translation is to enhance the accessibility of the Islamic text for the English-speaking reader, who may not be familiar with Muslim scripture. For the same reason, the city of Makkah will be identified as 'Mecca', and Madinah as 'Medina'. On the other hand, I will refer to the Koran as "Qur'an," as is common in modern literature.

I would like to thank all those who freely gave their time for consultation, interviews and conversations, and thus greatly contributed to this book. They include Prof. Peter Awn, Dean of General Studies at Columbia University; Dr. Francis E. Peters, Professor of Middle Eastern Studies at New York University; Prof. Elaine Pagels of Princeton University, the author of the bestseller *Beyond Belief: The Secret Gospel of Thomas*; Prof. Khaled Abou El Fadl, Professor of Islamic Law at UCLA; Prof. Jean-Pierre M. Ruiz of St. John's University; Prof. Bruce Chilton of Bard College, author of the bestselling *Rabbi Jesus*; Dr. Thomas K. Tewell of the Fifth Avenue Presbyterian Church in New York; Dr. Jacob Neusner, Professor Emeritus at Bard College and author of countless authoritative works on Judaica; Dr. Afaf Marsot, Professor Emeritus of Middle Eastern Studies at UCLA; Rabbi Peter J. Rubenstein of the Central Synagogue of New York; Sheikh Abdul Aziz Bukhari in East Jerusalem; and Rabbi Reuven Firestone, who is Professor of Judaism and Islam at USC. It goes without saying that any errors in the narrative are mine, and mine alone.

Finally, words cannot begin to express my gratitude to my wife Cathie, who has been my faithful companion and indefatigable muse during our many journeys through the Middle East.

Jean-Pierre Isbouts
Santa Monica, CA

Introduction
The Journey of Three Faiths

Arab and Jewish children in Issawiya, a Palestinian neighborhood in Jerusalem.

This book will attempt to show how Judaism, Christianity and Islam not only originated from a common source – the earliest strands of monotheism in Syria-Canaan as exemplified by the story of Abraham – but that in the process, each of these movements were profoundly influenced by the literary and cultural conditions in which they originated. Given this assumption, I will also argue is that these traditions largely agree on the essential precepts of their scriptural narrative, and that the differences between them are largely determined by the unique socio-cultural context in which each of these movements came about.

To make this argument, I will not only rely on archaeological and literary evidence, but also try to tell this extraordinary story -- indeed, in many ways an *untold* story -- through the prism of *both* the Bible *and* the Qur'an (or Koran). To many readers, this will come as a surprise. These readers may be shocked to learn that many stories in the Bible and the New Testament, including those about Adam, Joseph, Moses and Jesus, also appear with great frequency in the Qur'an, though often in a different context. For example, the Creation accounts in Genesis and the Qur'an are quite similar, though with different emphases, which reflect the unique cultural and historical milieu in which each narrative originated. As such, this book is arguably the first to compare the stories of the Bible and the Qur'an side by side, and in the context of the evolution of their faith traditions.

View from Mount Sinai, where according to tradition, the Pentateuch (the first five books of the Hebrew Scriptures) was revealed to Moses

What are these scriptures? Throughout this book, I will distinguish between three sources: the Hebrew Scriptures (which Christian call 'The Old Testament'); the Christian New Testament; and the Qur'an of Islam.

THE HEBREW SCRIPTURES are composed as follows:

- The *Law* or *Five Books of Moses* (the Torah proper) that consist of Genesis, Exodus, Leviticus, Numbers and Deuteronomy; these Five Books are often referred to by their Greek name *Pentateuch,* meaning 'five scrolls.'
- The Books of the Prophets (*Nevi'im*), including the *former* prophets (Joshua, Judges, I and II Samuel, I and II Kings) and the *latter* prophets (including, among others, Isaiah, Jeremiah, Ezekiel and the Twelve Minor Prophets); and
- The Writings (*Ketuvim*) which include the Psalms, Proverbs, the Book of Job, the Song of Songs, Ruth and others.

Of all these, the Book of Genesis is of paramount importance. Genesis establishes the notion that God is a force of moral good, that he is passionately devoted to the well-being of mankind, and that to vouchsafe such, he will reveal his will to messengers and prophets. All three attributes, as we will see, are a radical departure from the predominant pagan beliefs and practices in Mesopotamia and Egypt.

THE NEW TESTAMENT (NT) is the principal book of scripture for Christians, encompassing some 27 volumes. The core of the NT is formed by the four Gospels of Matthew, Mark, Luke and John that describe the life and deeds of Jesus. The other key elements are the *Book of Acts of the Apostles,* which covers the early development of the Christian Church; the *Letters* or 'Epistles' attributed to St. Paul that offer a broad range of guidelines in the interpretation of faith in Jesus Christ; additional apostolic letters; and the apocalyptic *Book of Revelations.*

THE QUR'AN is the scripture of Islam. The Qur'an is a written record of divine revelations that the prophet Muhammad received over a period of some twenty-two years in the city of Makkah (Mecca) and then in Yathrib, later called Madinah (or Medina). There are 114 chapters in all, each conveying one particular revelation. Chapters are called *suras* and are arranged by length: the longest chapters can be found at the beginning, whereas the shortest suras are contained near the end. This is not a chronological arrangement, for the shorter chapters are actually among the earliest revelations. In fact, the very first revelation is contained in verses 2-6 from sura 96, *Al-'Alaq* ('The Clot'). The Qur'an does not constitute a chronological saga, like Genesis, or a biographical narrative in the tradition of the gospels, but rather a collection of individual sermons, spoken by God and revealed to Muhammad. In doing so, the Qur'an often harks back to stories that are very familiar to both Jews and Christians, featuring messengers and prophets (*anbiya* and *rusul*) from Adam and Abraham to Moses and even Jesus.

In referring to these three books, we must understand that scripture is foremost a document of faith, not history. Consequently, we must recognize the need for what the theologian John Dominic Crossan has called *exegetical excavation*: the understanding that copying and redacting has added layers (or *strata*) of commentary or theological interpolation. These layers were often added by pious men, both clerics and scribes, eager to "explain" the original source tradition to the unenlightened reader, as was common in Late Antiquity.

However, such additions can often obscure the intent of the original source. If it is our goal to understand the true meaning of these biblical stories in the context of their time, we must probe through these layers and try to find the original meaning of what history has passed on to us. This, of course, is by no means an exact science. No one could ever claim to know for certain whether his or her interpretation is correct. But then again, that is precisely what makes the effort so appealing.

To better understand the context in which the three scriptures originated, we will also look at literary sources that either predated these books, or originated in the same geographical and cultural milieu. Examples are the Sumerian myths and king-lists; Babylonian narratives and legislative sources; Assyrian reliefs of conquests; tablets from Syria-Canaan, as well as the extensive library of ancient Egyptian records. From the 5th century B.C.E. onwards we will also refer to Greek, Persian and subsequently Roman texts, while pre-Islamic literature will help set the stage for the rise of Islam.

This Assyrian wall panel from the Central Palace in Nimrud shows the army of Tiglath-pileser III laying siege to a city in Syria-Canaan, as described in the biblical Book of Kings

In addition, we will use Jewish, Christian and Muslim texts that evolved in the wake of the three scriptures proper, including texts not included in the Jewish and Christian biblical 'canon', such as the Jewish Mishnah; Gnostic texts; and the wealth of material found in the Islamic *Hadith* ('Sayings of the Prophet') and other *Tafsir* literature. Both form part of an extensive body of Muslim commentary that originated as early as the 7th century C.E.

Equally important source for our story, however, is the growing body of archaeological evidence recovered in Egypt, Mesopotamia and Israel/Palestine. Throughout our narrative, we will come across some amazing finds that seem to confirm the historicity of stories we otherwise might have dismissed as biblical legend. This includes evidence of Semitic tribal movements into Egypt during times of famine; the presence of Ramesside garrison cities akin to those described in *Exodus*; proof of repeated military invasions by Assyrian and Babylonian overlords in Israel; and architectural details of New Testament settings like Herod's expanded Second Temple. Sometimes the archaeological record may fill gaps in the biblical record, as in the case of the role the newly excavated city of Sepphoris may have played during the 'lost years' of Jesus' adolescence.

Mosaic floor from the ancient city of Sepphoris

Equipped with this fascinating body of evidence, this book will begin by describing the genesis of monotheism in the land of Canaan (later known as Palestine). We will recognize the truly revolutionary character of this nascent movement, squeezed between the polytheistic traditions of Mesopotamia and Egypt. Furthermore, our investigation will indicate that the cult of *El*, of one God, may have been sustained by a number of tribes throughout the region. This will become of vital significance after Jacob's tribe re-settled in the Goshen district of Egypt and its cult of *El* was gradually subsumed by Egyptianization. We will find that Moses' pivotal role as the savior of proto-Judaism may have been due to the fact that Moses (or tribal leader(s) like him) were not Egyptian, but quite possibly Kenite in origin. Indeed, the enigmatic role played by the priestly figure of 'Jethro' may indicate that the Kenites (as well as other native tribes) had remained faithful to the 'pure' strand of Abrahamaic monotheism while the Jacobite tribe languished on the Nile.

MOVING INTO THE PHASE of Joshua's 'Conquest', we will discover that the Israelite 'invasion' of the Promised Land was a good deal less violent than the Book of Joshua suggests. Archaeological evidence indicates a gradual infiltration of Canaan by Hebrew tribes and clans, with most of the military activity confined to contested areas of prime agricultural importance, such as Jericho and the Jezreel Valley.

I believe that this time was perhaps the high mark of the early Jewish experience. Quite possibly, these early settlers, bound together by the need to defend their homesteads against native marauders in a strange land, found a sense of *Sabra* solidarity that was lost with the coming of the monarchical period. Always fearing attack from Canaanite or Philistine tribes, struggling to cultivate the land on their ancient *kibbutzim*, these Hebrew clans were sustained by a range of cultic practices. These practices may first have been recorded in the early 10th century B.C.E., and were then absorbed and codified during and after the Babylonian Exile, culminating in the Deuteronomic Laws of the 6th century B.C.E.

Hazor, one of the reputed sites of Joshua's "conquest"

As we enter the monarchical period, we will find that the 'Golden Age' of David and Solomon was perhaps less magnificent and powerful than the scribes of the Davidic tradition want us to believe. For one thing, the reputed wealth of Solomon was based on coercive policies, including the use of forced labor, which did not survive beyond the king's reign. Once Solomon was placed in his tomb, his storied empire fell apart along tribal fault lines. Thus weakened, the warring fiefdoms of the North and South were ready prey for the emerging colossus from Mesopotamia.

THE HEBREW SCRIPTURES TELL US that the end of the monarchy was due to the alarming frequency with which the Hebrews would turn to pagan cults. Archaeological evidence seems to bear this out. Well into the 6th century and beyond, we find evidence of pagan shrines of either Canaanite, Philistine or Syrian origin throughout the territory of ancient Israel. As it happens, Israel's great misfortune (and the source of its former wealth) was that it was placed at the cross roads of the great caravan routes of Antiquity. Foreign merchants, artisans and mercenaries came and went, often seducing the locals with their exotic and sensuous cultic practices. That same geographical position, however, also made ancient Israel inevitably the battleground in the power play between the empires of Egypt and Assyria/Neo-Babylonia. Economically exhausted, vexed by internecine strife, the Jewish kingdoms did not stand a chance against the aggressive militarism from the East.

The Babylonian Captivity gave Judaism the respite it needed to complete the work begun under King Josiah: the comprehensive codification of the Pentateuch, the 'Mosaic Laws' that had emerged among the tribes since their gradual settlement into the Promised Land. In a way, these Laws filled the political vacuum created by the loss of Jewish autonomy, and sustained Jewish religious identity even as successive overlords chipped away at its sense of nationhood.

And then we once again find the Jewish nation in crisis. First deprived of independence, the Jews now see the very vestiges of their faith under assault. The conquest and reign of Alexander the Great may have been short-lived, but the Hellenistic influence that followed in his wake was not, and it is this Hellenism that proved to be deeply subversive of Jewish values, religious practices and way of life. With Greek-educated rulers came Greek fashion, Greek architecture, philosophy, language and art. For example, the Mosaic Laws forbade graven images and emphasized modesty. Greek culture, on the other hand, *reveled* in imagery, and particularly depictions of the nude human body. Worse, Greek cultural imperialism brought once again the curse of polytheism.

Jerash, the biblical Gerasa located in modern Jordan, was one of the ten cities of the 'Decapolis,' a center of Greek or 'Hellenistic' culture

When the Seleucid king Antiochus IV enforced a vigorous program of Hellenization throughout Judaea, the people revolted under leadership of Judas "The Hammer" Maccabeus, and briefly recaptured the illusion of an independent Israel. But his successor, Jonathan, made a fatal mistake. Drunk with victory, he allowed himself to be appointed both king *and* high priest. For the pious Jews, this was infamy of the highest order. Priests could not be appointed at will; according to the Torah, the High Priest was chosen from the direct descendants of Aaron, Eleazar, and Phineas. Jonathan and his successors, however, persisted in usurping the holiest position of Israel. It was as if, in our modern day, the Roman Catholic Pope would henceforth be appointed by the ruling political party of Italy.

A wedge was being forced into Jewish society – a wedge between the Jewish masses and the increasingly autocratic priesthood; between Hellenistic and observant Jews; between peasant and urban communities; between have's and have-nots. The fabric of society began to tear at its seams. This social polarization was further aggravated when Judaea became a Roman province. Organized economic exploitation by the Romans led to land appropriation and a steep drop in the standard of living in agricultural regions such as Galilee.

In this period of fear and uncertainty, Jewish solidarity gave way. The hallowed institutions of its faith began to crumble. For the first time, Jews broke away into sects, pitting Pharisees and Essenes against the Sadducees. In fact, the movement of John the Baptist rejected Temple sacrifice altogether (as did, quite possibly, his disciple Jesus); others, like the Zealots, prepared for armed insurrection.

What these 'dissident' movements had in common was a fervent desire for a complete break: a total *regime change* in favor of a new, theocratic society headed by a Messiah, heir to King David. That this was not going to be a 'velvet revolution' was obvious. A complete and all-consuming apocalypse was needed to wipe away the filth and corruption from the sacred soil of Jerusalem. How this apocalypse would come about was not entirely certain; what was clear, however, was that people had to repent and return to God, lest they be swept up in this vast tsunami of divine vengeance.

In this context, we will see that contrary to Gospel tradition, Jesus was very much a man of his time – a product of contemporary Judaism in his own right. Jesus, in fact, sought to reform Judaism through a return to the quintessential tenets of Deuteronomic Law: obedience to God, compassion for one's fellow man; and respect for social justice in the land. A pupil of John the Baptist, Jesus inherited John's charismatic leadership and baptism metaphor of repentance.

But Jesus rejected the cardinal doctrine of John's *mishnah*: that the divine kingdom could only be brought about by a terrifying, catastrophic deluge. Jesus, who grew up in a small rural village bearing the stigma of a *mamzer* of uncertain paternity, had developed a very intimate concept of YAHWEH as a loving *Abba*. He could not accept the image of a wrathful, Old Testament God who once again would drown mankind in blood. In Jesus' vision, responsibility for building the kingdom began with one's self. Through acts of kindness and devotion, each man and woman would "pass on" the good news of God's love until the Jewish community had healed itself from within.

The northern shore of the Sea of Galilee, the center of Jesus' ministry

As Jesus' following began to grow, people wondered if perhaps *he* was the Messiah. This was not surprising; other prophets, like John the Baptist, had been asked the same question, so desperate were the thousands of Galileans who had been dispossessed and displaced by Herod's rapacious tax regimes. But Jesus gently rebuffed such labels; he knew the political danger of the word *Mashiach*, and possibly had seen with his own eyes how John the Baptist had been dragged away by Herod's henchmen before his movement became too powerful. No matter how hard some scholars have tried to depict Jesus as a political revolutionary, his 'kingdom' manifesto had no geo-political agenda; it was a message for Jews, living within a Jewish society. In the end, it did not matter. Like his mentor John, Jesus was arrested on grounds of sedition, and executed as a political agitator who had challenged the sovereign rule of Rome.

After the crucifixion of Jesus, the Jesus Movement sputtered on like so many other reform movements before him, now bereft of its charismatic ruler, Worse, the ministry of Jesus had been so unbelievably short – anywhere from 12 to 18 months – that his followers had hardly begun to grasp what Jesus' *mishnah* had been all about, let alone commit it to paper. Perhaps as a result, the movement began to break apart into factions, much as Judaism itself had broken into distinct sects during the intertestamental period.

First, there was the core 'Palestinian' movement based in Jerusalem, which clung to the memory of Jesus as a Jewish Reformer, and quite possibly the Messiah. Emboldened by reports of his resurrection, these Jewish proto-Christians continued to worship in the Temple and observe the Laws of the Torah. But they were increasingly ostracized by other, non-Christian Jews because of their allegiance to a man who had been condemned and executed as a political terrorist. The 'Christian Jews' were shunned from synagogues and community life, until the Sanhedrin, the Jewish Privy Council, condoned an all-out persecution against the Jesus cult. James, the brother of Jesus and head of the Jerusalem church, was thrown to his death by an angry mob.

QUITE A DIFFERENT JESUS MOVEMENT, however, had begun to coalesce around a Jewish Pharisee and intellectual named Paul. Raised and educated in sophisticated circles in the city of Tarsus,

Paul saw an opportunity to evangelize the Jesus Movement – that is to say, a *Europeanized* version of this movement – in the Greco-Roman cities of Asia Minor. Paul knew that the official Roman religion, once the anchor of Rome's greatness, had become morally eviscerated by rampant materialism and the ludicrous farce of imperial cults. Inhabitants of the Roman Empire, particularly the vast majority of workers and slaves, yearned for a religion that could bestow hope and meaning to the senseless injustice of everyday life. The cult of Jesus could bring such hope. The vision of a compassionate and merciful Father who offered redemption to all, regardless of social class, had enthralled the masses of Galilee; it could do the same among the disenfranchised millions of the Roman Empire. There was only one problem. This potential market for the Jesus Movement was Gentile, not Jewish. And Jesus himself had always insisted that his message was for Jews and the "lost sheep of the house of Israel" only. During his missionary work, he had avoided the Gentile cities of Galilee as much as possible.

Paul then made a decision that paradoxically sealed the fate of the movement in Palestine proper, yet boosted its appeal in the Roman Empire hundred-fold. Paul unmoored the Jesus movement from its Jewish foundation, and indeed its very Jewish identity. He assured his Gentile followers they would *not* have to practice circumcision, would *not* have to eat kosher food, and *not* follow the *Taharat HaMishpacha*, the laws of family purity – and in fact, dispense with the Mosaic Laws altogether. Jesus' death, said Paul, had superseded the Laws. Far from being a tragic and shameful end to a promising career, Paul argued, Jesus' crucifixion had actually been *planned* all along by God the Father. Jesus was the *über*-paschal lamb, the last sacrifice ever to be made to YAHWEH. The evidence lay in Jesus' resurrection. By bringing Jesus back to life, YAHWEH had accepted his sacrifice and restored him to his heavenly throne as his rightful Son. All Paul's followers had to do was be baptized, and thus be cleansed by the same Holy Spirit that had sustained Jesus through his life, death and resurrection.

NOT ALL PROTO-CHRISTIAN COMMUNITIES accepted the theology of Paul. There were a number of dissident groups who claimed that this was not at all what Jesus had talked about. His *misnah,* they argued, was not about his death, but the teachings of his life. And those teachings envisioned a Kingdom of God as a state of grace within men and among men, as a reflection of the Kingdom of Heaven. To emphasize the physical, corporeal suffering of Jesus, as Paul did, was to miss the whole point of his teaching. The body – even Jesus' body – was nothing but a temporary hull for the power of the *pneuma,* the Divine Spirit. What Christians had to do instead, these dissidents argued, was to focus on the divine Spirit within oneself, and through meditation reach a higher level of consciousness – or *gnosis,* the Greek word for knowledge – that would bring them closer to God.

Modern scholarship has coined the rather unfortunate term of *Gnostics* for these dissident groups, and what we know about them is largely due to the chance discovery of some of their secret texts in 1945, sensationalized in Dan Brown's Book "The Da Vinci Code." But it is probably safe to say that in the 1st and early 2nd centuries C.E., these dissident groups were still a powerful Christian force to be reckoned with – not in the least because they drew their inspiration from apostolic figures such as Peter and Mary Magdalene, who had known Jesus intimately, instead of Paul, who had never met Jesus in the flesh.

In the meantime, a cataclysmic event had taken place. The long-simmering resentment of Roman occupation, which had produced two peasant revolts around the beginning of the 1st century, erupted in an all-out rebellion against Rome in 66 C.E. The revolt was led by a faction of the Zealots, but gradually almost all sectors of Jewish life were subsumed in the uprising. The war lasted four years and ended in the destruction of Jerusalem, including the just-completed Second Temple complex begun by Herod the Great.

The Western Wall in Jerusalem is part of the Herodian wall that once supported the Second Temple platform. Today it is the holiest site in Judaism

The destruction of the Temple was perhaps the most traumatic experience in the history of Judaism. It ended the long tradition of the sacrificial cult as the principal redemptive feature of cultic life, and led to a renewed focus on Scripture and scriptural exegesis – producing the era of 'Rabbinic Judaism.'

CONSEQUENTLY, AS THE FIRST CENTURY entered its final quarter and the Temple of Jerusalem lay in ruins, both Christianity and Judaism were compelled to redefine themselves. The original Jesus Movement had fragmented into a number of different sects throughout the Mediterranean basin, each claiming to be the true followers of Jesus. As the conflict between these factions escalated, each of the principal 'wings' – the 'liberal' wing of the 'Gnostics' versus the 'orthodox' wing of the Pauline tradition – turned to written 'gospels' to propagate their doctrines, using biographical details of Jesus as well as citations from Hebrew Scripture to make their case. The biographical data were extent, because they had continued to circulate in the form of oral traditions (such as the Passion story) as well as 'sayings documents' (such as *The Gospel of Thomas* on the 'liberal' side, and the hypothetical *Quelle* document on the 'orthodox' side).

Mark, arguably the first of the Pauline evangelists, arranged the acts and sayings of Jesus in a chronology that propelled the whole impetus of the story towards the climax of crucifixion. The other canonical Gospels followed his example; Matthew and Luke, in fact, copied as much as sixty percent of Mark's story into their own narrative. The Gnostics, not to be outdone, produced a body of scripture of their own, including such documents as the *Gospel of Thomas, the Gospel of Philip* and even a *Gospel of Mary*.

LOOKING BACK AT THE TURBULENT 1ST century, then, we will find that Christianity was a branch off the tree of the Torah – but a branch that was subsequently grafted onto the trunk of Greco-Roman culture. For Paul's Christians (as well as for the Gnostics), the Torah was no longer the vessel of obedience, but merely the vehicle of proto-Christian revelation and prophecy. The Torah's role as the supreme covenant with God was now supplanted by the covenant theology of Christ's Redemption. In the process, the Jesus movement changed from a Jewish reform movement to a new form of monotheism, a new *religion*: indebted to Judaism, but embracing all of mankind.

In the battle of these Christian doctrines, the Pauline or 'orthodox' movement eventually emerged triumphant (possibly due to their superior organization, based on a strict clerical hierarchy, as Elaine Pagels has argued). But Gnostic dissidents – now branded 'heretics' – continued to vex the Mother Church. The restless Greek mind could not resist debating the paradox of the corporeal and spiritual presence of Jesus. Despite vigorous persecution by the newly Christianized Roman emperors, these dissidents – such as the Nestorites and Arianites -- continued to stake their claims. Many of them sought refuge in Arabia, where the long arm of the Byzantine Empire could not reach them. Here, they settled along the caravan routes that crisscrossed the peninsula, tending to pilgrims and merchants in a life of pious *caritas*. As we move to Part III of this book, it was here, in these desert hostelries, that a prosperous merchant from Mecca may have heard about the tenets of Christianity – and the ongoing schisms that continued to vex the Christian Church.

Muhammad, by this time, was still a pagan; his city was, in fact, an important center of pagan pilgrimage. Right in the heart of Mecca was the *Ka'bah*, a cube-like structure in which local tribes venerated a pantheon of greater and lesser divinities, including a chief god called *Allah*.

This alabaster clan figure from Southwestern Arabia may give us an idea of pre-Islamic idols

But Arabia was tormented by strife – vicious, internecine strife, that pitted tribe against tribe, clan against clan, sometimes family against family. Muhammad, a compassionate and intelligent man, must have despaired of his nation's perennial state of civil war. His travels throughout the peninsula had brought him in contact with Jewish traders as well as emissaries of the Byzantine and Persian empires. Consequently, Muhammad must have known about the political systems that existed outside of Arabia, and perhaps recognized the unifying power of their indigenous religions. Blessed with a life of leisure thanks to the wealth of his wife, Muhammad surrendered himself to long periods of meditation, trying to grapple with his destiny and that of his tormented people.

I believe that Muhammad was impressed with the strength of Jewish faith; of how the Torah – as well as the Talmud -- sustained the far-flung Jewish Diaspora communities and bound them together. Perhaps it was the moral clarity of monotheism that struck him, in much the same way as he may have been moved by the selfless compassion shown by Christian monks in their desert outposts. Reflecting on these two great religions, it was no great leap of faith to imagine what his own Arabian people could accomplish, if only they, too, could be unified under the single banner of a great and omnipotent God.

Lost in meditation on Mount Hira, Muhammad experienced the first of his revelations in 610 C.E. Little more than twenty years later, all or Arabia had become one under Islam.

AND SO, as we come to the end of our journey, we can draw some conclusions. One is that the history of Judaism had a profound impact on both Christianity and Islam. Notwithstanding the Pauline re-orientation of Jesus on the needs of the Gentile world, Jesus's *mishnah* is unthinkable without the urgent issues of his day: Temple worship, observance of the Law, and social justice as defined in the Deuteronomic tradition. If

Jesus took issue with the priorities of the Law, he never abandoned its guiding spirit. At the end of the day, he remained the Son of Man, the angelic herald of the Book of Daniel who looks beyond Israel's coming cataclysm to a better and more humane world.

By the same token, I would argue that proto-Islam in many ways represented a focus on a covenant theology not dissimilar from early Judaism. Early Islam, like ancient Judaism, was focused on one people – the Arab nation – in the fulfillment of its manifest destiny under God. At the same time, Muhammad rejected the clerical hierarchy system of Christianity – possibly because of the inherent conflict with secular authority – in favor of a 'flat' governance model where wisdom and justice was dispensed by enlightened imams, in the same way that Talmudic knowledge and counsel was administered by the rabbinate.

Muhammad also embraced much of the *kosher* legislation that had sustained the health of the Jews in the harsh climate of the Near East. In creating houses of worship, Islam eschewed the sanctified church model of Christianity in favor of an assembly hall, similar to a synagogue, where men and women, separated by sex, could worship together. But one aspect of Christianity Muhammad would adopt without qualification – its emphasis on charitable works and the compassion for one's fellow man. Not surprisingly, Islam thinks of *Isa* or Jesus as God's greatest prophet after Muhammad, on a par with the great prophet *Musa* (Moses). The Qur'an also reserves great reverence for Mary, and adheres –with Roman Catholicism – to belief in the virginal conception of Jesus. In fact, the figure of Jesus would continue to inspire centuries of Muslim literature and *belles lettres.* According to one such tradition, it is Jesus, not Muhammad, who will appear on the Last Day to herald God's judgment.

What emerges from the pages of this book, then, is the story of three faiths who each set out on their journey from one common source: the unquestioned, unqualified faith in one divine Being as first revealed to a tribal chieftain in Syria-

Canaan. As belief systems, each of these faiths would arrive at quite different solutions, molded by their geographical location, tribal culture and historical condition. But at the end of the day, as this book may testify, all followers of these faiths still find their roots in Abraham.

‌   ∞

Chapter One
The Story of Creation

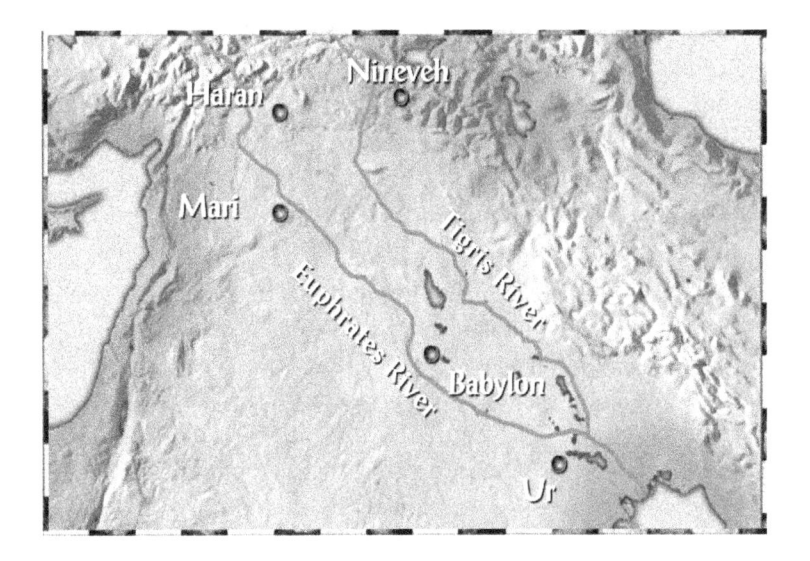

If there is one thing that distinguishes the Near Eastern faith traditions from those of Asia, it could be their preoccupation with origins. The Hebrew and Christian Bible, as well as the Qur'an, the Holy Book of Islam, are deeply concerned with the beginning of time and the creation of the earth. This is perhaps not surprising when we remember that in the region where monotheism first originated -- Mesopotamia -- this preoccupation was as old as civilization itself. Mesopotamia is a Greek word that means "the land between the two rivers." These two rivers were the Euphrates and the Tigris, both majestic bodies of water that originate in Turkey and navigate the thousand miles of dry plateau of ancient Iraq before emptying themselves in the Persian Gulf. This river system, so unique in the parched climate of the Middle East, encouraged hunter-gatherers of the 10th millennium B.C.E. to settle down and devote their energies to domestication – both of animals as well as crops. But as things go in this part of the world, safeguarding a harvest was no mean feat. Unlike in Egypt, where the Nile could be expected to rise every year to spread the fertile richness of its silt far and wide, the land of Mesopotamia had no such blessing. The Euphrates and the Tigris stubbornly refused to adhere to any set schedule of inundation. Years might pass without any flooding whatsoever, leaving the land between bereft of water. And then, without warning, the rivers might suddenly rise, swollen by the runoff from snow and rainfall in the northeastern mountains of Turkey, and deluge the land, destroying everything in its path.

No wonder, then, that these prehistoric farmers desperately sought to anticipate Nature's wiles by placating her and forestalling her wrath – through sacrifice. As a result, the earliest deities worshipped in Mesopotamia – first in the earliest city-state of Eridu, and later in the splendid civilization of Sumeria – were creatures believed to be responsible for the myriad functions of agriculture. Inanna, the Earth Mother, was the goddess of fertility and its corollary, sexual love. Baal was revered as the Lord of Rain and Dew. Enki was the god of fresh water; An, the ruler of the heavens. Inanna, the Babylonian Ishtar, was also Baal's consort; if they quarreled and eschewed the marital bed, or so it was believed, rains would stop and the land would lay dry. So persistent was this belief that well into the period of Israel's Dual Monarchy, observant Hebrew farmers would continue mate with prostitutes in local shrines of Ishtar on the sly, just to be sure that no harm would come to their fields.

In time, the roles of these local deities coalesced into what we could perhaps call a "national religion" that spawned shrines, temples and a dedicated priesthood throughout the Sumerian realm. With such organized worship came a scriptural narrative, including a Creation epic, that is perhaps one of the oldest extant descriptions of the origins of man. This Creation epic has come to us in the form of Akkadian tablets dating from the 1st

millennium B.C.E. However, since the story contains many characters from the familiar cast of Sumerian gods – including Enki, Enlil and Ea – it is likely that the epic is much older, dating either to the Old Babylonian period (2nd millennium B.C.E.) or the Sumerian period itself.

Early farmer dwellings in Mesopotamia were probably not dissimilar from this mud-brick hut in today's Iraq

According to this epic, then, the earth was first formed when the god Marduk was charged by all other gods to defend their heavenly pantheon from the evil schemes of Tiamat, the ocean goddess. But Marduk exacted a heavy price for his service: if he did emerge victorious, all gods would have to accept him as their supreme leader. The gods consented, Marduk headed into battle, and in the process succeeded in vanquishing Tiamat. He tore the ocean goddess in two, and used the pieces to create the earth and the firmament. Next, the epic tells us,

> "He constructed stations for the great gods,
> Fixing their astral likeness as constellations.
> ……...
> The Moon he caused to shine, the night (to him) entrusting.
> He appointed him a creature of the night to signify the days:
> ………
> Thou shalt have luminous horns to signify six days,
> On the seventh day reaching a [half]-crown.
> When the sun [overtakes] thee at the base of heaven,
> Diminish [thy crown] and retrogress in light.
> ………
> [And Marduk said:]
> I will establish a savage, 'man' shall be his name
> Verily, savage-man I will create.
> He shall be charged with the service of the gods.

As such, this Babylonian creation epic set a pattern that we would find again in both the Bible and the Qur'an. First, the firmament and the earth are created as separate entities. Next, time is instituted as the essential measure of life, anchored in the seven-day week. Then, the sun and the moon are placed in the heaven, followed by living creatures, the last of which is man.

Genesis, the first book of the Hebrew Scriptures, thus originated in a cultural milieu where the idea that heaven and earth were created out of nothing, simply by divine command, had been valid for over a thousand years. But when did the Genesis version of this creation story first emerge? The answer is, of course, a hotly debated issue. Orthodox Jews and fundamentalist Christians believe that Genesis and the other four books of the *Torah*, the "Law" (also known as the Five Books of Moses), were dictated by God to Moses on Mount Sinai. According to this interpretation, the books are therefore *ipsa verba dei*, the literal spoken word of God, in much the same way that Muslims believe the Qur'an is the faithful recording of words revealed by God's agency to Muhammad. Biblical scholars respect this view, but can point to over a hundred years of scholarly research that suggests that the stories of Genesis originated over time – through oral traditions, told around campfires at night, until they could be committed to paper.

In fact, scholars suggest that the *Torah* represent a collection of at least four different strands of oral narrative, the oldest of which – known as the 'J' strain, for *Jahweh* (or Yahweh in German) – originated in the tenth century B.C., around the time of King David's reign. It is because of the presence of these different oral strands, skillfully woven into the tapestry of the Mosaic Laws by scribes many centuries later, that we have sometimes conflicting accounts about the creation of Adam and Eve, the events in the Garden of Eden, and what followed after the Expulsion.

The opening chapters of the Book of Genesis, called *Beresh't* in Judaism (meaning "In the beginning," the Book's first three words), are devoted to the biblical story of Creation. "In the beginning," says Genesis, "the earth was without form, and void; and darkness was upon the face of the deep" (G 1:2). So it had been before the beginning of time, and it was only when "the Spirit of God moved upon the face of the waters" that things began to happen, the water rippled, light broke through the cloak of darkness, and life stirred beneath the seas.

The Qur'an, the Holy Scripture of Islam, agrees with this vision of Creation. In fact, it is possible to place both stories side by side and observe some striking parallels:

Genesis
In the beginning... the earth was without form, and
void; and darkness was upon the face of the deep.
And the Spirit of God moved upon the face of the waters.
(G 1:1-2)

Qur'an
For it is He who created for you all that is in the earth, and He directed Himself to the heaven.
(Q 2.29)

Genesis
And God said, Let there be light.....
Let there be lights in the firmament
of the heaven to divide the day from the night...
(G 1:14-16)

Qur'an
He created the heavens and the earth
in six periods of time, and He is firm in power;
He throws the veil of night over the day,
which it pursues incessantly;
and (He created) the sun and the moon and
the stars, made subservient by His command"
(Q 7:54).

The 13th *sura* or chapter adds that "it was God who raised the heavens without any visible support, and assumed His throne, and ordered the sun and the moon (so that) each one runs its appointed course. He regulates all affairs, and clarifies all signs that you may be certain of meeting with your Lord" (Q 13.2).

"And then," Genesis continues, "the earth brought forth grass, and herbs yielding seed after his kind, and the tree yielding fruit, whose seed was in itself, after his kind, and God saw that it was good" (G 1:12). The Qur'an further specifies the individual plants and trees that were created at this time. "And in the earth there are tracts side by side, and vineyards, fields of corn and date-palm trees, some with one root and others with multiple roots, yet all are watered with the same water, though We make some bear more excellent fruit than others" (Q 13:4).

By and large, then, the Creation accounts in Genesis and the Qur'an are quite similar, though with different emphases, which reflect the unique cultural and geographical milieu in which each Book originated. One specific difference between Judaism, Christianity and Islam pertains to the specific days on which God did his work, because that determined the day that should be considered "holy" and a day of rest. For the Jewish tradition, the day on which God rested is the Sabbath, from Friday sundown to Saturday sundown. For Christians, it is Sunday. The 13th century book *Qisas Al-Anbiya,* or "Stories of the Prophets," on the other hand, argues that Ibn Abbas, one of Muhammad's Companions, said that "the beginning was on a Saturday and the ending on a Friday, so that the taking of His seat was also on a Friday, and for that reason we keep it as a holy day." Furthermore, Ibn Abbas remembered that at one point Muhammad called Friday "the mistress among the days," because on this day "Adam was created, on it his spirit was breathed into him, he was wedded, he died, and on it will come the Final Hour. No human ever asks his Lord for anything on Friday but that God gives him what he asks." Therefore, Muslims chose Friday as their holy day of prayer (*Jumu'ah*).

And thus the earth and the heavens were created in six days; and on the seventh day, God rested. But by then, a man named Adam was already walking in the Garden of Eden.

Chapter Two
Adam and Eve in Paradise

The Creation of Adam, from Michelangelo's Sistine Chapel ceiling frescoes, painted between 1508 and 1512

Once all of Creation was in place, says Genesis, God decided to make man, in his own image, after his own likeness. To do so, he "formed man of the dust of the ground, and breathed into his nostrils the breath of life; and man became a living soul" (G. 2:7). The same story is told in the Qur'an. God "created him from dust, then said to him, Be, and he was" (Q. 3:59). Elsewhere, in chapter 7, the Qur'an is more specific, suggesting that this primordial dust was impregnated with divine sperm: "Do you disbelieve in Him Who created you from dust, then from a small seed, then He made you a perfect man?" asks sura 18 (Q. 18:37).

Other suras indicate that Adam was made from clay or mud. In one verse, God says that "I created [Adam] with my own hands," as if Adam was molded from clay by a potter (Q 38:75). Later writings would go even further, and add that the soil with which Adam was made came from the four corners of the earth, so that Adam's body was truly in harmony with all points in the world. The important distinction, Islamic commentators assert, is that Adam was formed from *matter,* in contrast to angels, who were made from light; and demons (*djinn*), who were made from fire.

AS SOON AS ADAM IS made, says the Qur'an, God convenes all the angels of his heavenly realm (angels being equally prominent in Islamic Scripture as in Jewish and Christian writings). God tells this council of angels that "I am about to place a *vice-regent* on earth," using the term *khalifa* or Caliph (later also used as "replacement," the title assumed by Muhammad's successors). God even insists that the angels prostrate themselves for Adam, thus placing Adam, as the First Man on earth, on a higher plane than the angels themselves.

Naturally, the angels vehemently protest. "Will You place someone (on earth) who would create disorder and shed blood, while we go on intoning Your litanies and sanctify Your Name?" they complain bitterly. But God responds, "I know what you do not know," and that is that angels, while beautiful and selfless, primarily exist to praise and glorify God (Q 2:29). Man, on the other hand, has been endowed with something unique and truly divine: free will. This quality carries with it the germs of all kinds of trouble, even violence and war; but for Islam, that is mankind's ultimate moral challenge. In the Qur'an, therefore, the story of Adam and Eve illustrates one of its pivotal themes: that each man, endowed with free will, needs to overcome his own hubris and find the way to submission to God.

The angels eventually agree to do God's bidding and submit to Adam – all, except one character named *Iblis.* Iblis is, of course, the Islamic equivalent of Lucifer, the Satan (or *Shatan* in Muslim literature) who broke with God to establish his own dark universe. "I am better than [Adam]," says Lucifer in sura 7; after all, "You created me of fire, and him you created out of clay." For this intransigence, Lucifer is banned from God's presence, but not from the story of mankind. In fact, the Quranic God explicitly allows Satan to tempt Adam, his offspring and all of mankind for all time until Judgment Day, because without temptation, without the polarizing forces of good and evil, having a free will would be pointless. Thus the Qur'an sets up the glory and tragedy of the human race: how, throughout life, man and woman are challenged to make moral choices and remain true to God. Satan removes himself from the scene – though not for long.

ACCORDING TO THE BIBLE and the Qur'an, Adam is put to work right away. The world is teeming with animals, and none have been named yet. So for days on end, poor Adam labors as he tries to come up with an appropriate name for every species that God presents to him. "And so, Adam gave names to all cattle, and to the fowl of the air, and to every beast of the field," says Genesis (G. 2:20). "And the cattle are made lawful for you," says the Qur'an (Q. 2:30). Giving something or someone a name, in Antiquity as well as 6th century Arabia, implied *acceptance*. When in Genesis Abraham "names" Ishmael, the child of his concubine Hagar, he implicitly accepts Ishmael as his son. Hence, by naming the elements of Creation, Adam welcomes and embraces all of the living creatures and accepts their meaning and relationship to Nature.

But Adam is lonely; with even the lowliest species having both males and females, he keenly feels the need for a companion himself. So God causes Adam to fall into a deep sleep; and while he slept,

> ".. he took one of his ribs,
> and closed up the flesh instead thereof;
> And the rib, which the LORD God
> had taken from man, made he a woman,
> and brought her unto the man." (G. 2:21-22)

The Qur'an agrees:

"of the same (kind) did He make his mate,
that he might dwell with her;
so when he covers her she bears a light burden (Q. 7:189)

Eve – *Hawwa* in Arabic – is not mentioned in the Qur'an by name, but chapter 30 reminds its listeners why she was created:

He created mates for you from yourselves,
so that you may find rest in them, and He
put between you love and compassion (Q. 30:21)

Does the Quranic phrase "of the same (kind)" mean that Eve was made from Adam's rib, as Genesis asserts? Some of the *Tafsir* literature would reject this notion. "Is God unable to create her except out of Adam's rib?" asks one account, and adds, "[God] held a clay and mixed it with his right hand … so He created out of it Adam and part of it was left untouched, so He created Eve out of it." In this view, Eve was molded by God from the same primordial life-giving clay, rather than from any part of Adam himself, thus putting her on a par with her male counterpart.

Adam is delighted with his beautiful mate. Together, they are led by God into a beautiful Shangri-la called the Garden of Eden, with "every tree pleasant to the sight, and good for food." Many centuries later, after the Exile, when Persian influences began to make themselves felt on the Genesis tradition, the Garden of Eden acquired a new name: *paradise*. The term is rooted in the Old Persian word *pardis*, which means "walled (or protected) enclosure," usually referring to park-like estates maintained for the king's comfort. The Garden of Eden was green, lush and filled with water – essentially everything that the desert was not. For beneath the Garden, says the Qur'an, "flow rivers. Perpetual is the fruits thereof and the shade therein."

One Islamic tradition suggests that Paradise was not located on earth but in heaven, so that when Adam was expelled from

Paradise, he literally *fell* to earth – and landed on the spot that is today is marked by the Dome of the Rock in Jerusalem.

This detail from Hieronymus Bosch's 'The Garden of Earthly Delights' (1504) depicts Eden as a place of bountiful physical pleasures

Another tradition has Adam descending to India, while Eve is sent down to Jeddah. Eventually, they make their way to Arafat near Mecca, where they are finally reunited. Genesis, on the other hand, suggests that the Garden was located in Mesopotamia:

> Genesis:
> A river flows out of Eden to water the Garden, and from there it divides and becomes four branches. The name of the first is Pishon; it is the one that flows around the whole land of Havilah... the name of the second river is Gihon; it is the one that flows around the whole land of Cush. The name of the third river is Tigris which flows east of Assyria. And the fourth river is the Euphrates.

(G. 2: 10-14)

We know the Tigris and Euphrates, of course, but where was Gihon and Pishon? Some scholars believe that these streams can be detected in satellite photographs of a dry riverbed system near Wadi al-Batin. The land of 'Cush' has been tentatively identified with the Horn of Africa. But regardless of the final identification of these places, one thing is clear – Eden must have been inspired by the primordial bounty of Mesopotamia in ancient times.

A modern photograph of Wadi al-Batin, part of the dry riverbed of Wadi Al-Rummah in Saudi Arabia.

GOD BIDS ADAM "and his wife" to dwell in the garden, "and eat from it a plenteous food wherever you wish" (Q 2:35). There is but one exception, and that is what Genesis calls "the tree of good and evil." In the Quranic version, Adam and Eve receive the same injunction. "Do not approach this tree," says the Qur'an, "for then you will be of the unjust." The type of the tree is not specified, though later commentators would suggest that it was either a vine, an ear of grain, a fig tree or simply a tree bearing delicious fruit.

In the Bible, this is when the serpent comes slithering onto the scene, cozying up to Eve and asking her, "Did God say, 'You shall not eat from any tree in the garden?'" (G 3.1). No, Eve corrects the serpent in her naiveté, "we may freely eat of the fruit of the trees in the garden, but of the fruit of the tree which is in the garden's midst, God told us we cannot not eat of it, nor even touch it, lest you die." The serpent rolls his eyes and says, Come on now, surely you won't die. And then he reveals the secret of *why* God doesn't want Adam and Eve to partake from the tree: "for God knows that on the day you eat thereof, your eyes shall be opened, and you shall be as gods, knowing good and evil" (G 3:3-5).

In the Qur'an, a similar story unfolds, though it is not the serpent who tempts Adam and Eve, but Satan himself. "Shall I guide you to the tree of immortality and a kingdom that will never perish?" Satan asks the couple (Q 20:120). Satan then explains that "Your Lord has forbidden you this tree so that you may not both become two angels, and become of the immortals" (Q 7:21).

Knowledge or immortality – which would be a greater temptation? John Milton's *Paradise Lost,* echoed in Philip Pullman's novel *The Golden Compass,* would argue for the former. By pursuing knowledge and science unfettered by doctrine or ideology, man may lose his innocence but become conscious of himself and his role in the universe. Immortality, on the other hand, offers life without death, but a life wholly committed to the glory of God, together with all other angels. Which is better? In the Qur'an, Satan urges the couple to eat, assuring them that "most surely I am a sincere adviser to you."

The tree as the sacred symbol of life was current in Babylonian and Assyrian mythology, as evidenced by this Assyrian wall relief from Nimrud, ca 860 BCE

In the Bible, it is Eve who succumbs to the serpent's temptation. As soon as she has eaten from the tree, she makes sure that her mate does so as well, to assuage her guilt. But the end result is the same: "as soon as they tasted from the tree," the Qur'an says, "their evil inclinations became manifest to them, and they both began to cover themselves with the leaves of the garden."

God is shocked that they have shown themselves to be so gullible to Satan's evil scheming. "Did I not say to you that Satan is your open enemy?" he cries in the Qur'an. Adam and Eve agree that "we have been unjust to ourselves." "If you don't forgive us and have mercy on us," they plead, "we shall certainly be the losers" (Q 7:22-23). In the Qur'an, in other words, both the man and the woman accept blame for what they've done, and in solidarity with one another hope for God's forgiveness.

In Genesis, on the other hand, Adam cannot resist making a last-ditch attempt to shift the blame to his young wife, and by extension to God, who came up with this female creature to begin with. "This woman whom you gave me," he says, "she gave it to me." God thereupon questions Eve, who readily passes the blame onto the serpent.

And so, Adam and Eve have lost their claim on innocence by striving for attributes well beyond the realm of their peaceful little dream world in Eden. Mankind's first couple, once so full of promise, is evicted from the Garden, to till the land "by the sweat of your brow," as Genesis puts it, and to give birth "in sorrow and pain." Devoid of their earlier child-like innocence, Adam and Eve become aware of their nakedness – and sexual attraction. And, says Genesis, "the Lord made garments of skins for the man and for his wife, and clothed them" (G3:21). "We have indeed sent down clothing to you to cover your shame," says God in the Qur'an, though with some sense of fashion as well as propriety: "clothing for beauty as well as clothing that guards (against evil)" (Q7.26).

BUT THERE IS HOPE. As God sends Adam and Eve "from this state," he promises them that "whoever follows my guidance, no fear shall come upon them, nor shall they grieve." The Muslim *Tafsir* writings emphasize the "right of return," the idea that believers who have led a moral life will be allowed back into Paradise. According to one account, Muhammad said that "it is the paradise that God promised for His faithful after life for their deeds."

The Islamic concept of Paradise or "the Garden" (*Jannah*) as a reward for those who have lived a moral life is, regrettably, a subject of some controversy, given the notion put forth by some fundamentalist imams that *shahids* or suicide bombers will be allowed immediate passage to this paradise, without having to wait for the Day of Judgment.

The root of this idea can be traced to the 1980-1988 war between Saddam Hussein's Iraq and Revolutionary Iran. At the time, the Ayatollah Khomeini issued a finding that soldiers who gave their life fighting the Iraqis would be considered *shahids*, with free passage to Paradise. The Arabic word *shahid* means 'witness', but is most often used as 'martyr'. The theological basis for Khomeini's finding was that Saddam Hussein was a tyrant, and that therefore soldiers who died fighting this tyrant were akin to the great Shi'ite martyr Husayn ibn 'Ali, who died fighting the "tyranny" of the Ummayad caliph Yazid. Khomeini cited sura 3 in the Qur'an:

> "Think not of those who are slain in Allah's
> way as dead.
> Nay, they live, finding their sustenance in
> the presence of their Lord; They rejoice in
> the bounty provided by Allah. (Q 3.169)

Khomeini's edict has been used by extremist imams ever since to justify the use of suicide bombers in attacks on Western forces in the Middle East, or acts of terrorism around the world. These imams, however, ignore the fact that suicide is expressly forbidden in the Qur'an. Sura 4, *An-Nisaa* ('The Women') warns the believers "not (to) kill yourselves, surely God is most Merciful to you" (Q 4:29). According to a Hadith, Muhammad himself said it even more clearly: "He who commits suicide with something, will be punished with the same thing in Hell." By the same token, says the Qur'an, entry into Paradise is reserved only for those who:

> "....spend their days (benevolently) in ease as well as in straitness, and those who restrain (their) anger and pardon men; and God loves the doers of good (to others)... Their reward is forgiveness from their Lord, and gardens beneath which rivers flow, to abide in them, and excellent is the reward of the laborers. (Q 3:134-6)

In other words, the Qur'an agrees with the Christian tradition that "the righteous" shall be granted access to paradise after their resurrection on the Day of Last Judgment (*Yawm ad-Din*).

That being the case, are there any important differences between the Muslim and Christian concept of paradise? Most certainly; to most Christians, paradise is a place of perfect spiritual harmony with God. For Muslims, on the other hand, the pleasures of paradise are physical and tangible, as described in great detail in the *Tafsir* literature.

For example, regardless of their age at death, all men will be 32 years old– the same age as Jesus upon his Ascension. Men and women will be clothed in gorgeous garments adorned with previous jewels. Banquets will be served around the clock, served by beautiful youths, and enjoyed in the company of loved ones – provided they too have led an exemplary life. And, says the Qur'an, "We shall mate [the believers] with companions pure, most beautiful of eye" (Q 52:20). These "beautiful companions" (*Houri*), of "modest gaze," are the controversial beautiful creatures that some Hadith refer to as the seventy-two "wives" or "virgins." The interpretation is far from universal. Other Hadith (the Arabic word can be used both in the singular and plural) claim that all women, regardless of age, will simply be restored to their age of youth and beauty. "Lo!", says one, "We have created them a (new) creation and made them virgins, lovers, equal in age."

The Qur'an also differs from the Bible in applying the meaning of the story of Adam and Eve in Paradise. For Genesis, the expulsion from the Garden of Eden marks the Fall of Man, a loss of innocence that is only redeemed by God's covenant with Abraham and Moses. For Christians, the story of Adam and Eve identifies the moment mankind was branded with original sin, "and through sin death," as Paul would write to the Romans. "And thus," Paul continues, "death pervaded the whole human race – until the coming of Christ, and his sacrifice on the cross" (*Romans*, 5:12).

The Qur'an rejects this Christian idea of original sin. Man cannot be flawed from the start, Islam argues, because he was created by God; therefore, whatever sin he may commit is strictly his own doing. "Catholics from Augustine on down had focused on sin as something that separated humanity from the divine," says Peter Awn. "They believed that as a result of the fall of Adam and Eve, our human natures were deformed simply by being born. Islam, on the other hand, refuses to affirm that interpretation. The Qur'an argues that their mistake literally becomes the model of all of our lives. So Adam and Eve don't become the symbols of the deformation or the corruption of human nature, but are emblematic of the battle between good and evil that humans will have to fight all their lives."

What is also remarkable about the Quranic version is the absence of any attempt to place Adam above Eve, or to "frame" Eve for having started the tragedy with the forbidden fruit to begin with, as some Christian authors have tried to do. In the Qur'an, no distinction is made between either the position of Adam and Eve or their degree of complicity, which is remarkable for a religion often maligned for its treatment of women. Instead, Satan makes his "evil suggestion" to Adam and Eve both, simultaneously, and both will share equal responsibility for the consequences.

Chapter Three
Cain and Abel

Modern-day shepherds in Egypt seem almost indistinguishable from their Stone Age predecessors

As we have seen, sometime around 10,000 B.C.E. the people of the Near East experienced a major psychological transformation. Traditionally, man's principal occupation – the gathering of food for himself, his mate and their offspring – was focused on hunting game or finding edible crops that grew in the wild. But eventually, man grasped that there was a different way to secure survival; that he, in a way, could take control of his destiny by growing crops or husbanding animals himself. This transformation didn't happen overnight, of course. Many early farmers continued to hunt to complement their diet. But over time, these farmers gained sufficient experience and confidence to know that seeds, properly sown and watered, could sustain their families. They *settled down* to focus on tilling their land and keeping their cluster of domesticated sheep, goats or cattle. Others decided to gather such domesticated animals in large quantities, in *herds*. This forced them into a nomadic lifestyle, since no single plot of land could sustain a large herd. These nomads would travel from field to field, ever in search of fresh pastures.

The typical Near Eastern contrast between nomadic shepherds and settled farmers is illustrated by the story of Cain and Abel, which appears in both the Bible and the Qur'an. The narrative begins when Adam and Eve have been ousted from the Garden of Eden and Adam has settled as a farmer, to "till the land from which he was taken" (G3:23). Adam thereupon "knew his wife Eve, and she conceived and bore Cain, saying, I have produced a man with the help of the Lord." The name of this boy, 'Cain,' is one of the wordplays of which Genesis is so fond, for *qayin* means "that which has been acquired or produced." Naturally, Cain (or *Qabeel* in Arabic) grew up to become a farmer like his father. "Next," Genesis continues, "she bore his brother Abel," a name that by contrast means "Emptiness," for Abel (or *Habeel* in Arabic) is destined to become a shepherd and spend his days roaming the great stretches of empty, uncultivated land.

ONE DAY, WHEN BOTH BROTHERS have come of age, they decide to present an offering to the Lord, to thank him for their good fortune. Cain, naturally, presents the fruit of the soil, the best share of his crops, whereas Abel picks "the firstlings of his flock, and of the fat thereof" (G 4:2-4). The Lord accepts Abel's animal offering, but refuses Cain's fruit of the earth.

This may strike us as rather strange, but in fact, Genesis is illustrating a typical Stone Age social conflict between farmers and nomads. Farmers lived in settled communities, close to their fields and wells, which were jealously guarded against roving nomadic shepherds and their large, thirsty flocks. In the Bible, stories of conflict over land and wells are legion; the story of Abraham, for example, is replete with disputes related to land and water resources. The same was true for the *Hijaz*, the southeastern region of Arabia, as we will see in a later chapter.

The story of *Qabeel* and *Habeel* must therefore have resonated with Muhammad's audience as well. "Tell them the story of the two sons of Adam, when they both offered an offering, but it was accepted from one of them and not from the other," says the Qur'an (Q5:27). And indeed, in the Genesis story, God sides with the nomadic shepherds: he "had regard for Abel and his offering, but for Cain and his offering he had no regard."

The Qur'an has an explanation for God's choice. Cain's offering was disfavored because his heart was filled with envy and sin. "God only accepts from those who guard (against evil)," the Qur'an tell us. And so, shortly thereafter, when the brothers were both in the field, "Cain rose up against Abel his brother, and slew him" (G 4:8).

In Genesis, this terrible event takes place without any preamble or argument; it is, quite simply, an act of premeditated murder – the first instance of homicide in the Bible. The Qur'an, on the other hand, enhances the story with extensive dialog, a phenomenon that we will see again in many stories to come. The dialog opens with Cain announcing his murderous intent to Abel.

"I am going to kill you," he says.

"If you plan to raise your hand to kill me," Abel responds, "then I for one am not going to raise my hand against you. Truly, I fear God, the Lord of the worlds." And if Cain kills him anyway, Abel continues, "I hope that you will bear the sin committed against me, and your own sin, so you become one of the inmates of fire [i.e., Hell], for this is the reward of the unjust."

But Cain's mind is made up. He "rationalized the killing of his brother," the Qur'an continues, "and so he killed him; and he became one of the losers."

As soon as Abel lies dead on the ground, a raven appears to help Cain "(dig) up the earth, so that he might show him how he should cover the dead body of his brother." The infamy of murder must be hidden as soon as possible. But the raven's appearance fills Cain with indignation. "What?" he says; "do I lack the strength that I should be like this crow, and cover the dead body of my brother?" And so, the Qur'an concludes, "he became one of those who look back in regret" (Q 5:27-31).

Genesis provides the next scene in this family tragedy. Cain has hastily buried his brother in the ground, but the Lord is on to him. He questions Cain, saying "Where is Abel, your brother?" To which Cain responds, with words that capture the essential moral dilemma of all human experience: "What? Am I my brother's keeper?"

"The voice of your brother's blood cries out to me from the ground," God retorts: "and now you are cursed from the earth, which has opened her mouth to receive your brother's blood from your hand" (G 4:9-11).

With that, God casts Cain out the land, and out of his favor. Cain is now a "marked man," for Abel's blood is "crying out" for revenge. Ancient tribal law demanded that the unlawful murder of one of its own had to be avenged. Failure to exact any form of retribution was considered a sign of weakness that made the tribe appear vulnerable. Consequently, a killer was fair game.

In Genesis, God appears to facilitate this revenge by casting Cain out of his settlement, making him a "fugitive" on the run, exposed and stripped of his tribal protection. Cain pleads with God, saying that "my punishment is greater than I can bear!" Bereft of his clan's sanctuary, "anyone who meets me may kill me!" (G 4:10-14).

For the Qur'an, however, the story of Cain and Abel illustrates the essential struggle between good and evil, between a murderer and his innocent victim. "For this reason did We prescribe to the children of Israel (*Banu Isra'il*) that whoever slays a soul, unless it be for manslaughter or for mischief in the land, it is as though he slew all men," the Qur'an states, "and whoever keeps it alive, it is as though he kept alive all men." In other words, the Qur'an regards an unlawful killing akin to a crime against humanity. It is a profound statement that those who, in our modern times, perpetrate acts of terror in the name of Islam, should do well to take to heart. In the *Tafsir* literature, several Muslim commentators have gone as far as to argue that even a killing in self-defense is prohibited. The caliph 'Uthman is said to have followed this commandment when a group of assassins succeeded in breaking into his palace in Medina in 656. He refused to offer any resistance, and thus was killed without a struggle, in imitation of Abel.

In Genesis, God then decides that one murder is enough, and that the killing of Abel should not lead to a vicious cycle of familial revenge. Though Cain has been condemned to roam the world as an outlaw, a fugitive, he will not be harmed. "Whoever slays Cain," says the Lord, "vengeance shall be taken on him sevenfold." And to underscore the fact, "God put a mark on Cain, so that no one who came upon him would kill him (G 4:15).

Here, as in the Qur'an, God shows himself to be a source of mercy or *rachman* – the word is virtually the same in Hebrew as in Arabic. And so Cain went away and settled in the land of Nod, quite literally "the Land of Naught," a place of aimless wandering. There he marries a woman who will bear him a son named Enoch. Enoch then "built a city, and named it Enoch after his son Enoch."

THIS IS THE FIRST TIME THAT Genesis refers to "a city." By now, farmer settlements had sufficiently coalesced to deserve the appellation of a community. Genesis tells us that Cain's offspring included a man named Jubal: "he was the ancestor of all those who play the lyre and pipe" (G 4:21). A lyre and flute were among the precious objects that the British archaeologist Sir Leonard Woolley discovered in 1922 in a tomb near Tell al-Muqayyar, north of Basra in today's Iraq. The beautiful lyre was decorated in lapus lazuli, showing lions devouring a deer or a ram, and capped with the golden head of a bull, his horns fashioned from ivory. The tomb belonged to an elaborate set of Royal Graves, the resting place of kings of the Third Sumerian period (ca. 2400 B.C.E.). In those days the city near Tell al-Muqayyar was called Ur – presumably the birthplace of a man named Abraham.

ஐ

Chapter Four
A Tribal Chieftain named Abraham

A Sumerian game board from about 2600 B.C.E.

From about 3500 B.C.E. onwards, Mesopotamia would witness the rise of the first great civilization known to man: the culture of Sumer. This Sumerian society, as we will see shortly, was made up of several city-states, including the royal city of Ur. It is here that Bible and archaeology interconnect for the first time. For just as archaeologists pinpoint the origins of human culture in Ur's Sumerian civilization, so too does the Bible appear to place the family of its first great protagonist, Abraham, in this city. Abraham (or *Abram* as Genesis still calls him at this point) was the son of Terah; he had two brothers, Nahor and Haran. But unfortunately,

> Genesis
> Haran died before his father Terah in the land
> of his birth, in Ur of the Chaldeans. (G. 11:28)

Beginning with Abraham, then, the stories of Genesis begin to interlock with actual history. From here on, it seems, we are dealing with real people, with the full panorama of human emotions, as husbands and wives struggle to build a future for their children.

So, who was Abraham? Who was this man, this 'father of monotheism,' who would become the wellspring of the three great faiths? As the Bible tells us, the family of Abraham may have hailed from one of the great urban centers of Sumer. Ur's history begins in the 5th millennium. Encouraged by the fertility of the Sumerian alluvial plane, man had learned to grow crops and breed domesticated animals. Thus agriculture began to develop, but it was limited in scope. The early Sumerian farmers found that plots had to be in close proximity to the river or its tributaries, in order to secure sufficient water for their crops. This severely limited the yields, which compelled some bright-eyed farmers to think of a solution -- the obvious one being a network of small canals that could carry the water further inland. The problem was that such an elaborate irrigation system could not be undertaken by a handful of farmers alone. It required planning, equipment, resources and capital -- in sum, it required *organization*. Thus, the need for widespread irrigation spawned the development of a farmers' co-operative framework across the Sumerian planes. This cooperative was so successful that before long, Sumer became the breadbasket of Mesopotamia. So lush were its vineyards and so fertile its groves, that it did not stretch the imagination to, indeed, imagine Sumer as the Garden of Eden on earth.

This bounty freed up other villagers to concentrate on other tasks, such as producing pottery, weaving or construction. Soon, yields were such that even after satisfying the needs of an entire village, there was sufficient agrarian surplus to sell to other communities nearby. This stimulated the development of local trade. Around 3500 B.C.E., Ur's trade had grown to such a degree that the city, happily perched on the crossroads between Asia and Africa, became the dominant presence in the region.

With trade came the necessity of accounting, of listing products, quantities and price. To that end, traders began to impress small tables of soft clay with symbols representing the type and quantities of goods purchased. The result was a primitive script of pictures or pictograms, essentially abbreviated symbols of a particular product, number or value. Through daily use, these pictograms became stylized into a proper alphabet, known as cuneiform script. 'Cuneiform' refers to the wedge-like pen or stylus with which the stylized symbols or "letters" were impressed into the soft clay.

A cuneiform tablet recording a transaction for jugs of beer, indicated by the vessel-like symbols with pointed bottoms

So successful was the revolution of cuneiform script that it was adopted by virtually all other developing language groups in greater Mesopotamia, including Akkadian (the root of both

Babylonian and Assyrian dialects), Hittite, Elamite and other tongues. The innovation possibly reached as far as Egypt, where the early Sumerian script may have been the model for an indigenous pictogrammatic alphabet known as hieroglyphic.

What made the development of the cuneiform script so significant is that it used *clay*, rather than papyrus or any other perishable material. Baked clay is incredibly durable and virtually impervious to the effects of time. Entire libraries from the ancient world, filled with paper scrolls, have been lost to fire, floods or willful destruction; but clay endures. A fire only serves to harden it further. This is why the period of 3,000 years in which cuneiform script was used offers us an invaluable window on the history of Mesopotamia. The British Museum, the Louvre and countless other museums are literally stocked with thousands of records pertaining to kings and warriors, conquests and trade, and the cycle of destruction and re-building -- all of which will figure prominently in our story.

Of course, all this trade and activity in Ur and other Sumerian cities was bound to lead to an accumulation of wealth. Wealth, regrettably, leads to envy. So it was with the nomadic tribes bordering on Sumer, who were eyeing the region's prosperity with keen interest. Soon, the budding Sumerian communities fell victim to vicious cross-border raids, and instinctively reached out to one another for protection. The pastoral settlements coalesced into cities that could be walled in and thus more easily defended. Eventually, these new cities decided to elect a leader to take command of a local militia and organize defensive works.

As each city grew, so too did the prestige and power of its elected communal leader, known as a *Lugal*. By 2750 B.C.E., Sumer had become a nation ruled by the first of a dynasty of Kings, named *Men-barage-si*. These kings wasted no time in setting up a feudal system of local chieftains, who ensured a steady flow of taxation to sustain the king's army and his luxurious lifestyle.

The king also took charge of organized, state-sponsored worship. As we have seen, religion had always played an important part in Sumeria. Despite the sophistication of its irrigation technology, a good harvest was by no means a sure thing. Drought, flooding or climatic changes could doom the farmer's yield and jeopardize the economy of the city state.

In fact, around 2,900 B.C.E., the region was struck by a massive flood. Mesopotamia had experienced major flooding before, but never on a scale such as this. So traumatic was the experience that it became a pivotal event in Sumerian mythology, its history reckoned as periods before and after the flood, just as Noah's flood in Genesis would mark a major transformative moment in the history of mankind. While excavating the royal palace at Ur near Tel-al-Muqayyar, north of Basra in today's Iraq, British archaeologist Sir Charles Woolley found a 10 foot layer or *stratum* of pure clay -- clear evidence of a massive flood that all but wiped out large stretches of cultivated land.

Not surprisingly, then, the stories of the Flood in the Bible and the Qur'an share many common features with their Sumerian precedent. The most famous account of the Sumerian flood is found on a tablet from Nippur, dating from the 18th century B.C.E. and sometimes referred to as the Eridu Genesis, though the original story may be much older. According to this narrative, the gods Enlil, Enki and Ninhursag create man in the form of "black-headed people," and grant them kingship, whereupon the first five cities (or "cult-centers") of Sumeria are formed. But soon the gods develop second thoughts. They decide to wipe out mankind with a huge flood.

The Athrahasis Epic, a cuneiform tablet written in Old Babylonian, ca. 1635 B.C.E.

Though part of the text is missing, a later version, known as the *Atrahasis Epic*, can help fill in the blanks. One deity, the water-god Enki, takes pity on the humans. He leaks news of the impending calamity to a man Atrahasis, and urges him to build a boat. This vessel, the god tells Atrahasis, should be filled with all of his possessions, including animals and birds. Next,

> All the windstorms, exceedingly powerful,
> attacked as one,
> At the same time, the flood sweeps over the cult-centers.
> After, for seven days (and) seven nights,
> The flood had swept over the land,
> (And) the huge boat had been tossed about by the
> windstorms on the great waters,
> Utu came forth, who sheds light on heaven (and) earth.
> (And) Ziusudra opened a window of the huge boat.

The famous *Gilgamesh Epic* also contains the story of a catastrophic flood. Once again the gods decide to eliminate the tiresome humans, and this time it Gilgamesh's ancestor Utnapishtim who is destined to be saved. Utnapishtim follows the counsel of the God Ea and builds a large ship. He then gathers up his family and all the beasts of the field, and waits for the waters to subside.

It will be obvious to the reader that the narrative outline of both epics returns in the story of Noah. The meaning of the name "Noah" is not entirely clear. In the Jewish tradition, 'Noah' is believed to derive from *niham,* meaning "he gave comfort to his people," whereas the Islamic name *Nuh* (based on the verb *naha*) is believed to mean "he wailed for his people" – an indication of where the Quranic version is going to take us.

In Genesis, the story begins when men "began to multiply on the face of the earth," as in the case of its Sumerian precedent. But their multitudes is not what provoked God's ire; their behavior is. Man's "wickedness was great," says the Bible, and "every imagination of his heart" was filled with evil thoughts. Now God "regretted that he had made man on earth, and it grieved his heart. And the Lord said, 'I will destroy man whom I have created from the face of the earth...' But Noah found grace in the eyes of the Lord" (G 6:1; 5-8).

In the Qur'an, the story of Noah and the Flood is also treated with great prominence. Noah's name appears forty-three times, but for a different reason. Unlike the Genesis tradition, where he is treated as a righteous and God-fearing man, Noah is revered as one of Islam's principal prophets. Like Lot and Moses, as well as the Arabian prophets *Hud* and *Salih*, he is called a "prophet of warning," tasked to warn his sinful audience of great impending punishment from which they can only escape through repentance and submission to God.

This theme must have resonated with Muhammad, particularly during the early years of his ministry in Mecca, where his preaching met with overt hostility. In the Qur'an, its principal theme is Noah's strenuous efforts to convert his fellow citizens, and the stubborn refusal of his listeners to heed his words. So important is Noah to the early phase of Muhammad's revelations that elements from the story return in twenty-six suras, with one, *Nuh* ('Noah' in Arabic), devoted entirely to the theme of Noah and the Flood.

In Genesis, God tells Noah to build a boat, a very large ship, an "ark of cypress wood." God even provides detailed specifications of how this ark should be built: "This is how you are to make it: the length of the ark three hundred cubits, its width fifty cubits, and its height thirty cubits. Make a roof for the ark, and finish it to a cubit above ... And of every living thing, of all flesh, you shall bring two of every kind." (G 6:14-19). These measurements appear to correspond closely to the design provided by the god Ea to Utnapishtim in the Gilgamesh Epic: "These are the measurements of the barque as you shall build her ... Let her beam equal her length, let her deck be roofed like the vault that covers the abyss; then take up into the boat the seed of all living creatures." Interestingly enough, there is no provision for a rudder or a sail in the Genesis description, which scholars believe may suggest that the ark was not meant to be navigated – merely carried by the waters under the protective hands of God.

We are not given any measurements in the Qur'an, but *Tafsir* commentaries fill the gap by suggesting that Noah used wood from a tree that had grown for 40 years, until it was some 300 cubits high. Some accounts suggest the boat was rectangular, while others describe it as a round bowl. In one of the stories told by al-Kisa'i, the apostles urge Jesus to raise Noah's son Shem, so that he can give Jesus detailed information about the ark's design. Jesus is told that the lowest deck was for animals; the second deck reserved from human beings, and the third deck contained the birds.

Whichever design these traditions may have had in mind, there is irrefutable evidence that large cargo ships did ply the waters of the Mediterranean and the Red Sea as early as the Old Kingdom in Egypt (ca. 2500 B.C.), as detailed wall paintings suggest. This would put these vessels in the same time frame as the earliest Babylonian epics. The oldest shipwrecks that have actually been recovered from the Mediterranean date from the

Late Bronze Age (1550-1200 B.C.E.), which still predates the earliest written version of Genesis by several hundred years.

An Egyptian miniature boat, Middle Kingdom, 11th dynasty, ca. 2000 B.C.E.

In the Qur'an, the ark begins to take shape. The people who pass by Noah's house see the old man at work on his boat, and laugh at him. "Laugh all you want," Noah says, "for surely we will laugh at you" (Q 11:38). While this scene does not appear it Genesis, it is familiar from several rabbinic writings, where people mock Noah with equal gusto.

At last the great ship is finished, and God says, "Carry in it two of all things, a pair, and your own family – except the non-believers" (Q 11:40). And, says Genesis, Noah went in with his sons, his wife, and his sons' wives, "and a pair of every living thing of flesh, male and female; every kind of birds, and every kind of cattle, and every kind of creeping thing" (G 6:19-20).

Just as great fountains begin to well up from the deep, and the windows of the heavens let loose a torrent of rain, an incident occurs that is only related in the Qur'an. In the sura *Nuh*, Noah had urged God to cleanse the earth of all who had rebuffed him, saying, "my Lord, leave not one single unbeliever on the land!" (Q 71.26). But now, as the waters begin to rise, Noah is shocked to see his own son Canaan back on shore. Canaan has refused to embark with the rest of his family.

Noah is deeply vexed. "O my son!" he cries out, "embark with us, and don't remain with the nonbelievers!" But his son thinks he has a better plan. "I will find refuge on a mountain, which will protect me from the water," he says, with the utter self-confidence of youth. Noah is beside himself. "No one can save you from God's punishment, except those upon whom He shows mercy," he cries. But once again, Noah's warnings go unheeded. A large wave comes between them and carries Noah's son away, his fate now certain (Q 11:42-43). Desperate to save him, Noah makes one final appeal to God, as any father would: "My Lord! Surely my son belongs to my family, your promise is true!" But God rejects his plea. "Noah," God says sternly, "he obviously is no longer part of your family, since his deeds speak for themselves. Therefore, do not ask of Me what you do not understand" (Q 11:45-46). The boy drowns, the victim of his own folly.

AND SO, THE GREAT FLOOD comes to pass. First a cauldron of boiling water is poured out over mankind. Next, God "sent the clouds pouring rain on them in abundance," says sura 6, "and We made rivers flowing beneath them. Thus they were destroyed because of their faults" (Q 6.6). All of the earth was covered with water, and every living thing, man and woman, and every kind of animal, every plant and tree perished in the deluge. "All in whose nostrils was the breath of life," says Genesis, "of all that once roamed on dry land, was now dead. Only Noah remained alive, and those that were with him in the ark" (G 7:22-23).

At last, the Qur'an tells us, God decreed that it was enough. He said, "O earth, swallow your water; O cloud, clear away. And the waters did abate; and the matter was decided." And when the last of the rivers had receded, "the ark rested on Mount Judi" (Q 11:44). *Al-Judi*, today called Djudi in Turkish, is the name of a mountain range in southeastern Turkey, close to the border with Iraq. But it is not clear whether the Quranic 'Judi' actually refers to this Turkish location. Several Muslim commentators have sought to place it in Arabia proper, close to Mecca. That has not stopped many pious Muslims from visiting Mount Djudi in Turkey, as countless plaques and votives attest.

Genesis, on the other hand, claims that the ark came to rest "on the mountains of Ararat" (G 8:4). *Harê Ararat,* the plural of "mountains of Ararat", has often been mistaken for the singular *mount Ararat,* the name given to the tallest mountain on the border of Turkey and Armenia. Mount Ararat is in fact a volcano, which rises to an elevation of some 17,000 ft. This mountain continues to enjoy visits as well, in this case from scores of Christian tour groups, in the firm belief that this is where the ark once stood. But in truth, the exact location of the mountain described in Genesis is equally uncertain. In fact, the Book of Jubilees states that the ark came to rest in a different peak in the Ararat mountain range, called Lubar.

View of Mount Ararat from Khor Virap in Armenia
(Courtesy, Seçkin resimler)

DESPITE THE DESTRUCTION CAUSED by these great floods, the Sumerian civilization continued to prosper. Temples dedicated to the principal gods rose from the plains, paid for out of the national purse. These temples not only contained statues representing the gods, but also figurines of the human faithful – perhaps to assure these gods that they were attended by round-the-clock worship.

These statuettes show both male and female worshippers dressed in fringed skirts or gowns, and with clasped hands -- no doubt a Sumerian gesture of deep-felt piety. The eyes are large and exaggerated, often marked with a thin trace of paint, while the men invariably wear long and carefully stylized beards. Some of these oldest figures date from around 2700 B.C.E. and are now in the Antiquities Museum of Iraq in Baghdad.

Statue of Ebih-Il, a priest at the temple of Ishtar in Mari, about 2400 B.C.E.

Many of these Sumerian temples used the motif of a stepped pyramid or *ziggurat*. One such structure stood in the Sumerian city of Uruk (or Erech in the Bible). It was perched on a walled-in sacred enclosure measuring 1000 acres -- an astounding feat in the 3rd millennium B.C.E. In the heart of this fabled city, whose enormous walls are extolled in the *Gilgamesh Epic*, stood the square tower, which tapered upwards to support a vast square platform at its summit, accessible through ramps.

A thousand years later, another square pyramid of truly massive proportions rose in Ur, dedicated to the moon god Nanna. This ziggurat, now partly restored, still stands at Tell al-Muqayyar in southern Iraq. It was built in the time of king Ur-Nammu (2112 - 2095 B.C.E.), and remained standing up to the Persian conquest in the 6th century B.C.E.

The partly restored ziggurat of Ur, ca. 2100 B.C.E.

Ur was then superseded by Babylon as the religious and political center of Mesopotamia, and under king Hammurabi it rose as the capital of a vast new Babylonian empire. Here rose another ziggurat, this time dedicated to the god Marduk (whom we previously encountered in the *Epic of Creation*). So renowned was this towering temple platform that it was carefully restored by Nebuchadnezzar II in the 6th century B.C.E. Most scholars therefore assume that this ziggurat may have formed the inspiration for the Tower of Babel story.

In the Islamic tradition, the story of Babel begins once Noah has settled in Babylon after the flood. The Hadith tradition reports that many generations later, two fallen angels, Harut and Marut, were condemned to serve time in Babylon as prisoners. But once in the city, the angels began to study the arts of magic, and were soon able to infect the people of Babylon with their evil sorcery.

What kind of black magic were these angels accused of practicing? A new and mysterious art -- the art of building tall buildings, such as a tower, or a *ziggurat*. This is what the people of Babylon or *Babel,* in their infinite pride and hubris, immediately proceed to erect. "And they said, 'Let us build a city and tower'," Genesis tells us, "whose top may reach unto heaven; and let us make a name for ourselves" (G11:4). The name 'Babylon' is derived from the Akkadian *bab-ili,* or "gate of the gods."

Up to this point, says Genesis, "the whole earth was of one language, and of one speech," but that changed when "the Lord came down to see the city and the tower which the children of men had built." Rather than destroying this monstrous structure, God adroitly "confounded their language," so that they did not understand each other's speech. "They learned from them the means to sow discord between man and wife," the Qur'an says; "and they learned what harmed them, not what profited them" (Q 2:102). Confused, unable to communicate, the proud builders left the city to be "scattered abroad" (G 11:1-8). The name of the city was "Babel," says the Bible, one example of the many double-entendres that this Genesis tradition is fond of, since the word *babil* means gate, while *balal* in Hebrew means 'sowing confusion', like the English *babble*.

It is interesting to note, however, that the first association between a ziggurat and linguistic confusion is not made in the Bible, but in a Sumerian myth about the very first ziggurat, the one in Uruk. According to this legend, king Enmerkar of Uruk was busy assembling his huge platform when a shortage of materials compelled him to demand supplies from tributary lands. To ensure that they heeded his royal order expediently, he invoked the god Enki to ensure that all of the populated regions in his realm worshipped in the same language; and that if they refused his decree, the god Enki should disrupt their linguistic unity by way of revenge.

NEITHER THE QUR'AN NOR the Bible actually describe the destruction of the Tower of Babel, though it is inferred that the project was left unfinished. And so it appears, as a hulking ruin, in countless drawings and paintings, most famously the magnificent vision of Pieter Brueghel the Elder from 1563, inspired by depictions of the Coliseum in Rome.

The Tower of Babel, by Pieter Brueghel the Elder (1563)

But later Islamic authors offer a more satisfying end of the story. The renowned 10th century author al-Tabari tells us that the Tower of Babel was originally built by the mythical king Nimrod, great-grandson of Noah (whom Genesis also cites as the builder of Babylon), and that the tower was subsequently destroyed by God. At the same time, al-Tabari writes, the primordial language of humankind was fragmented into no less than seventy-two different tongues. Another author, the 13th century Muslim commentator Abu al-Fida, argues that only one man was allowed to keep his primordial language, since he had not participated in the construction of the infamous tower. This language, Abu al-Fida writes, was Hebrew. Jewish traditions would agree. The name of this righteous man was Eber, and as Genesis tells us, he was the ancestor of a man called Abraham.

SUMER'S ARCHITECTURAL TALENTS, HOWEVER, were not limited to the building of temples alone. The royal tombs in Ur, for example, feature fully developed arches some 3,000 years before the appearance of Roman architecture. The so-called 'Royal Standard', a block of wood decorated with scenes in copper and lapis lazuli, shows us another Sumerian invention: the wheel-borne wagon.

The 'Royal Standard of Ur', ca. 2600 B.C.E.

It was still an awkward contraption to be sure, this solid wooden wheel (the spoked wheel did not appear until 1800

B.C.E.), but with it the Sumerians had established a form of transportation that endures to this day.

Perhaps the greatest legacy of Sumerian civilization was its revolutionary concept of a moral code -- a body of laws that governed and sustained a just and peace-loving society. This Sumerian code, the fruit of hundreds of years of human experimentation, was first written down and codified by a Babylonian warrior king named Hammurabi, who ruled over Sumaria after its absorption in the First or 'Old Babylonian Empire from 1792 to 1750 B.C.E. It was Hammurabi who collected, organized and documented the extant laws of the region, and made them known on *stele* or stone pillars throughout the Empire.

GIVEN THE RICH HISTORY OF Sumer, it is perhaps not by accident that Genesis places the origins of Abraham in Ur. After all, Ur had stood at the very beginning of that great experiment of human civilization. But why would Abraham's father, "a man called Terah", pack up his family and leave Ur for an uncertain fate in a distant land?

Recent excavations and cuneiform tablets can give us a clue. As early as 24th century B.C.E., Sumer was overrun by a Semitic group of people known as the Akkadians. The Akkadian king, Sargon of Akkad (2334-2279 B.C.E.) was the first to consolidate the region's city-states into one cohesive empire. Sargon did not establish his residence in Ur or any of the other cities down south, but further north in Akkad, close to the future site of Babylon. One reason for this move, scholars believe, was the growing realization that the irrigation system of the Sumerian plain was in decay. The far-flung network had led to excessive evaporation and increased saline levels. Cuneiform records from the period show a dramatic drop in crop yields. Entire estates may have been abandoned.

We do not know if Sumer's decline spurred Sargon to expand his kingdom, but we do know that Sargon began a policy of aggressive conquest that would set the precedent for nearly two millennia of brutal aggression by Mesopotamian rulers, from Sargon to Ashurbanipal. Sargon's grandson Naram-Sin (2254-2218 B.C.E.) followed in his footsteps, as evidenced by the magnificent *stele* that is now the prized possession of the Louvre in Paris. It shows the triumphant king at the top of a mountain summit under the protection of two astral deities, reveling in his victory over the Lullubi (a group of people who lived at the border of today's Iraq and Iran). Proudly holding his bow and arrow, the king looks down on his victims, who are either dead or dying – the first of many Babylonian representations of brazen military conquest.

Stele of Naram-Sin (2254-2218 B.C.E.)

Stylistically speaking, the Louvre stele is carved with unprecedented naturalism. The naked torso of the king is carefully moulded so as to suggest living flesh, articulated by muscle and bone -- a far cry from the stiff, stylized 'temple worshippers' we saw earlier.

The stele only marks one of Naram-Sim's spectacular victories. By 2218 B.C.E., at the end of his reign, the First Babylonian Empire encompassed all of Assyria, Syria and major parts of Turkey. The orientation of these conquests was no accident, for it followed the direction of the main international caravan routes.

As we have seen, trade had become an important factor in Mesopotamian economy. Sumer had been able to barter its large agricultural surplus (including woven textiles) in exchange for goods it did not have, specifically raw materials like metal, wood and precious stones. To sustain this growing import/export business, Sumerian traders established trading posts along the principal caravan routes.

Around 2150 B.C.E., the Akkadian period came to an end under pressure of a new invasion of foreign tribes, known as the Guti. The central government system once established by Sargon dissolved, and the ancient Sumerian city-states were able to re-establish themselves as the dominant centers of power. But this Neo-Sumerian period was relatively short-lived. Even while the city of Ur prospered under the reign of Ur-Nammu (2112-2095 B.C.E.), a new wave of Semitic tribes began to filter into the Mesopotamian plain. Historians refer to them as the Amorites. By the time of the last ruler of Ur, king Ibbi-Sin, the Amorites were powerful enough to subdue many of the city-states and put an end to the Third Dynasty of Ur.

Rivalry between these foreign clans led to a long period of civil war. In time, these warring citystates would congeal to a new and powerful entity, ruled by a new dynasty of Babylonian kings; but around 1900 B.C.E., this stabilizing power had not yet come about.

SOME SCHOLARS BELIEVE THAT it was around this date, between 1900 and 1850 B.C.E., that many inhabitants of Ur decided to abandon the city. Quite possibly, Terah was one of them. Perhaps he was a merchant who had seen much of his trade evaporate in the turmoil of war between the Amorite tribes. This is perhaps the reason why he gathered his family, his servants and his flock, and set out in search of shelter and safety.

The Bible says that Terah settled in the region of today's southern Turkey. It was a natural choice. Some 300 years after Sargon, there were still several flourishing Sumerian trading posts located here. Recent excavations have brought to light one such colony near Kayseri in central Turkey. Using pottery shards, archaeologists were able to date the site to 1920 B.C.E. – mere decades before the putative date of Terah's journey.

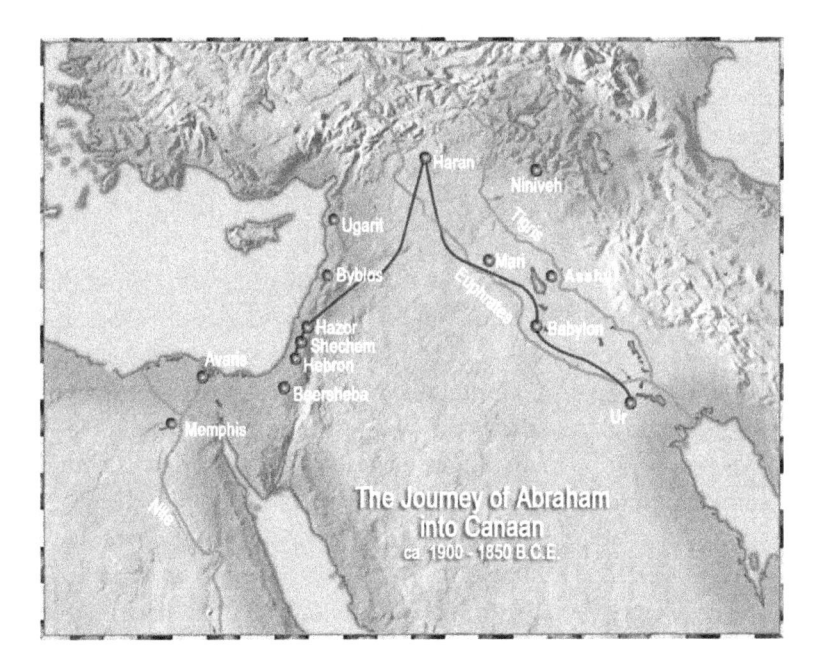

The Journey of Abraham into Canaan ca. 1900 – 1850 B.C.E.

To reach his destination, Terah probably took the principal trade route between Ur and the Mediterranean. For many centuries, this road had been the main conduit of trade between Mesopotamia and the Egyptian Empire, with a steady flow of gold, silver and obsidian going one way, and textiles, cereals and other agricultural products going the other. Several times per month, great caravans would gather and embark on the long journey towards the Turkish border. From there, they would turn south along the Mediterranean coast, through the land of Canaan, and on to the very frontiers of Greater Egypt.

But Terah did not go this far. His destination, as the Book of Genesis tells us, was Haran. This city was located on the left bank of the Balikh river, a tributary of the Euphrates, near today's frontier between Turkey and Syria. It was likewise populated by Amorites who spoke a local Semitic dialect called Akkadian, and worshipped many gods of Sumerian origin.

Haran was a fertile place at the time, with vast stretches of cedar forests that were the envy of the ancient world. The climate was temperate, and the meadows were green. Terah's flocks, exhausted from the long journey through desert land, grazed and were content. It was a good land, and perhaps that's why Terah decided his family should settle here for good. But it was not to be.

IN TYPICAL MESOPOTAMIAN FAMILY clans like Abraham's, the father, the *patriarch* ruled supreme. It was he who chose the place where the families would pitch their tents; who planned the daily routine of herding and grazing, and supervised the men going about their various tasks. He was also chiefly responsible for maintaining friendly relations with other nomadic groups around them.

In the Qur'an, however, the relationship between Abraham (or *Ibrahim*) and his father (here called *Azar*) is deeply strained, The reason is Azar's continued worship of his tribal idols. Abraham decides to question his father's friends, who obviously have a bad influence on Azar. "What are these images that you so desire to worship?" he asks. "Why," they respond, "we found our fathers worshipping them," so why shouldn't they? "Well," says Abraham laconically, "then certainly both you and your fathers were seriously mistaken" (Q21:52-54). Elsewhere in the Qur'an, Abraham confronts his father and says, "Why do you worship that what can neither hear nor see, nor avail you in the least?" The father angrily retorts, "What, do you dislike my gods, Abraham? If you do not desist, I will cast you out and send you away for a while." But Abraham decides to leave on his own accord.

In Genesis, the story of Abraham's clash with his father's family over idol worship is not explicit. Nevertheless, some form of a "break" is implied when God speaks to Abraham for the very first time, and tells him to "go from your country *and your kindred* and your father's house to the land that I will show you" (G 12:1, my italics). While there is no record of a dispute (and in fact, Abraham's father Terah has passed away at this point), the decision to abandon one's clan, one's land and one's rightful heritage is certainly a rather reckless move when viewed in the context of Babylonian customs. Abraham was his father's rightful heir, and as such responsible for the continuing prosperity of his family, his herds and his clan. Yet Abraham is prepared to turn his back on them, and follow an uncertain path to Canaan, down south, as his Lord has instructed him. For God has given him the promise that "I will make of thee a great nation."

But how unprecedented is Abraham's God, who is called *El* in Genesis? Cuneiform tablets discovered in 1929 among the ruins of the ancient city of Ugarit, near Tell Ras Shamra, Syria, help us to place the Abrahamaic *El* in the context of other deities in Syria and Canaan. In Ugaritic mythology, a divinity named *El* was the supreme head of the pantheon of gods, father of creation, not unlike the role of the pagan *Allah* in pre-Islamic Arabia. Even Baal, the god of Rain, Dew and Wind who controlled the fate of the harvest, was subservient to the authority of *El*:

> To El of the Sources of the Floods
> In the midst of the headwaters of the Two Oceans
> At El's feet he bows and falls down,
> Prostrates himself, doing him homage

Seen in this context, Abraham's worship of the pre-Israelite *El* may be less radical than we might otherwise assume. It is also noteworthy that God does not, as yet, inform Abraham that he is the *only* God, as the God of Moses, YAHWEH, will insist much later in the biblical narrative. The essential difference between the Ugaritic *El* and the Abrahamaic *El*, however, is that God takes a passionate interest in Abraham and his progeny – unlike Syriac-Canaanite deities, who cared little for the aspirations of ordinary human beings. Thus the story of Abraham is truly the starting point of the great narrative arc of the Pentateuch and the Deuteronomistic history -- the story of how across the span of hundreds of years, from the fields of Haran to the walls of Jericho, God's promise would ultimately be fulfilled.

IN GENESIS, THE STORY CONTINUES with Abraham, his wife Sarah (still called *Sarai* at this point) and his nephew Lot traveling down south with their slaves, their herds and possessions until they arrive in Canaan, the land later known as Israel. The land of Canaan, or *kena'an* in the Bible, is a small sliver of land perched between the river Jordan and the Mediterranean Sea. Egyptian records of the time refer to it as *Retenu*. The nomadic tribes who dwelled there are contemptuously described as 'Sanddwellers' or *Habiru* – which may, or may not, be the root of the word 'Hebrew.' In fact, the word Canaan was already current in Mesopotamia as early as the 16th century B.C.E., because the words *eres-kena'an* ('land of Canaan') are found in a cuneiform inscription dedicated to the ruler of Alalakh, *Idri-mi*, uncovered by Leonard Woolley in the late 1930's.

The Canaan of Abraham's time was a sparsely populated place with just a narrow strip of lush valleys surrounded by hill country. Most of the urban settlements were located closer to the coast, but Abraham preferred to stick to the hills, moving down from Hazor (just north of the Sea of Galilee) to Shechem (the Egyptian *Sekmem*) in the heart of the Samarian Mountains.

View of the Samarian Mountains near the biblical Shechem (today's Nablus)

Modern excavations have revealed that ancient Shechem was located at Tell Balata, southeast of the city known today as Nablus, across the hills of Gerizim and Eval. Shechem was a prosperous place, and Abraham paused here to erect an altar to his God *El*. God rewarded him by reiterating his promise, that "to your offspring I will give this land" (G. 12:7). A large temple platform is still visible today, but it dates from the 13th century B.C.E., and is most likely dedicated to Baal, the pre-eminent fertility god of Canaan.

From Shechem, Abraham continued down the Judean hills on his way to Beersheba, possibly passing through a small settlement which ancient Egyptian records refer to as *Rushalimum*. Many centuries later, this tiny village would blossom into the holy city of Jerusalem.

As we follow Abraham's itinerary in Genesis, it soon becomes clear that the chieftain is careful to avoid the urban centers. He seeks the solitude and safety of the high country along the Jordan, where passing nomadic tribes would hardly raise an eyebrow. Abraham was not out for conquest or territorial claims; he did not want any trouble. He simply followed the path that God had shown him, until his heart would tell him that he had arrived.

After a sojourn in Egypt (during which, in one of the more morally ambiguous passages of Genesis, Abraham consents to his wife sleeping with Pharaoh in return for a massive booty of slaves and livestock), they return to Bethel. But once they're settled, it soon becomes clear that the land they occupy cannot possibly sustain the many herds and slaves they have acquired in Egypt. Abraham and his nephew Lot discuss the matter, and agree to separate. Abraham magnanimously gives Lot first choice of the land. Lot considers his options, and decides to settle in the lush valley of the Jordan River, close to the Dead Sea, for "(he) saw that the plain was well watered everywhere like the garden of the Lord." Of course, Genesis adds, "this was before the Lord had destroyed Sodom and Gomorrah." Fatefully, Lot thereupon moves his tent "as far as Sodom," even though, as the Bible warns, "the people of Sodom were wicked, great sinners against the Lord" (G 13: 5-13). Abraham himself opts to remain in the highlands of Canaan, even though its soil is hard and dry, and vegetation, such as it is, depends on the uncertain frequency of rainfall or the occasional well.

Once the two families have split, the Lord comes and gives Abraham the covenant that will reverberate across millennia to the headlines of today: "for all the land that you see I will give to you and to your offspring forever.... Rise up, walk though the length and breadth of the land, for I will give it to you (G 13:15). And Abraham gets up, packs his tent, and moves down south, to Hebron, which in later years will serve as the southernmost boundary of Israelite settlement in the Promised Land. Today, the city is still one of the most hotly contested places in the Israeli-Palestinian conflict.

For many years, Abraham and Sarah live in Hebron, surrounded by their herds and their servants, enjoying their wealth in the sunset of their lives. They are content, except for one thing. Abraham and Sarah are childless.

Chapter Five
Ishmael and Isaac

Abraham urgently needs a son, an heir. If he dies childless, his tribe will be rent by internal strife, with many pretenders jockeying for power. Vexed by this quandary, Abraham and his wife Sarah fall back on a custom as old as the Babylonian lands whence they came from. An Assyrian marriage contract from the 19th century B.C.E., for example, stipulates that if the bride cannot bear children within the first two years of marriage, she must purchase a slave woman as a "surrogate mother," to bear a child for her husband. And indeed, in Genesis it is Sarah who suggests this arrangement to her husband, and then selects a suitable surrogate from her train of maids.

According to this stele listing the Laws of Hammurabi (of which only the top is shown), a barren wife is expected to procure a concubine to beget children for her husband (1750 B.C.E.)

And, as it happens, among the many slaves whom Sarah and Abraham brought back from Egypt is a comely Egyptian girl named Hagar.

Hagar then becomes a key protagonist of the story in both the Bible and the Qur'an. In the Islamic tradition, her prominence is so great that multiple legends are told about her origins in the *Tafsir* literature. According to one tradition, Hagar (or *Hajar* in Arabic) was not a slave girl in Pharaoh's retinue, but his daughter. Perhaps this is inspired by the reference in Genesis that Pharaoh thought Sarah was Abraham's sister, rather than his wife, and slept with her. By way of compensation, the king then gave his daughter Hagar to Abraham in marriage. The point of this legend, naturally, is to establish Hagar as Abraham's legitimate spouse, rather than his concubine.

Another Muslim tradition adds a refinement to this story, in that Hagar was originally the daughter of the King of Maghreb, who in turn was a descendant of a prophet named Saleh. According to the Qur'an, this prophet (who is sometimes equated with Shelah, son of Judah in the Bible) lived nine generations after Noah, and tried to convince his fellow citizens to abandon their idolatry, as Abraham did. Unfortunately, the king of Maghreb was killed by Pharaoh, who then took the princess Hagar as a slave. But because of her noble blood and bearing, Hagar soon became one of the leading women at Pharaoh's court. Pharaoh thereupon gave Hagar to Sarah, to give to Abraham.

The purpose of these traditions is manifold: one, to affirm Hagar's high social standing despite her status as a slave in the Bible; two, to place her in line with one of Islam's earliest prophets, thus establishing her religious credentials; and three, to document the legitimacy of her union with Abraham, and thus by extension that of her offspring.

IN GENESIS, ABRAHAM, ever the dutiful husband, has no objection to what Sarah suggests. He takes the girl to his tent and proceeds to sleep with her. In due course the girl finds out she's pregnant. Everyone is overjoyed, Hagar included. She soon realizes that she is now an important personage, for she quite literally carries the future of the clan in her belly. This is heady stuff for a young teenager, and so we're not surprised to learn that little Hagar begins to develop an attitude, and "looked with contempt on her mistress" (G 16:4). Here is a triangle as old as human passion itself. What is Sarah to do? Naturally, she fights back; she goes to her husband and prevails on him to get rid of this girl. Abraham, not known for firmness in domestic matters, meekly agrees.

And so the poor girl, her belly swollen with child, is sent to the desert where she undoubtedly would have perished, where it not for the intervention of an angel of the Lord. This angel finds Hagar near a spring (since natural wells often have a sacral significance in both the Bible and the Qur'an), and urges her to swallow her pride and submit to her mistress. The angel also tells her that she will bear a son; "you shall call him Ishmael, for the Lord has given heed to your affliction."

This notion that the Lord has heard her plight is enshrined in the boy's name: *Ishmael*, a contraction of *El* (the Lord) and *shama'* (hears), means "God hears (me)". And then the angel makes an astonishing promise, saying that the Lord "will so greatly multiply your offspring that they cannot be counted for multitude" – a promise which shortly will be extended to Abraham's other son Isaac as well (G 16:1-13). Later on, this pledge to Ishmael will be reiterated by God himself:

> As for Ishmael, I have heard you;
> I will bless him and make him fruitful and
> exceedingly numerous;
> He shall be the father of twelve princes, and I will make
> Him a great nation. (G 17:20-21)

Thirteen years go by before God re-appears to Abraham to conclude his covenant. "I will make nations of you, and kings shall come from you," God tells Abraham. This covenant is sealed with the act of circumcision; henceforth, all male children born from Abraham's issue, starting with Ishmael, are circumcised on the eighth day after birth (G 17:6; 10-14). In the Jewish faith, this rite of *Brit milah* has been faithfully observed from that very day; but it is also observed by many Muslims. Circumcision (*Khitan* in Arabic) is not required by the Qur'an, but the Hadith report that Muhammad himself was circumcised, and that the Prophet insisted that his sons undergo the rite by the seventh day after birth as well.

Today, the question whether circumcision as an Abrahamaic rite is obligatory for Muslims is fiercely debated, usually along factional lines. The majority consensus among Muslim scholars is that whereas circumcision is recommended, it is not considered mandatory, since such a commandment is missing from the Qur'an. Even so, Islamic circumcision is widely practiced, though usually not shortly after birth. In many Islamic cultures, boys are circumcised between the ages of seven and twelve, as part of an elaborate puberty rite, which also involves the young boy reciting from the Qur'an.

SHORTLY AFTER THESE EVENTS, Abraham has pitched his tents in the plain of Mamre, a wide and fertile valley close to a Canaanite shrine dedicated to the Syrian god *El*. While his servants are tending to his flocks, Abraham is dozing in the heat of the afternoon, sitting just under the overhang of his tent, when three strangers appear before him. It is a momentous visit, for the message brought by these strangers will have a tremendous impact on our story and indeed, the future of Judaism and Islam. Not surprisingly, the visit is described in vivid detail in both Genesis and the Qur'an. Abraham, says Genesis, "looked up and saw three men standing near him." With typical Near Eastern hospitality, Abraham rushes out to greet them, well aware that the strangers must be thirsty and perhaps in need of food. "Let a little water be brought, and wash your feet, and rest yourselves under the tree," he urges them in the Qur'an (Q18:1-4). "Peace, they said, and Peace, said he, and made no delay in bringing a roasted calf" (Q 11:69). And Abraham "took a calf, tender and good, and gave it to the servant who hastened to prepare it," Genesis adds.

When the strangers are seated and everyone in the camp is running around making preparations for this impromptu lunch, one of the visitors clears his throat and casually asks, "Where is your wife Sarah?" And (Abraham) said, "There, in the tent." Then one said, "I will surely return to you in due season, and your wife Sarah shall have a son" (G 18:9).

In both Scriptures, this prophecy leaves Abraham and Sarah dumbfounded. After all, the couple was well advanced in age, and, the Bible adds, "it had ceased to be with Sarah after the manner of women." Sarah cannot help herself and begins to laugh. "She laughed when We gave her the good news of Isaac and his son Jacob," the Qur'an says. "After I have grown old and my husband is old, shall I have pleasure?" she wonders in Genesis. But the strangers, who are obviously angels sent by the Lord, are quite serious. "Do you wonder at God's bidding?" they ask Sarah in the Qur'an. "Is anything too wonderful for the Lord?" Genesis adds.

Sarah looks the strangers in the eye and is suddenly afraid to have given offense. "I didn't laugh," she assures them quickly, and the angel says, "Oh but yes, you did laugh" (G 18:11-15; Q 11:71-73). It is not meant as a retort, but as a prophecy; for the child that Sarah will bear in nine months' time will be called Isaac, *Ishaq* in Arabic and *Yishaq* in Hebrew, which means "he who laughs."

In due course, Sarah does conceive and presents Abraham with a boy. When the child is eight days old, Abraham circumcises his son and gives him his name, *Isaac*. According to ancient custom, giving a child his name (and his patronymic) was an act by which a man accepted a child as his. "Praise be to God, Who has given me in old age Ishmael and Isaac," Abraham exults in the Qur'an; "most surely my Lord is the Hearer of prayer" (Q 14:39).

But not all is well in the Abraham household. Genesis tells us how one day, when Isaac has grown to be a toddler, Sarah spots him playing with his half-brother, Ishmael. Seeing the two children together raises the urgent question of the family's birthright: who will inherit the leadership of the clan – and by extension, the covenant with the Lord?

Sarah decides that the only way to settle the question is to evict Hagar and Ishmael from the clan. "Cast out this slave woman with her son," she tells Abraham peremptorily; "for the son of this slave woman shall not inherit along with my son Isaac." And, Genesis continues, "the matter was very distressing to Abraham on account of his son," as we can well imagine. How to choose between these two sons whom Abraham loves in equal measure? But God intervenes. He tells Abraham to do as Sarah suggests, for "it is through Isaac that offspring shall be named for you." But Abraham should not be concerned for Ishmael, for, says God, "I will make a nation of him also, because he is your offspring" (G 21:1-13).

His conscience thus somewhat assuaged, Abraham breaks the news to Hagar. She and her son will have to go. On the morning of her departure, he rises early, just to ensure that she and her son will be well provisioned for the long journey back to Egypt from whence she came. Hagar and her teenage son duly set off into the wilderness, but as everyone should have known, the young girl has no experience in desert survival, nor in charting her course through the wilderness of Sinai. Her voyage is doomed. She has barely passed Beer-sheba (where Abraham himself will settle soon) when she finds herself utterly lost. After several days of aimless wandering, Hagar collapses near some shrubs. There is no more food and water; the sun is beating mercilessly on their heads. Ishmael is semi-conscious. She cannot bear to see her own son die, so she gently places him in the shade of a nearby tree. The child rolls over and moans softly, his lips parched and cracked with thirst. Hagar falls to her knees and cries. It is a heartbreaking scene.

Hagar and the Angel, by Giovanni Battista Tiepolo (1732)

Fortunately, the Lord has not forgotten about Ishmael and his mother. An angel of the Lord calls out from heaven: "Do not be afraid; for God has heard the voice of the boy where he is. Come, lift up the boy and hold him fast with your hand, for I will make a great nation of him" (G21:15-18). God opens Hagar's eyes, and she spots a well of water nearby. They rushed over and drink to their fill.

Thus fortified, Genesis assures us, "the boy grew up in the desert and became an expert with the bow. He lived in the wilderness of Paran" (G 21:20-21). *Paran* is a region in the northeastern part of the Sinai peninsula, close to the large oasis of Qadish Barnea, which in turn was about a week's journey from the Egyptian border at Pelusium. When the boy reaches maturity, Hagar may have traveled down this road to procure a wife for her son, for as Genesis tells us, she "got a wife for him from the land of Egypt."

In the Islamic tradition, however, things work out differently. Hagar is never mentioned by name in the Qur'an, but stories about her are plentiful in the various Hadith. According to one tradition, Abraham accompanied Hagar and Ishmael into the desert and led them as far as Paran (or *Faran* in Arabic). However, this particular Paran is not located in Sinai but in Arabia proper – close to the future city of Mecca. Once in Paran, God decides to test Abraham and orders him to leave Hagar and his son. Abraham reluctantly does so, and before long, the Genesis scene is repeated as Ishmael is dying of thirst, and Hagar frantically searches for water.

As it happens, the valley where Hagar and Ishmael find themselves is ringed by towering peaks. In her desperation, Hagar runs between two mountains, al-Safa and al-Marwa, climbing them repeatedly in the hope of finding a well. When she climbs the mountain a seventh time, the angel Gabriel finally intervenes. He strikes the earth with his staff, water pours forth, and Hagar and her boy are saved (though in another version, Ishmael strikes his foot on the soil to release the spring). This sacred well still exists in Mecca today. It is called Zamzam, and the rite of walking between the two mountains seven times, known as the *sa'y*, is re-enacted every year as part of the *hajj*, the pilgrimage to Mecca.

SOON AFTER HAGAR HAS LEFT the clan, God decides to put Abraham to another test. This poignant episode, which appears in both the Bible and the Qur'an, is referred to as the Binding of Isaac, or the *Akedah* in the Jewish tradition, and *Dhabih* in Arabic. God says to Abraham, "take your son, your only son Isaac, whom you love, and go to the land of Moriah, and offer him there as a burnt offering on one of the mountains that I shall show you" (G22:2). Abraham is deeply shocked, but he does as he is told.

In Genesis, he goes about the preparations for this horrific sacrifice without telling anyone. He then takes a donkey, for Moriah is a three-day march north of Hebron; later, Jewish and Islamic tradition will associate Mount Moriah with Temple Mount in Jerusalem.

In the Qur'an, however, Abraham cannot restrain himself. "O my Son!" he cries; "I have seen in a dream that I must sacrifice you; what do you think of that?" But Ishmael is calm. Despite his young age, he is ready to subject himself (*muslim*) to the will of God, whatever that may be. "Father," he replies, "do what you are ordered; if it is God's will, you will find me patient and ready" (Q 37:102).

In Genesis, Abraham, his son and two servants now set out on their tragic journey. When Abraham spots Mount Moriah in the distance, he orders the two servants to wait with the donkey; "the boy and I will go over there; we will worship, and then we will come back to you." But as soon as Isaac and his father begin the climb, Isaac senses that something is amiss. "Father," he asks, "the fire and the wood are here, but where is the lamb for a burnt offering?" Abraham responds, "God himself will provide the lamb for a burnt offering, my son." They arrive at the designated spot, and Abraham busies himself with building an altar and creating a wooden pyre. Then, no doubt with tears in his eyes, he binds Isaac, and places him on the altar on top of the wood.

This moment, so laden with drama, has produced many wonderful legends in the *Hadith* literature. In one story, the boy asks his father to pull the ropes tight, so that he will not be able squirm. In another, the young victim tells Abraham to push his clothes away from the spot where the knife will strike, so that Abraham can return the garments to his mother without any evidence of blood. Abraham thereupon kisses his son, and his tears run freely.

In Genesis, Abraham raises his knife. But just as the blade is about to plunge in the child's body, an angel intervenes.

"Abraham!" the angel calls out, "do not lay your hand on the boy or do anything to him, for now I know that you fear God." In the Qur'an, it is God who calls to Abraham, and says, "You have indeed shown the truth of the vision; and so we will reward the does of good. This was indeed an important test." (Q 27:104-6). The Abraham of Genesis then spots a ram caught in a thicket by its horns. He takes it, and offers the animal up to God instead (G 22:13). As the Qur'an puts it: "And so We ransomed him with a mighty sacrifice" (Q 37:107).

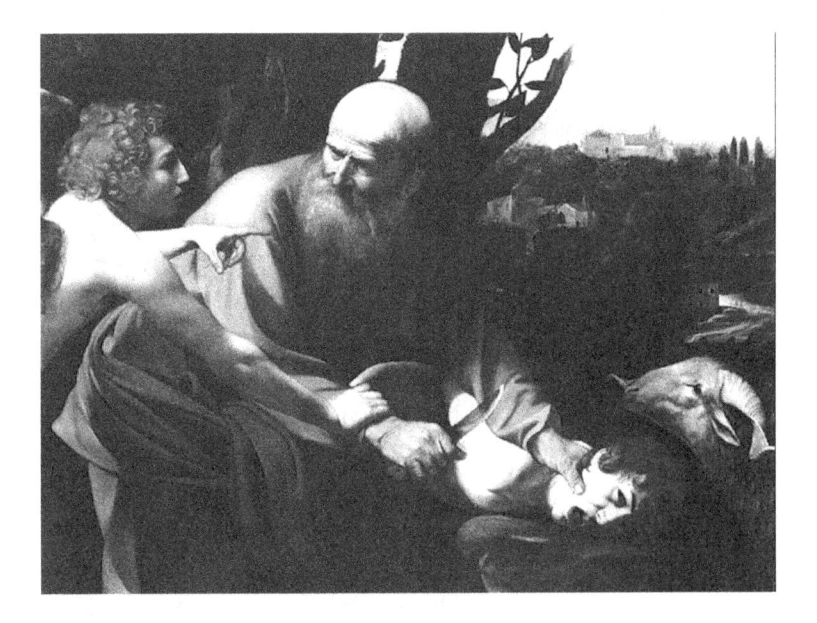

Caravaggio, The Sacrifice of Isaac (1603)

As many authors have pointed out, the story of Abraham sacrificing his son is one of the great episodes in the biblical tradition. It is told with immense skill and great sensitivity for Abraham's obvious distress. And yet it is filled with horror. How on earth, we wonder, could God ask such a terrible thing: to sacrifice one's child, one's own flesh and blood?

The answer is that child sacrifice *in extremis* was common in the Stone Age. In Ur, for example, human sacrifice often took place at the death of an important lord or his consort. When excavating Ur's Royal Tombs, the British archaeologist Sir Leonard Woolley discovered that important figures were invariably accompanied in the grave by anywhere from six to eighty servants, put to death at the moment of their lord's internment. Since there was no sign of fatal injuries, Woolley theorized that these servants drank poison, or a sleeping drug, before being entombed. But there are many examples of human sacrifice in the Bible as well.

During the war between Moab and the kingdoms of Israel and Judah, for example, when it "became clear that the battle was going against him," the king of Moab "took his firstborn son who was to succeed him, and offered him as a burnt offering on the wall." Child sacrifice was also practiced as part of the Phoenician cult of Ba'al, known as Moloch in Canaan. The Torah had to explicitly forbid Jews to "give any of your children to devote them by fire to Moloch, and so profane the name of your God" (Leviticus 18:21). Nevertheless, young children were still being sacrificed as late as the 7th century B.C.E., in the Valley of Hinnom below Jerusalem, as Jeremiah attests (Jer 32:35).

A cryptic reference in the Qur'an suggests that Arabia before Islam was no stranger to child sacrifice either. "Thus were the idol worshipers duped by their idols," says sura 6, *Livestock,* "to the extent of killing their own children." The point of Abraham's sacrifice in the Qur'an, then, is essentially the same as in Genesis: God puts mankind on notice that he will not tolerate such cruel and inhuman practices. But the story also serves to emphasize the theme of obedience, of supreme and total submission to God's will, even if it meant the killing of someone whom Abraham loved above all. Love for God must trump all other bonds.

But which son is the Qur'an referring to: Isaac or Ishmael? The boy is unnamed, and many early commentators accepted, perhaps based on biblical precedent, that the victim was Isaac. Later writings inferred that the Qur'an is talking about Ishmael, for it is only further down in this same sura that we hear that "We gave him the good news of Isaac, a prophet among the good ones" (Q 37:112). Since the son's willingness to be sacrificed ultimately sealed him as the one and true progenitor of God's chosen people, many Muslim commentators have argued that the Qur'an is talking about Ishmael as the father of God's nation under Islam; if it had been Isaac, the line would have favored Judaism and Christianity. "[There is] no doubt that *Ishma'il ben Ibrahim* (Ishmael son of Abraham) is a father for the Prophet [Muhammad] and his Household," says Al-Hasani Al-'amili in his *The Prophets, Their Lives and Their Stories*; "for if Ishmael was slain, then all of this holy tree would have been lost." Indeed, so important is the episode of the near-sacrifice in Islamic tradition that it is celebrated every year as part of the *Eid ul-Adha* festival. During this festival, Muslims roast the meat of a sheep, cow or camel, and share it with their family, as well as the poor and needy.

RELIEVED BEYOND MEASURE, Abraham packs up his donkey, and returns to his family. They move to Beersheba, where they live in peace, content to see the herds prosper. Until one day, the harsh climate of the Negev becomes too much for the ailing Sarah. Abraham pulls up the stakes of his tent and returns to the gentler climate of Hebron, where breezes from the valley cool the city on the hill. But Sarah never quite recovers; eventually, she dies in Abraham's arms. Deeply saddened, Abraham looks for a suitable tomb, and settles on the Cave of Machpelah.

When many years later, Abraham dies as well, he is interred in a tomb close to her. Abraham's son Isaac, his wife Rebekah and grandson Jacob all find their final resting place here, making the Cave Machpelah the family tomb of the patriarchs.

*The Cave of the Patriarchs in Hebron, including the walls
erected by King Herod (late 1st century B.C.E.)*

The Cave of Machpelah is still believed to exist - it is one of very few archeological sites that are associated with the figure of Abraham, and perhaps the oldest shrine in Judaism. Located in Hebron, it was venerated for many centuries until in the 1st century B.C.E., Herod the Great built a vast mausoleum over the site. Allowing for various additions, this Herodian structure has remained largely intact to this day. Herod conceived the shrine as a vast wall surrounding the six principal tombs of the cave. The entire mortuary compound originally measured some 215 ft by 115 ft, adorned with flat Hellenistic pilasters reminiscent of those that surrounded the Second Temple in Jerusalem. The same finely chiseled masonry, hewn with almost machine-like precision, can be seen on the recently excavated walls of the Herodian complex on the bottom of Temple Mount.

During the Byzantine period, the mausoleum became a Christian basilica. After the Islamic conquest, it was converted to a mosque. In the 9th century C.E., the Fatimid caliphs built a new entrance in the northeastern wall and added domes to cover the tombs of Abraham and Sarah. They also added a large hostel for pilgrims.

In Crusader days, the inner shrine was once again converted to a church. These Crusader columns and capitals were then put to use in the construction of the Islamic pulpit, after Salah al-Din reconquered Hebron and the Cave became a mosque once again.

It today's charged political climate, it has remained a controversial site – not in the least, perhaps, because the Cave is equally revered by Jews, Christians and Muslims.

Chapter Six
Joseph in the Land of Pharaoh

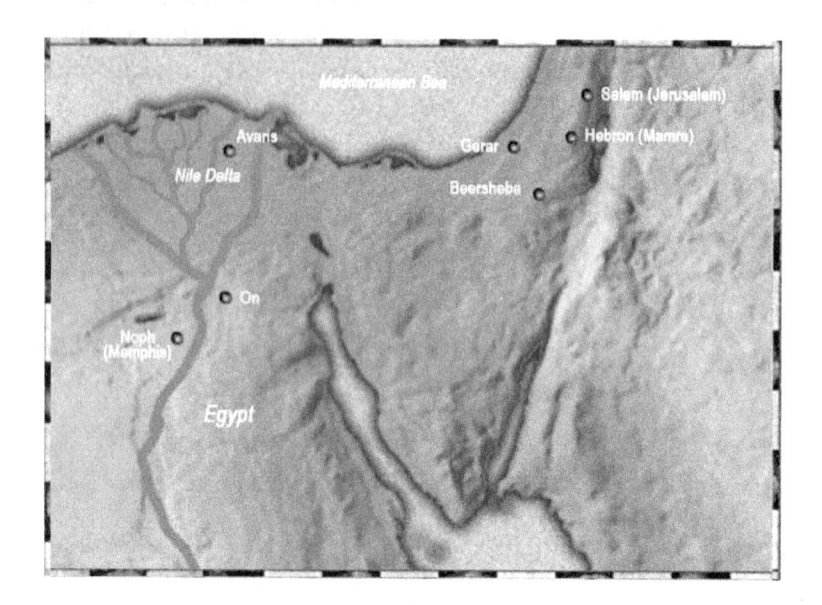

[Map showing the Nile Delta, Egypt, and surrounding regions with labels: Mediterranean Sea, Avaris, Nile Delta, Gerar, Salem (Jerusalem), Hebron (Mamre), Beersheba, On, Noph (Memphis), Egypt]

After the death of Abraham, the patriarch's covenant with God passes to his son Isaac. Isaac marries a woman named Rebekah and has two sons: Jacob and Esau. Esau, the older of the two, is a strong and virile young man who delights in the hunt and is often gone for days on end. Jacob, on the other hand, is content to be with his herd, nurturing and shepherding his flock from one pasture to another. Here again, Genesis offers us the two principal paradigms of the early Stone Age: the hunter-gatherer vs. the domesticated shepherd and farmer.

Rebekah is told in a dream that it is her second son Jacob who should receive the birthright from his father, rather than his older brother Esau. And so it comes to pass. When Isaac is old and virtually blind, Rebekah uses an elaborate ruse to deceive her husband, who duly gives his blessing to Jacob.

Naturally, when Esau returns from one of his hunting trips, he is upset. Jacob has to flee his wrath, and ultimately winds up in the city of his ancestors, the trading post of Haran. Here, God once again affirms his covenant: that Jacob and his offspring shall have God's favor.

Haran turns out to be a fortuitous choice for Jacob. In the house of his uncle Laban, he meets a cousin named Rachel. Rachel is a beautiful young woman, and Jacob falls in love with her. Unfortunately, Laban does not want to see his beautiful daughter leave for an uncertain fate in a distant land, and he comes up with every possible excuse to keep Jacob in Haran. He even compels Jacob to marry his older daughter Leah first. Only after many years of service is Jacob finally allowed to marry his sweetheart Rachel, and take her and Leah back to Canaan.

By this time, however, Jacob has twelve sons by four different mothers. These twelve sons will go on to become the founders of Israel's Twelve Tribes. This is why Jacob is seen as the founder of Israel; indeed, it is God who changes Jacob's name to 'Israel' later in life.

Unfortunately, as often happens with families of multiple unions, there is envy among the children. Jacob's older sons by his first wife Leah -- Reuben, Simeon, Levi, Judah, Issachar, Zebulun and Dinah -- feel that Jacob and his wife Rachel lavish too much love and favor on Rachel's own son, Joseph (or *Yusuf* in the Qur'an). Joseph is the youngest, and the son of the woman whom Jacob truly loves; naturally, he is the apple of his father's eye. Oblivious to his favoritism, Jacob dotes on his son while Joseph's envious brothers watch in silent anger.

One day, Jacob decides to present Joseph with a gift: a beautiful coat, erroneously translated in the King James Bible as a "coat of many colors." The word *passim* actually denotes a "coat with long sleeves," a rare luxury for a family of shepherds. The brothers are furious. They firmly resolve that this upstart needs to be taught a lesson. All they need to do is wait for an opportunity to take 'little Joe' out of the house and put him in his place.

This is when Joseph starts having some very strange dreams. These visions only reinforce the impression that Joseph is a spoiled brat, for they seem to suggest that Joseph is placed well above the station of his brothers.

> *Genesis*
> And he said unto them, Hear, I pray you,
> this dream which I have dreamed:
> For, behold, we were binding sheaves
> in the field,
> and, lo, my sheaf arose, and also stood
> upright;
> and, behold, your sheaves stood round about,
> and made obeisance to my sheaf.
> And his brethren said to him, will you indeed
> reign over us?
> or will you indeed have dominion over us?
> And they hated him yet the more for his
> dreams, and for his words.
> (G 37:6-8)

But Joseph, in his naive enthusiasm, is deaf to their grumbling. In the Qur'an, Joseph then has another dream. He runs to his father and says, "O my father! Surely I saw eleven stars and the sun and the moon -- I saw them making obeisance to me" (Q 12.4). But Jacob understands what's going on, and urges Joseph to keep these dreams to himself: "O my son! Do not relate your vision to you brothers, lest they devise a plan against you" (Q 12.5).

Nevertheless, when Joseph hears that his brothers have taken the flocks up north, to pastures near Shechem, he decides to follow them, eager for their company. This is the moment that his brothers have been waiting for. They throw him in a well; some brothers are of a mind to kill him, right then and there. Fortunately, Judah intervenes and suggests a lesser penalty. It so happens that a caravan of merchants is passing by on its way to Egypt. The Bible calls these merchants 'Ishmaelites', although in all probability no particular meaning was intended; for the scribes of the 7th century who committed the oral traditions of Genesis to paper, 'Ishmaelites' was simply another synonym for 'Arabic tribes'. Later on, Genesis will refer to Joseph's captors as 'Midianites' -- meaning, Bedouin-type tribes living in the Midian.

The brothers know that the Egyptian nobility is always looking for able-bodied slaves. Why not sell Joseph, get rid of him and make some money in the bargain? And so, Genesis notes, Joseph was sold for 20 shekels or "silver pieces" -- which, according to contemporary inscriptions, was indeed the going rate for a mature male slave. The brothers are pleased. They watch as Joseph is led away to Egypt and a life of servitude.

Velázquez, 'Jacob Receives the bloody coat of his son Joseph' (1630)

But what shall they tell their father, who no doubt is anxiously awaiting Joseph's return? The brothers decide that Joseph has had an unfortunate accident. They spill some blood from a goat on Joseph's garments, and bring it back to Jacob, shedding crocodile tears all the way. "A beast has taken him away," they exclaim. Jacob wails and collapses in grief. "And all his sons and all his daughters rose up to comfort him," Genesis tells us, "but he refused to be comforted, and said, now I will go down into the grave mourning my son" (G. 37:35).

JOSEPH THEN ENTERS A LAND that, roughly around 1650 B.C.E., is still the greatest and most powerful nation the ancient world has ever seen. For an astonishing 1500 years, this immense Kingdom has prospered as a unified nation led by hereditary rulers or 'Pharaohs'. Boosted by the wealth of its fertile Nile Delta as well as the mines of Sinai and northern Africa, Egypt is a cultural and economic magnet, the center of a trade network that reaches as far as Greece in the North and India in the East.

The principal engine of Egypt's creativity is the cult of the dead. Ancient Egyptians believed in an afterlife that could only be secured by careful mummification of the body and the prodigious accumulation of luxury goods that would accompany the soul during its stay in the underworld. As a result, Egyptian artisans always had a limitless appetite for raw materials: timber for coffins and furniture, marble and granite for sarcophagi, silver, bronze, gold and other precious stones for adornment. Most important of all, the mummification process required the use of a number of exotic chemicals, some of which could only be procured abroad. The biblical story of Joseph has a strong basis in fact when we read that Joseph's captors carry 'balm and myrrh' to Egypt, for these were precisely the items used for mummification and the sprinkling of incense in the temples.

Eventually, Joseph is sold as a slave into the household of Potiphar, the captain of Pharaoh's Guard. Potiphar takes a liking to Joseph. Even though Joseph is evidently a *Habiru* or 'Sanddweller', Potiphar detects a keen intellect in the boy's eyes. In due course, Joseph becomes the head of the domestic staff, supervising the cooks, the maids, stable hands and personal attendants.

In 1650 B.C.E., the pyramids of Giza were already a thousand years old

Joseph has become a very handsome young man, and he soon catches the eye of Potiphar's wife. The Qur'an offers an anecdote of Joseph's beauty that is not found in the Bible. With such an attractive young lad in the house, the women in the city were bound to gossip, saying, "the wife of Potiphar seeks to seduce her slave boy; surely he has affected her deeply." Potiphar's wife, who is called Zuleikha in the Qur'an, decided to exact her revenge. She invited these women to lunch in her house. As soon as they sat down with a knife in their hands, ready to partake of the meal, she said to Joseph, 'come and join us.' "And," says the Qur'an, "as soon as they saw him, they were speechless, and cut their hands (in amazement)" (Q 12:31-32).

But the fact is that Zuleikha is indeed very attracted to Joseph. "It came to pass after these things," Genesis tells us, "that his master's wife cast her eyes upon Joseph" (G 39:7). "And she," says the Qur'an, "made for him, and he would have made for her, were it not that he had seen the manifest evidence of his Lord" (Q 12.24). "And so he refused," Genesis says. But Potiphar's wife is not so easily ignored. "She caught him by his garment, saying, Lie with me; and he fled" (G 39:12). The Qur'an agrees. "They both ran to the door and in the struggle she tore his shirt at the back. Then they met her husband at the door" (Q.12.26).

Imagine Potiphar's surprise. Zuleikha quickly cries: "What is the punishment of him who intends evil to your wife, except imprisonment or a painful chastisement?" Joseph retorts: "It was she who sought to seduce me against my will!" (Q.12.25). Who is Potiphar to believe? Naturally, he sides with his wife. And so, Joseph's master "took him, and put him into the prison" (G 39:20).

Many scholars have pointed to striking similarities between the story of Joseph and Zuleikha and the ancient Egyptian fable of "The Tale of Two Brothers", found on the Orbiney Papyrus. This story relates how Bata lived in the house of his older brother Anubis and his wife. One day, the brothers were ploughing a field when it transpired that they had run out of seed. Bata was sent home to get some. Anubis' wife was waiting for him. "O, you work so hard," she purred; "every day I see how strong you are. Why not lie down with me for an hour? I will give you pleasure, and also make you some fine clothes." Bata is too loyal to his brother to even consider such a proposal. He refuses, and leaves. Of course, Anubis' wife now fears that Bata will tell her husband, and decides on a pre-emptive defense.

She covers herself with paint and mud, and pretends that she has been violently abused. When Anubis comes home, she lies prostrate in their bedroom and cries that Bata insisted on sleeping with her. Naturally, the poor Bata can protest as much as he wants, just as Joseph loudly proclaimed his innocence. The "evidence" of the torn garments is too compelling to ignore.

Many moons pass as Joseph languishes in prison. But, as we will recall, the young man had a special gift: the ability to interpret dreams, not only his own but also the visions of others. In Egypt as well as in other cultures throughout the Middle East, this was a critical faculty. People believed that gods often revealed important matters to mortal beings in their dreams. Interpreting the true significance of a vision, no matter how strange or bizarre, was considered a priceless art.

Joseph's gift is now put to good use. It so happens that Pharaoh's Royal Cupbearer and Royal Baker are thrown in prison. One night, both men have dreams. The Cupbearer sees three branches, from which he takes grapes and presses them into Pharaoh's cup; and the Baker dreams of three cake-baskets, from which the birds eat at will. Joseph believes he can interpret these dreams. The Cupbearer will be restored to his position in three days, he says; but the Cupbearer will be put to death.

It comes to pass just as Joseph has foretold. Three days later, Pharaoh changes his mind and the Cupbearer is restored to his position. Just as the fortunate official is released, Joseph in the Qur'an reaches out to him "and said to him whom he knew would be delivered: remember me with your lord ...!" (Q. 12.42). Of course, human frailty being what it is, "the chief Cupbearer did not remember Joseph, but forgot him."

TWO LONG YEARS MUST PASS. Joseph slowly withers away in prison. But then, it is Pharaoh who has a vision. He dreamt that he stood by the river, "and behold, there came up out of the river seven fat cows; and they fed in a meadow. And, seven other cows came up, lean and thin; and the thin cows did eat the seven fat cows. Then Pharaoh awoke" (G 41:1-4).

Pharaoh instantly summons his political advisors. The Qur'an tells us, "the king said: .. O chiefs! Explain to me my dream, if you can interpret the dream" (Q. 12.43). But all of Pharaoh's councilors are flummoxed. "Can nobody interpret this dream for me?" Pharaoh cries out in frustration. Then, belatedly, the Cupbearer remembers.

Reading the Bible and the Qur'an side by side, the story unfolds as follows:

Seven cows in a river, from an Egyptian wall relief in Saqqara, Old Kingdom, 6th dynasty, ca. 2240 B.C.E.

Genesis
There was with us a young man, a Hebrew; and he interpreted to us our dreams. Then Pharaoh sent and called Joseph.... (G 41: 9)

Qur'an

Joseph! O truthful one! Explain to us seven fat cows which
seven lean cows devoured. (Q. 12.46)

Genesis
And Joseph said: the seven good cows are seven years
of great plenty throughout all the land of Egypt.
(G.41:25-29)

Qur'an
Then there shall come seven years of hardship
Which shall eat away all that you have beforehand
laid up in store for them. (Q. 12.48)

Genesis
Now therefore let Pharaoh look out a man discreet and wise,
and set him and let him appoint officers over the land, and
let them gather all the food of those good years that come."
And Pharaoh said unto Joseph, I am Pharaoh,
and without thee shall no man lift up his hand or foot in
all the land of Egypt. (G 41:44-45; 33-35)

Qur'an
And Joseph said: then grant me authority over the
resources of the Earth for I shall conserve them well,
and will know how to exploit them. (Q. 12.56)

Thus, the son of a tribal chieftain, a sand dweller, a *Habiru*, is appointed to Grand Vizier, the second highest office in the Egyptian empire, comparable to the position of Prime Minister in modern monarchies. Genesis is full of astounding events, but this certainly strains credulity. Is it conceivable that a young man of such low origins, sold as a slave, could rise so rapidly to power?

A number of scholars have sought to place the story of Joseph's ascent in a period known as the Hyksos dynasty. The years between 1720 and 1650 B.C.E. were a time of great turmoil in Egypt. When the death of King Amenemhet III left Egypt bereft of a legitimate successor, nomadic immigrants from Syria and Northern Canaan rose in rebellion. Their power slowly spread across the Nile Delta, so that by the late 1700s they all but controlled Lower Egypt. The Egyptians called these nomadic chieftains "Hyksos" (*Hikau-khoswet*), meaning "Desert Princes". The Hyksos then initiated a rival dynasty of Pharaohs of their own, starting with King Sheshi around 1665 B.C.E., which would rule for over a hundred years. Throughout this time, the original Egyptian aristocracy lived in exile in the city of Thebes. As further proof of their Semitic heritage, the Hyksos brought with them a new chief god, named Seth -- the Hyksos name for Baal, Lord of Rain and Dew.

It is tempting to think that the new Hyksos rulers would welcome ambitious young men of intelligence and skill who, like themselves, were Semitics from the East. Certainly, a Hyksos King would feel far more comfortable with a young lads from the East than with the local cadres, who undoubtedly viewed the newcomers with contempt.

There are two important clues that corroborate this thesis. The Hyksos made their summer residence near the mouth of the Nile, in a city called Avaris. It so happens that Avaris lies in the region identified by scholars as the Biblical Goshen -- the same territory where four centuries later, the book of Exodus would place Joseph's descendants, the Israelites, enslaved in bondage.

Second, the Hyksos brought with them an important military innovation -- the horse-drawn chariot. No doubt, such flying squadrons driven by arrow-flinging missileers were a key factor in the stunning series of Hyksos victories. And Genesis specifically states that Pharaoh allowed Joseph to "ride in the second chariot which he had" (Genesis 41:43).

Egyptian chariot, from the treasure of Tutankhamon, New Kingdom, 18th dynasty, ca. 1340 B.C.E.

If that is true, as some scholars have asked, why isn't there an Egyptian record of the appointment of so exceptional a figure? Why isn't there an inscription marking Joseph's appointment? One reason may be that after the Lower Kingdom was reconquered by the armies from the South, all the vestiges of Hyksos rule, including monuments, effigies and tablets, were summarily destroyed.

Meanwhile, it comes to pass as Joseph has foretold. The Nile fails to rise for seven years in a row, and famine spreads over the land of Egypt. As Egyptian records tell us, this was not an exceptional event. "My heart is heavy over the calamitous failure of the Nile floods these past seven years," writes King Djoser, the Pharaoh of the stepped pyramid in Saqqara, in a now-famous inscription on the island of Sehel near Aswan., which may actually date from the Ptolemaic era. And if Egypt is having trouble feeding its people, imagine the conditions in Canaan. Palestine's vegetation was nourished not by rivers and streams, but by annual rainfall. During seven years of drought, the situation would be infinitely worse than in Egypt. And so it is not surprising that Genesis now cuts back to Canaan, where many tribes pack up their families and trek west, to Egypt. "And all countries came into Egypt to Joseph for to buy corn," says Genesis; "because the famine was so sore in all lands." (G 41:57)

Now it is the turn of Joseph's brothers to prepare for the long journey. Will the Egyptians grant them a share of the precious stores amassed by their powerful Grand Vizier? Jacob is not so sure. With much of Egypt suffering as well, he expects grain to fetch a hefty price. So he tells his sons, "Take some of the choice fruits of the land in your bags, and carry them down as a present to the man – a little balm and a little honey, gum, resin, pistachio nuts and almonds" (G 43:11). All of Jacob's sons prepare to journey to Egypt, except Benjamin, Jacob's other son by his beloved Rachel. Jacob simply cannot bear the thought of losing his youngest son as well.

After a long voyage, the brothers come at last into the presence of Joseph. The Grand Vizier is dressed in the ornamental garb of his high office, so naturally, as the Qur'an tells us, "[Joseph] recognized them as soon as he saw them, but they knew him not. And when he had made provisions for them, he told them: bring your brother on the father's side also" (Q. 12:59). Joseph wants to see his brother Benjamin. And just to make sure that the brothers abide by Joseph's wish, Genesis tells us that one of them, Simeon, must remain behind in Egypt as a hostage.

In the Qur'an, Jacob is desperate. He beseeches his sons, "How can I trust you with him, expecting anything different from that which happened when I entrusted you with his brother the last time?" But the famine persists, and Jacob has no choice but to send his sons back -- Benjamin included.

When they arrive in Egypt, Joseph invites them to his house, so that he can properly receive his "Hebrew" guests. The next day, the brothers -- who still have no idea why this Grand

Vizier takes such an interest in them-- are packed off to Canaan. Huge bushels of grain are straining the seams of their leather sacks. Even the money they paid to acquire the supplies has been returned to them. But what they do not know is that Joseph has also hidden his own silver goblet in one of the bags -- specifically, the sack that belongs to Benjamin.

Just as the brothers approach the border, they are overtaken by Joseph's steward. One of the Grand Vizier's precious goblets is missing. Benjamin's bag is found to contain the missing item. The young boy is promptly arrested and brought back to the capital. His brothers follow in despair. Once admitted in Joseph's presence, they plead Benjamin's innocence. Now Joseph can no longer restrain himself. He sends all of his servants from the room. Then he turns to his brothers, and in one of the most touching verses of Genesis, cries out: "*I am Joseph, your brother!* Your brother, whom you sold into Egypt." The brothers are shocked. Can this be true? Is this powerful Egyptian in truth their little brother Joseph? "Don't be angry with yourselves that you did sell me into slavery;" Joseph assures them, " for it was God's plan so that I could preserve you." Joseph then tells them to return to Canaan and bring their father Jacob to Egypt. They should settle in this land, he tells them, "and you will dwell in the land of Goshen" (G 45: 9-11).

The brothers embrace and weep. Before long, they head back to Canaan, and return to Egypt with Jacob and his household in tow. As Joseph promised, they are settled in the plain of Goshen. Here, as Genesis tells us, they "shall be close" to Joseph's house. Arguably, this would imply that Joseph himself lives in Goshen, possibly in the vicinity of the Hyksos capital of Avaris.

But where exactly was this mythical city of Avaris? Digging near the ruins of Tanis in the 1930's, Pierre Montet of the University of Strasbourg discovered a treasure trove of temples and sculptures, as well as granaries and storage facilities.

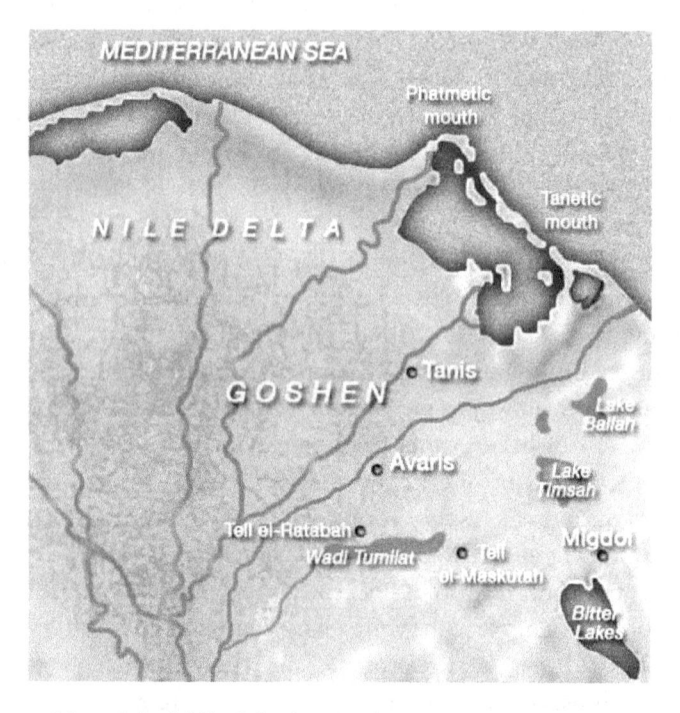

Map of the biblical Goshen in the eastern Nile Delta

The ruins seemed to corroborate the Genesis story perfectly. Only later, archaeologists determined that Tanis was actually built *after* the rule of the Hyksos, during the New Kingdom.

More recently, scholars have associated Avaris with the complex of Tell-el-Dahba, located close to the village of Qatana-Qantîr. Here, an Austrian team excavated an elaborate palace adorned with frescoes that have a remarkable resemblance to the bull-leaping frescos of the palace of Knossos in Greece, built around the same time of the Hyksos rule. According to Manfred Bietak, the Austrian archaeologist in charge of the dig, Tell-el- Dahba was part of a vast complex of palaces and granaries, located close to a tributary of the Nile.

As such, the place would have been an ideal central repository for Joseph's precious stores.

Ruins of Tanis, 21st dynasty, ca. 970 B.C.E.

Over time, the Nile tributary silted away and the court was forced to move elsewhere. According to Bietak, this is when the city of Tanis was built; but by then, the name of Joseph was only a memory. Or not even that, as we shall see.

According to Genesis, Jacob lived his final years surrounded by Joseph and his sons. When he died, Joseph buried him in true Egyptian fashion. He had Jacob embalmed; but conform his father's wishes, the body was sent back to Canaan, to be buried in the Cave of Machpelah, alongside his father Isaac and his grandfather Abraham.

Chapter Seven
Musa in the Desert

Though many of the ancient tributaries have disappeared, the biblical area of Goshen, in today's eastern Nile Delta, is still sufficiently lush to accommodate large herds of sheep

Some 100 years pass in relative peace and security. The Hyksos Kings in Avaris consolidate their power. Joseph's children marry and beget children themselves, as do the children of his brothers who dwell in the fertile fields of Goshen. They learn to till the land in the Egyptian fashion, planting crops after the floods of the Nile have receded, leaving the soil rich and plump with fertile nitrates. Like their Egyptian neighbors, the sons of Joseph go fishing in the nearby lakes, or hunt for duck and geese in the marshes. Because, as Joseph knows, "every shepherd is an abomination to the Egyptians" (G 46:34).

And how wonderful this Goshen land is! It is the "best of the land", assures Pharaoh in one of the final chapters of Genesis. (G 47:6). This is confirmed in a contemporary papyrus, written by a student named Pai-Bes to his instructor, Amen-em-Optet. "To live here is to enjoy a glorious life," the boy writes in the typical breathless prose of a teenager. "The pools are filled with fish, the lagoons are thick with birds; the meadows are covered with succulent grass."

The Egyptian Museum in Cairo has a large painted limestone slab, showing teenagers like Pai-Bes at a friendly wrestling match in one of the Delta's fertile marshes. The youngsters are divided over three boats, and each one is armed with a pole. The object of the game, it appears, is to push as many young men of the opposing teams into the water. This they proceed to do with lots of laughter and bawdy comments.

Sparring youngsters in boats, from Saqqara, Old Kingdom, 5th dynasty, ca. 2400 B.C.E.

"Feel that!" says one inscription, as a boy smacks his opponent with a pole. Their skiffs are loaded with fruits of every kind; the waters on which they sail are brimming with fish.

The situation down South, on the other hand, is not quite so happy. This is where the old aristocracy of Egypt, holed up in exile in their southern capital of Thebes, tries to hang on to its disenfranchised title of the 17th dynasty. The old lords are biding its time -- quietly plotting and waiting for the moment to strike.

The moment comes sometime after 1533 B.C.E., when a Southern warrior fleet floats down the Nile. Thus, the civil war begins, pitting the "Old Egypt" against the Syria-Canaan culture of the Hyksos. The Northern armies put up a fierce resistance, but eventually their forces start to give way. Pharaoh Ahmose I throws a siege around Avaris, capital of the Hyksos. After many clashes that leave thousands dead or dying in the hot sand, Ahmose emerges victoriously.

In 1567 B.C.E., the Hyksos take whatever treasure is left and flee back East, to Canaan and on to Syria. Now, all of the Nile Delta and the land of Goshen lies open to the victorious Egyptian armies. Triumphant, Ahmose I proclaims himself the ruler of a newly united Egypt. The 18th Dynasty has begun -- and with it, the New Kingdom of Egypt.

A new dynasty of Pharaoh has emerged: *warrior* kings, forged by battle, who vowe never again to suffer the humiliation of foreign occupation. Ahmose and his descendants of the Thutmosides dynasty make good on their vow. They raise new, professional armies, and build strongholds along the eastern border, the Upper Nile and the frontiers with Nubia, today's Africa. They then further bolster Egypt's security by creating a buffer zone of vassal states. Egyptian armies push deep into Canaan as far as Syria, ruling the new territories by proxy through local governors. This is the New Egypt, an Egypt brazen and strong, aggressively guarding its wealth and civilization.

The New Kingdom Pharaohs immediately indulge in their version of *destalinization* -- methodically erasing every vestige of the Hyksos occupation. Statues are toppled. Royal cartouches of Hyksos kings are carefully erased, and stamped over with the royal markings of the 18th Dynasty.

In 1290 B.C.E. a king called Seti I ascends the throne. The second King of the 19th Dynasty, Seti faces a major threat: Egypt's control of its vassal states, Syria and Canaan, is being challenged by the Hittite kingdom, located in Anatolia (today's Turkey). In response, Seti decides to increase the garrisons located on Egypt's border. This includes the construction of an all-new garrison city, which in later years will become known as *Pi-Ramesses-Meri-Imen*, 'The House of Ramses the Beloved of Amun', patron god of the Ramesside Dynasty. In fact, this garrison city is part of a vast new building program that leaves hardly a settlement along the Nile untouched. Seti has plans to erect three new temples in Abydos, several mortuary temples in Thebes and a huge Hypostyle Hall in the Temple of Amun in Karnak, which still stands to this day.

The Great Hypostyle Hall in the temple complex of Karnak, begun by Seti I and completed by Ramses II

Unfortunately, most of Egypt's able-bodied men are either at work in the fields or drafted in the vastly expanded Imperial armies. Where then to get the manpower to build all these wonderful works?

Not far from the city of *Pi-Ramesses* is the old city of Avaris, surrounded by the lush fields of Goshen. The area is populated by tribes of a vaguely Asiatic origin, who are busy tilling their fields and tending their flocks. Arguably, no one quite knows who they are, or when they settled in Egypt to begin with. And so, says the Book of Exodus, "there rose a Pharaoh who knew not Joseph" (E 1:8). Indeed - how could he? If indeed there had once been a document of Pharaoh's offer of asylum to Jacob and his tribe, it would have perished with all other Hyksos records during the New Kingdom purges. "And then," Exodus tell us, "[Pharaoh] said, Behold, the people of the children of Israel are more and mightier than we. Come and let us set taskmasters over them" (E 1:9). And thus, the descendants of Jacob and Joseph were forced into bondage.

After the death of Seti I, his son ascended the throne. Some records imply that this son was a co-regent with his father for the last three years of Seti's reign, though there is no conclusive evidence to support it. What we do know is this young man took the name of his grandfather, which was Ramses. Thus began the reign of Ramses II, perhaps the greatest of all Pharaohs of the New Kingdom.

Ramses II understood that the new garrison city near Avaris, begun by his father, could not possibly satisfy his grandiose military plans. His first decision was to rename the city, with all due modesty, after himself -- *Pi-Ramesses-Meri-Imen*. And then he ordered the construction of a second city, dedicated to his patron god Atum: Per Atum, or *Pithom* in Hebrew. This is where Egyptian records intersect with the biblical narrative, because the Book of Exodus confirms that the Israelites "built for Pharaoh treasure cities, Pithom and Raamses. And the Egyptians made the children of Israel serve in hard bondage, with mortar, and brick" (E 1:13-14). And this was the situation when a man named Moses -- *Musa* in the Qur'an -- appeared on the scene.

Panoramic view of the area identified by Manfred Bietak as the location of (Pi)-Raamses, near the modern village of Qantir in the Nile Delta

WHO WAS MOSES? "A Jewish writer once wrote that if Moses had not existed, it would have been necessary to invent him," says Baruch A. Levine, Skirball Professor Emeritus of Ancient Near Eastern Studies at New York University. No other mortal figure so encapsulates the history, the law and the *raîson-d'être* of the Jewish people as Moses. He is what Jesus is to Christians and the Prophet Muhammad is to Muslims: he is the quintessential figure, the Communicator with the Divine, the legislator of the Jewish faith. With him, the Covenant with God becomes both tangible and practical. As such, he is held in nearly equal reverence by Jews, Christians and Muslims.

"We have almost no evidence for his existence," Baruch Levine continues; "all of the sagas about his birth follow all the patterns of ancient narrative. But he's sort of that cornerstone, the foundation of it all."

Professor Khaled Abou El Fadl, an expert in Islamic law, agrees. "Unlike the Torah and New Testaments, the Qur'an is not primarily a book of historical merit," he says; "but there are two prophets who get the lion's share of historical material, and these are Moses and Joseph. Moses or *Musa* is a special case altogether. The reason is that he receives the *law*, in fact the very essence of the law, not just for Jews but for all mankind. That is Moses, and that is why we as Muslims hold him in great esteem."

Where does the story of Moses start? According to Exodus, it started with a bloodbath. Pharaoh woke up one day and decided that the Hebrew slaves were becoming too plentiful. He ordered that every male child born to the workers should be cast into the river. His soldiers moved to implement his terrible decree, and the Nile ran red with the blood of Pharaoh's innocent victims. This is when, says Exodus, "a woman conceived, and bore a son. And when she could not longer hide him, she made for him an ark of bulrushes" (E 2: 2-3). "Put him into a chest," God tells the mother in the Qur'an, "then cast it down into the river, and the river shall throw him on the shore; and there, one who is an enemy to Me shall take him up" (Q 20.39).

At that moment, Exodus continues, "the daughter of Pharaoh came down to wash herself at the river; she saw the child: and, behold, the babe wept. And she had compassion on him, and said, "This is one of the Hebrews' children" (E 2:5). "He will prove a source of joy for you and me," the princess tells her attendants in the Qur'an; "do not kill him; possibly he may be useful for us, or we may even adopt him as a son" (Q 28.10). "And so," says Exodus, "the child grew unto Pharaoh's daughter, and he became her son. And she called his name Moses, because she said, I drew him out of the water" (E 2:5-6;10).

Indeed, the story of Moses' infancy bears a remarkable similarity to the legend of King Sargon as an infant, first uncovered on cuneiform tablets from the old Babylon palace in Akkad. Sargon would eventually become the founder of the Semitic dynasty of Babylon in the 27th century B.C.E. But as a young child, his future as a royal prince was in doubt since he was an illegitimate child -- the son of a foreign princess named Enitu. Enitu feared for her child's life. As a result, Sargon tells us in the first person, "she put me in a box made of reeds, closed the lid with pitch, and put it in the river. The box carried me along and brought me to a man named Akki the water drawer. Akki adopted me and raised me as a son."

Moses is raised at the court of Pharaoh. But one day, Moses is visiting the workpits of the Hebrew slaves, toiling away to build the king's garrison cities, when..

Qur'an
... he found therein two men fighting; one of them
of his own people and the other from his enemies. (Q 20.15)

Exodus
And he looked around, and when he saw that there was no
one else, he killed the Egyptian, and hid him in the sand.
And when he went out the second day, two men of
the Hebrews were there; and they asked him,
why did you kill your countryman? (E 2:12-13)

Qur'an
At that moment there came a man from the far side
of the city running; and said: Moses, the nobles are
taking counsel together to put thee to death. Then
listen to me and depart from the city...
So Moses departed, fearful and alert, praying:
Lord, deliver me from the unjust people. (Q 20.21-22)

Something in Moses has snapped. When he finally comes to his senses, it is too late. The overseer lies slumped on the ground, dead. Moses understands he is in trouble; in fact, he decides to flee. This may strike us as odd. If Moses is truly the adopted son of Pharaoh, as the Bible suggests, killing an overseer may have incurred his father's wrath, but it is difficult to believe that Pharaoh would actually put Moses to death over this transgression. This has led to various hypotheses about the true nature of Moses, and the reason for his stay at the court of Pharaoh, which we shall examine in a moment. In the meantime, however, Moses has taken flight – into the wilderness of Sinai.

Here, exhausted by the long journey, he sits down to drink from a well when seven girls appear in the distance. They have come to haul water for the flock of their father, a man named Jethro. At that moment, a group of ill-behaved shepherds appear on the scene. They start to bully the girls. Moses comes to their defense, and the girls immediately tell their father Jethro about this handsome young Egyptian who has saved them.

Moses falls deeply in love with the most beautiful of the girls, named Zipporah. With Jethro's blessing, they decide to marry. In due course, Zipporah presents him with a son.

This is the story as the Book of Exodus presents it to us. It is a wonderful narrative, but it raises a number of questions. First, if Moses was indeed a palace courtier, how is he able to survive in the desert? How is he able to chart a course across one of the most desolate areas on earth, from Goshen to the Gulf of Aqaba, straight across the Sinai desert? And why does he choose to go to the Midian, located just across the Red Sea in what is today northwest Arabia – an area that until now has been largely ignored in the Genesis or Exodus narrative?

One theory I find particularly intriguing is the idea that Moses was no stranger to the desert and the Midian region at all; in fact, he was intimately familiar with it. The Midian, by this time, was one of the vassal territories of the Egyptian Empire. By necessity, these vassal regions were ruled by local chieftains, who understood the language and local customs, and could be relied on to deliver the annual tribute to the Egyptian Crown. Nevertheless, though these governors received a share of the annual tax, they were also in a perfect position to organize and launch a rebellion. It was therefore incumbent on Pharaoh to ensure the loyalty of the local viceroys. To gain leverage, many Pharaoh's "invited" the oldest son of each governor to come and be educated in the Egyptian capital, under the king's control.

As this theory goes, Moses may have been the son of a chieftain of the Midian, appointed by the Egyptian authorities to rule the territory on their behalf. It explains why Moses would be intimately familiar with the region, how he came to learn the ways of the desert, and why he fled to the Midian, rather than any other foreign territory, such as Canaan, which was much closer to Goshen. Most importantly, it explains *why* Moses had to flee after the murder of the overseer. Guest student or not, such a devious crime would certainly have met with a stiff retribution.

The Bible gives some important clues to buttress the idea of Moses have Midianite origins. The tribe of the Midian traced its origins to a son of Abraham's second wife, Ketura, whom he married after Sarah's death.

> Genesis
> Then again Abraham took a wife, and her name
> was Keturah. And she bare him Zimran, and Jokshan,
> and Medan, and Midian... (G 25:1-2)

Later in the Bible, we learn that a non-Hebrew prophet named Balaam referred to the Midianites as 'Kenites':

> Numbers
> He looked on the Kenites, and took up his parable, and said,
> Strong is your dwellingplace, and you put thy nest
> in a rock. (Num. 24:21)

The term 'Kenites' is derived from the word *Qain* or 'coppersmith' in Arabic. The tribe of the Midian, in short, was famous for its work in copper, which was found in richly veined mountain ores nearby – one more reason why this territory was ruled as one of Egypt's vassal states.

What the books of Genesis and Numbers suggest, in short, is that the Midianites were an offshoot of Abraham, just like the tribe of Jacob. It is possible that in the intervening centuries, they had remained faithful to the worship of one God, a deity named *El*. This explains why Moses felt a *kinship* when looking at the Hebrew slaves in Pi-Raamses.

The region to the east of the Gulf of Aqaba, in today's southern Jordan, has been identified as the biblical Midian

Perhaps the most powerful argument for this theory is the crucial role played by Jethro, Zipporah's father. Jethro, according to Exodus, is no mere shepherd; he is a *priest*. A priest of what? Quite possibly, he serves *El*, the ancient God of Abraham. Later, in Exodus 18:11, we learn how Jethro offers a burnt sacrifice to God. Moses' brother Aaron and "all the elders" then invite him to a meal and treat him with the greatest respect "in the presence of God". This is clear evidence that Jethro did not serve pagan gods.

If this is true, then the episode in the Midian is suddenly very significant. Through Jethro, Moses becomes the catalyst who restores the link between the Hebrew slaves in Egypt and the authentic cult of *El* in the Midian, thus reaffirming God's covenant with Abraham.

Indeed, it is only *after* Moses has been accepted in the household of Jethro that God "remembered his covenant with Abraham, Isaac and Jacob", looked down upon the slaves of Goshen, "*and took notice of them*" (E 2:24-25; my italics). It is as if the Israelites had simply disappeared off God's radar until such time that a young prince from the Midian would put the Egyptianized settlers in Goshen back in touch with the original Abrahamaic faith. For shortly thereafter, Moses receives his divine mission.

Chapter Eight
Moses and the Exodus

It is a hot day, and Moses has led his flock away from the scorching sun to the cool breezes around Mount Sinai. Suddenly, a strange phenomenon catches his eye, which is described in both the Bible and the Qur'an:

> *Exodus*
> and behold, a bush burned with fire, and the bush was not consumed. And God called out to him from the midst of the bush, and said ....
> (E 3:1-4)

> *Qur'an*
> Surely I am your Lord, therefore put off your shoes; surely you are in the sacred valley....
> (Q 20.11)

Exodus
And the LORD said, I have surely seen the affliction
of my people who are in Egypt, and have heard their cry
by reason of their taskmasters...
I will bring you up out of the affliction of Egypt
unto the land of the Canaanites ..
unto a land flowing with milk and honey
(E 3:7,17)

Qur'an
Now, Go you and your brother with My Message
and be truthful; Go you both to Pharaoh, and say:
we are apostles of the Lord;
therefore send the children of Israel with us
and do not torment them any longer!
(Q 20.42-43, 47).

Exodus
And Moses said unto God, Behold, when I come
unto the children of Israel, and shall say unto them,
The God of your fathers hath sent me unto you;
and they shall say to me,
What is his name? what shall I say unto them?
And God said unto Moses, I AM THAT I AM: and he said,
Thus shalt thou say unto the children of Israel,
I AM hath sent me unto you. (E 3: 13-14).

Like Muhammad in the centuries to come, Moses is reluctant to undertake the mission with which God has charged him. How is he to persuade Pharaoh to let the children of Israel go? "I will stretch out my hand," says the Lord, "and smite Egypt with all my wonders that I will do in their midst: and after that he will let you go." "But I am not eloquent," Moses protests again; "I am slow of speech, and of a slow tongue." YHWH has the solution. "What about your brother Aaron the Levite," the Lord replies; "I know that he can speak well" (E 4:10;14).

And so Moses, accompanied by his brother Aaron, travels back to Pharaoh's court in order to confront him.

In the meantime, Ramses II has not been idle. He is determined to put an end to the raids by the tiresome Hittites. In 1292, Ramses' forces meet the Hittites near the oasis of Kadesh. It is the largest clash of arms in the history of Egypt; but despite huge losses on both sides, no one can claim a decisive victory; and so it ends in a draw. Nevertheless, both parties, exhausted by the conflict, are persuaded to sign a non-aggression pact – the first such treaty in Antiquity. Ramses considers it a major victory. Soon, monuments and temples throughout the Empire celebrate this greatest of Ramses triumphs.

Ramses II smiting his enemies, 19th dynasty, reign of Ramses II, 1290-1224 B.C.E.

In the meantime, work on the garrison cities continues unabated. The Israelite slaves are hard at work when Moses and Aaron appear, telling them of their divine mission. The slaves are overjoyed; "they bowed down and worshipped," says Exodus. But would Pharaoh allow them to leave Egypt?

Moses and Aaron then confront the great king himself. "Thus says the LORD God of Israel," they tell Pharaoh, "Let my people go, so that they may hold a feast unto me in the wilderness. And Pharaoh said, Who is the LORD, that I should obey his voice to let Israel go? I know not the LORD, nor will I let Israel go" (E 5:1-2).

In fact, Pharaoh is so incensed over this impudent proposal that he orders punitive measures against the slaves themselves. "You shall no longer give the people the straw to make brick, as before," Ramses tells his taskmasters; "let them go and gather straw for themselves. But," he warns, " the tally of the bricks, which they made before, will not be any less. It is obvious that they have spare time; because they cry, Let us go [and] sacrifice to our God" (E 5:7-8). Moses' proposition has backfired.

What follows is the story of the Ten Plagues that YHWH rains down on Egypt to punish Pharaoh for his intransigence. The Nile turns to blood, locusts ravish the crops, an army of frogs swarms over the land, and the towns and villages are flailed by torrents of hail. For those who are familiar with the unique climate of Egypt, these natural phenomena are not as strange as they may seem. Sometimes, sedentary deposits from the Abyssinian lakes, or a toxic excess of algae, do stain the waters of the upper Nile a dark brown, or even a reddish color. Hailstorms, too, are not uncommon.

But it is the tenth and last plague that finally breaks Pharaoh's will. All of Egypt's oldest sons are killed by the angel of the Lord. The palace of Ramses II is not immune either. Before the coming of dawn, Pharaoh cradles the lifeless body of his oldest boy in his arms.

Once again, the subsequent sequence of events is told eloquently in both the Bible and the Qur'an:

Exodus
And the children of Israel did according to

the word of Moses; and the multitudes went up with them;
flocks, herds, and cattle; all the hosts of the LORD went out from the land of Egypt. And they took their journey from Succoth, and encamped in Etham, in the edge of the wilderness.
(E 12:35,41; 13:20)

Qur'an
But Pharaoh's people said: Do you leave Moses and his people to make mischief in the land and to forsake you and your gods?
(Q 7.127)

Exodus
And he took six hundred chosen chariots, and all the chariots of Egypt, and captains over every one of them.
(E 14:7)

Qur'an
And Pharaoh followed them with his armies, until they came upon them near the sea.
(Q 20.78)

Qur'an
And when he was drowning, Pharaoh said: 'Now I believe that there is no God but He on Whom the Children of Israel believe.'
(Q 10.90)

Did Pharaoh's chariots perish in the Red Sea? Virtually all scholars now agree that the Hebrew word *Yam Suph*, translated as "Red Sea" in the King James Bible, actually means "Sea of Reeds". There are no reeds to be found on the shores of the Red

Sea. But sandbanks, sometimes covered with growth, can still be found near the marshes of the Bitter Lakes, located in the heart of the litmus between Egypt and Sinai. As such, the Bitter Lakes lie directly in the path from Goshen to Sinai. It is likely that this is the spot where Moses chose to let his people cross, during low tide, when the sandbanks were exposed. Of course, the bottom of this marshland would be mud -- strong enough for a person, but certainly too soft to support Pharaoh's heavy armored chariots.

Reeds on the banks of the Bitter Lakes at low tide

AND SO WE ENTER THE STORY of Exodus proper - the long journey to the Promised Land. TheBible gives us a very accurate geographical description of the route, identifying each major stopping point near an oasis. The problem, of course, is that Moses does not seem to be heading to Canaan, the Promised Land, at all. If he did, he would have taken the same road that took Joseph to Egypt. Since the days of the Middle Kingdom, this road had been vastly expanded and modernized so as to accommodate the near-continuous columns of military traffic heading towards the vassal-states of the "Papyrus Curtain": the buffer zone of Canaan, Edom and Ammon. In later days this road, which skirts the Mediterranean Sea all the way into today's Gaza, was known as the "Way of the Philistines." Had Moses chosen this route, he would have reached the shade of the oak trees of Hebron in three months or less. Conversely, he could have taken the Way of Shur, which cuts straight across the Sinai and into the Negev. But Moses doesn't take these well-established routes, opting to head down south instead.

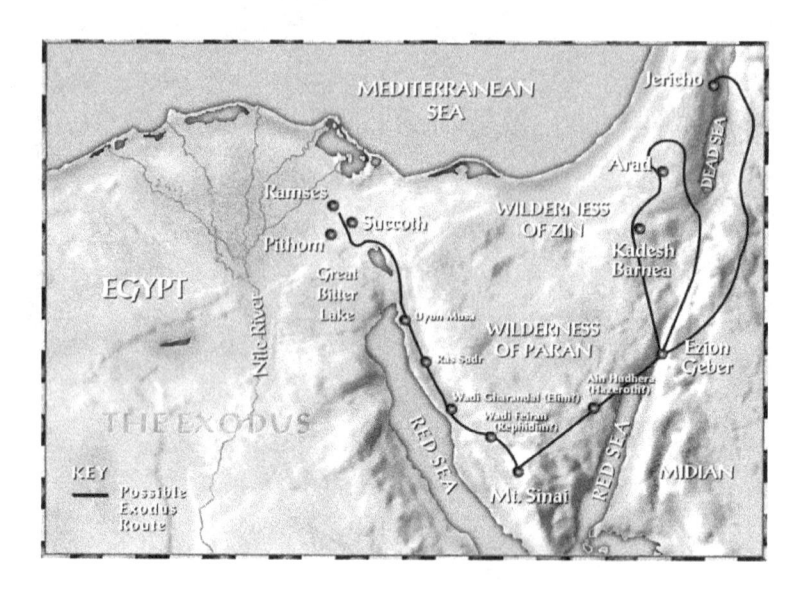

A reconstruction of the route of the Exodus

According to *Exodus,* Moses and his people traveled for three days without water until they came to the oasis of 'Marah,' where the water was 'bitter' (E 15:22-23). Tradition has identified 'Marah' with the small oasis of *Uyun Musa.* From Uyun Musa, the coastal road travels some 23 miles to Ras-as-Sidr, now a favorite weekend resort for middle-class Egyptians .

From here, Moses continued down south, in search of water. According to Exodus, he met with success after " they came to Elim, where were twelve wells of water, and threescore and ten palm trees: and they encamped there by the waters" (E 15:27). Where was Elim? Some scholars place Elim ('tamarisks') some five miles from Sarabit el-Khadim, in a small grove known as Wadi Gharandal. Moses then turned inland, straight across the desert of Sin. He is leading his people south-east, away from the Red Sea. Here, the ancient road east plunges into the mountains, around the towering hills of the Gebel Serbal and the Gebel Tarfa down to the Pass of Watia. And then, Exodus tells us, "all the congregation of the children of Israel journeyed from the wilderness of Sin, and pitched in Rephidim" (E 17:1).

The oasis of Wadi Feiran, often identified with the biblical Rephidim

Rephidim is the vast palm grove known today as Wadi Feiran, a vast stretch of trees surrounded by the majestic rise of the Sinai massif. This is where, according to Exodus, Moses struck a rock to fill the dried-up river bed of the wadi (E 17:6).

From here, it is but a short distance, a five day march, to Mount Sinai. Moses has brought his people to the place from where his mission started. Now, a happy reunion awaits. There, in the shadow of the great mountain, is Jethro the priest, who has brought Moses' wife Zipporah and his sons with him.

Mount Sinai is a forbidding mass of gray and pink granite that rises some 7000 ft above sea level. Today, most visitors start their climb just beyond the walls of the 1500-year old St. Catherine's Monastery, using a camel path that steadily winds its way to the summit. At first, this path is plunged in the shadow of the setting sun. But as the visitor draws near, a breathtaking panorama of desert and mountain peaks unfolds, bathed in gold and stretching as far as the eye can see -- beyond Sinai to the mountains on the Gulf of Aqaba, where ancient Midian was once located. Ninety minutes into his climb, the visitor arrives at the last and arguably hardest stretch: the thousand-or-so steps to the summit itself. Here is a small chapel, its weathered surface painted by the golden rays of the dying sun.

This, then, is where tradition places the momentous occasion when God presents his Ten Commandments:

Exodus
I am the LORD thy God, which have brought thee out of the land of Egypt, out of the house of bondage. You shall have no other gods before me. You shall not kill.
You shall not steal. You shall not covet your neighbor's house, nor his wife, nor his ox.." (E 20:1-17)

A chapel marks the summit of Mount Sinai

Inscribed on the tablets in Moses' hands is a code of ethics that will inspire Jews, Christians and Muslims in equal measure right up to our modern times. Or as the Qur'an puts it: "Moses, I have exalted you above the people of your time by My Message and My words. So take fast hold of that what I have given you and be grateful... and bid your people to hold fast" (Q 7: 145-146).

It is probably true, as some scholars have argued, that the Laws of Moses, which would evolve into the Books of Leviticus, Numbers and Deuteronomy, owe much to the Babylonian tradition of justice that previously produced the Code of Hammurabi. In the same way, it is not difficult to see similarities between the Ten Commandments and Egyptian law, with which Moses was undoubtedly familiar. In the Book of the Dead, for example, we hear of the so-called Negative Confession by which each Egyptian had to defend his actions before a panel of judges in the underworld.

".... I have not killed.

I have not caused pain;
I have not caused tears.
I have not deprived cattle of their pasture..."

But in all other aspects, the Mosaic Laws are unique. God is no longer the remote divinity, the El of a higher sphere. This is a compassionate God, a God who moves far beyond mere rituals of religious observance to spell out an entire code of conduct by which humanity will prosper.

"You shall not pervert justice; you shall not show partiality", Deuteronomy admonishes the future judges of Israel (Deut. 16:18-19). Merchants and traders are told to be fair and honest: "a full and just measure you shall have" (Deut. 25:15). Above all, every man and woman should be compassionate to the downtrodden and the marginalized. "You shall not strip your vineyard bare, nor shall you gather every grape," warns Leviticus; "you shall leave it for the poor and the stranger" (Lev 19:10). After all, Deuteronomy reminds Moses' followers: you were once like them. "Love the sojourner therefore; for you were sojourners in the land of Egypt" (Deut. 10:19).

Some time after the events on Mount Sinai, we find the people of Israel on the march again, this time heading towards Ezion-Gaber near today's Eilat. This was another center of Egyptian mining, and many scholars accept the statement in Exodus that guides from the Midian are now plotting the route. These guides take the caravan past the oasis of Hazaroth to the great oasis of Kadesh Barnea.

Since there is no road to Hazaroth, modern visitors must mount a group of camels and head straight into the wilderness. "I am firmly convinced that what the Bible calls Hazaroth is today En Gudra", says Yosi, a guide who has traveled the Sinai for 30 years. "*En* means 'water' in Arabic, and *Gudra* means 'green'. In this whole area, right across the route from Mount Sinai to Kadesh Barnea, there is nothing like it."

Standing at the edge of a crevice, he points into the distance. There, on the horizon in the shimmering heat, lies a clump of palm trees, surrounded by Bedouin huts. But before us yawns a huge drop to the desert floor -- the same deep canyon that, Yosi believes, the Israelites were forced to cross some 3000 years ago. We dismount and gingerly lead our camels down a steep path of rocks and boulders. The camels themselves seem unperturbed; alternatively chewing and belting out a roar of protest, they saunter down the path onto the desert floor.

Here, we mount our camels again and trod the remaining two miles to the oasis. A Bedouin family is waiting for us with fresh fruits and bread. "*Musa*, yes," our Bedouin host assures us, as if he still remembers the day; "*Musa* here, En Gudra." We look from under the tent flap to the endless reaches of the Sinai. From here to Kadesh-Barnea is another 100 miles - a march of two weeks, at least. There, the people of Israel tarried in the desert, growing strong, hardened by the climate, before their entry in the Promised Land can begin. But for Moses, it is not to be. On the eve of the Entry into the Promised Land, he climbs up to Mount Nebo to die, after one last glance down into the valley of Jordan. He is buried in an unmarked grave, further adding to the enigma that forever will surround this most hallowed figure in the Hebrew Scriptures.

Moses may have been a man of heroic proportions, a leader of great skill and courage, but he was also fallible and prone to doubt, like any other man. He was not assumed into heaven, like Elijah, nor granted a magnificent burial, like Jacob. In the end, Moses was just a man, buried in a simple grave -- and that, perhaps, is one reason why he is so revered by all the three great faiths.

IS THE EXODUS STORY BASED on an actual event? Some scholars have scathingly pointed to the absence of any reference to the Exodus in Egyptian records. Given that Egyptian kings did not make a habit of recording their defeats, this argument does not amount to much. On the other hand, there is ample evidence of tribal immigration into Canaan in the late 13th and early 12th centuries B.C.E. As we will see shortly, a number of foreign tribes settled in the highlands of Canaan in this period. Many of these shared a number of cultic practices that today we can tentatively identify with the Mosaic Laws, such as the avoidance of pig meat. We also know from Egyptian records that there were a great many Semitic "immigrant workers" living in Egypt *before* the Ramessides, as early as the Middle Kingdom, particularly on the farms and estates of the Nile Delta. It is therefore not inconceivable to imagine a steady migration from Egypt back to Canaan in the late 13th century B.C.E.

Why would these workers have decided to go back to their ancestral lands? Perhaps the increasingly racist and discriminatory policies of the Ramesside kings was one factor.

Detail of the stele of Merneptah (1207 B.C.E.)

In addition, the successful settlement of one tribe back in Canaan may have encouraged others to follow suit. The peace treaty with the Hittites, who had been the scourge of Syria-Canaan for many generations, may have been another factor why much immigrant labor in Egypt decided to return to their lands. In that sense, the story of the Exodus may have telescoped the mass migration of Semitic tribes and clans over many decades into one heroic narrative that exemplified the redemptive power of YHWH.

And in fact, there *may* be a record after all, in the form of the so-called Victory Slab of Pharaoh Merneptah, the son of Ramses II. The monument is dated around 1207 B.C.E. With the typical hyperbole that one expects from the House of the Ramessides, the inscription boasts that "Canaan is pacified and all its evil with it; the people of Israel are desolate, without offspring, Palestine has become Egypt's widow." It is the first mention of an entity called "Israel" on any document from Antiquity.

Chapter Nine
The Rise and Fall of Ancient Israel

A view of the Jordan Valley

For the next 1200 years, the Bible tells us, the Hebrew tribes established themselves in "The Promised Land," the territory of Canaan, where they slowly coalesced into a nation. This political entity, known as Israel, briefly flowered as an independent monarchy before its split into two rival states. These states, distracted by their mutual enmity, then became ready prey for the emerging militarism from the East, and the new superpower of Assyria.

This is the narrative as presented in the books of Joshua, Judges, Samuel and Kings. Recent scholars have argued that these books, together with the last book of the Pentateuch, the book of Deuteronomy, form part of a distinct literary group, given its consistent treatment of Israel's history through the prism of covenant theology. Referred to as "Deuteronomistic

History," these books -- though based on centuries-old oral and written traditions -- were probably edited during the reign of King Josiah in the 7th century B.C.E. Given that King Josiah ruled the southern state of Judah, this may explain the strong anti-Northern bias that runs through these narratives. What the Deuteronomistic History tells us is that Israel and its successor states prospered whenever they were faithful to the Lord's Covenant as detailed in the Mosaic Laws, but faced disaster and ruin whenever they succumbed to pagan practices.

On the one hand, the authors of these books have a point, because time and again the inhabitants in ancient Israel fall back on native pagan traditions, either to safeguard their harvests or in imitation of the many different cultures and religions that surrounded its territory and often exerted a powerful political and cultural influence. On the other hand, ancient Israel had the misfortune of straddling the crossroads of trade and military traffic between the two largest superpowers of its time -- Egypt and Assyria -- at a time of great upheaval and shifting alliances in the Near East.

IRONICALLY, CANAAN -- OR "PALESTINE" as it was known in later centuries -- was a rather unremarkable strip of land sandwiched between the Mediterranean Sea and the Arabian desert, cleft by a double ridge of mountains anchored to the river Jordan. It was a land of contrasts. While the hills of Galilee, the Carmel and Northern Samaria were green and lush with trees, much of the central lands were hot and dry, covered with soft limestone. Only the coastal regions enjoyed a fair amount of rainfall. Here, alluvial deposits had nurtured fertile soil where wheat could be raised for bread, grapes for wine and olives for oil. The only other main agrarian center was the Jordan valley, famous for its olive oil and dates, watered by that great river that flows steadily from the Sea of Galilee to the Dead Sea.

As in the days of Abraham, most Canaanite settlements were clustered in the Jordan valley proper, or near the coast. Here, in addition to agriculture, there was a fair degree of fishing, trade, light manufacturing (including the production of salt) and various other services that catered to the need of passing caravans. The dry highlands with their sparse vegetation were largely eschewed. These remained a perfect hideaway for unsettled nomadic tribes and other flotsam, drifting in from greater Mesopotamia.

Palestine, in sum, was not a particularly desirable territory. It did not have any rich minerals or precious metals, if we exclude the copper ores of Aqaba and the iron mines of the Transjordan. It did not have the sweet, lush gardens of Goshen nor the orange groves of Faiyum; the moist and fattened soil of the fertile crescent of Sumer, nor the pastoral beauty of the Garden of Eden. It was a rather unremarkable sliver of land with only a handful of fertile valleys, and those were jealously and fanatically defended by its inhabitants.

But this was the Promised Land; here were the first altars built by Abraham, the first tents pitched by Jacob, and the pastures where Joseph's brothers had tended their cattle. This was the land shown to Moses from Mount Nebo, and so this was the land that the Hebrews were determined to make their own, come what may.

The Book of Joshua tells us that the "invasion" of Canaan began with military assault on Jericho, strategically located near one of the principal crossings of the river Jordan. For six days, the new leader of the Hebrew tribes, a commander named Joshua, marched around the walls of the city, blasting away with their war horns, until the walls crumbled under the sheer acoustic stress of the "military brass" (Josh 6).

Ancient Jericho, located some 20 miles east of Jerusalem, is actually the oldest continuously inhabited city known to man. Settlers lived here as early as 9,000 B.C.E., evidenced by an impressive tower-like structure that scholars believe to be an early shrine to the local deity. What made Jericho was its complex of formidable defenses. Built as early as the 8th millennium B.C.E., some of these ramparts rose as high as 12 feet. But these powerful walls had been leveled long before Joshua's arrival, possibly by earthquakes in the 6th millennium.

The partially excavated walls of Jericho, ca. 2nd millennium B.C.E.

The Book of Joshua then proceeds to tell us of a military campaign whose success was matched by its cruelty. Joshua 'smites' his enemies with abandon, killing men, women and children with equal gusto. His army leaves a trail of scorched earth across much of Canaan. "And they smote them," the Book tells us, "so that they let none of them remain or escape" (Josh 8:22).

Archaeological excavations, however, suggest that such epic battle scenes may be the result of creative imagination on the part of 7th century biblical scribes. Many Canaanite settlements continued to live and prosper well past the presumed date of the 'Conquest'. In fact, the archaeological record suggests that the settlement of the Hebrew tribes in Canaan was a gradual process, with armed conflict mostly limited to the area immediately west of Jericho, and in the area of Hazor, north of the Sea of Galilee.

Hazor is the only Canaanite stronghold that bears signs of violent destruction during the years of the presumed 'Conquest', early 12th century B.C.E.

As the years passed, the Israelites began to experiment with a form of written script that would ultimately produce biblical Hebrew. This language evolved out of a common "indo-mesopotamian" language that was, by varying degrees, also spoken in Phoenician, Moabite and Edomite dialects.

Scholars do not agree as to whether this "proto-Hebrew" emerged during the time of the Patriarchs or as a result of the Conquest. It is clear, however, that after 1000 B.C.E., spoken Hebrew began to emerge as a distinct branch from the common source. To create a written form of Hebrew, the Israelites adopted the same linear alphabet first introduced to Canaan by the Phoenicians -- the same alphabet, in fact, that would be spread via Phoenician trade routes throughout the Mediterranean basin, including Greece.

For the next two hundred years, then, the confederation of the "twelve tribes of Israel" struggled to sustain a permanent presence in Canaan, tilling the land and herding their sheep. As these communities grew, tension with the Canaanite 'natives' increased. In many places there was a renewal of hostilities. The Bible depicts these cyclical clashes as God's punishment once the tribes neglected their religious duties as spelled out in the Mosaic Laws. Although many tribes were fiercely independent, they would usually rally to defend another tribe if it came under Canaanite attack. Sometimes, these tribes would elect a temporary leader or 'Judge', and with God's help resist the aggression -- a process that is described in the biblical Book of Judges.

Of course, these leaders were not 'Judges' in the legal sense. They were biblical *condottieri*, men chosen for their military acumen and initiative. The need for such professional commanders was clear. Militarily speaking, the Israelite tribes were quite inferior to Canaanites forces, which were equipped with such inventions as the armored chariots, developed by the Hittites and introduced into Egypt by the Hyksos. The Book of Judges tells us that Israel remained mired in the infertile hill country because "the Lord ..... could not drive out the inhabitants of the plain, because they had chariots of iron" (Jud. 1-19).

A turning point came when a female commander, known as Deborah, was finally able to defeat the predominant Canaanite ruler in the area, King Jabin of Hazor. Deborah and her commander Barak met the forces of Jabin near Megiddo, in the heart of the Jezreel valley. The Bible tells us that God unleashed a violent rainstorm that flooded the Jezreel Valley, turning the soft earth to mud. The heavy Canaanite chariots were soon mired in the muck, and its occupants were slaughtered. This event tipped the balance of power; for the first time, the fertile Jezreel valley was now in Hebrew hands.

The Jezreel Valley, the most fertile region in all of Israel

The tribes of Israel made good use of their new-found superiority. They built their settlements; dug cisterns to gather rainfall; funneled the water of the Jordan into a primitive network of irrigation canals, and slowly coached the first seedlings of crops from the uneven soil of this land.

And then, a new challenge appeared on the horizon. A wave of foreign invaders known as the 'Philistines' arrived on the shores of Canaan and settled in cities along the coastline, including Ashkelon, Ekron, Ashdod and Gaza.

Most scholars are inclined to link the Philistines to the Archaic period of Greece -- in particularly, the island of Crete. Jeremiah (47:4) claims that they hailed from a place called ' Caphtor.' Certainly, Philistine pottery bears a remarkable resemblance to painted jars found in the palace of Knossos in Crete. But the Philistines were not content to settle along the coastline. They wanted control of all of Canaan. To that end, they created a confederacy of the five principal coastal cities that became known as *Philistia* (from which the Greeks later derived the word "Palestine," the name for the region at large).

The Hebrew tribes were alarmed, but not unduly so; the battle for land had been a fact of life ever since they had arrived in Canaan. It was only when the Philistines launched a massive invasion of the Judean highlands, traditionally the heart of the Israelite territory, that the tribes realized their very survival was at risk. The elders of the twelve tribes agreed that for the first time, the Israelites needed to unify behind a common front, led by a single commander. They settled on a commander named Saul, son of Kish, of the tribe of Benjamin, who had distinguished himself by liberating the city of Jabesh-Gilead in the war against the Ammonites.

The election of Saul ultimately led to the establishment of a unified monarchy led by the House of David. In many ways, this development was inevitable. Unless the communities of these pioneer settlers united into a strong nation-state, the tribes would have no chance to rebuff the constant challenge of aggressive invaders.

The first king of this unified monarchy was David, a musician and singer who had been employed at the citadel of Saul in Gibeah, whose mood would darken with each report of new Philistine aggression. David, we are told, was a shepherd boy, the youngest son of Jesse whose singing lifted the spirits of all those toiling away in the fields of Bethlehem, where he was born. One day, reports filtered into Gibeah that the Philistines had revealed a new and terrible weapon. This was a giant named Goliath. No one in the Hebrew camp dared to challenge him -- except young David.

David rode out and met Goliath between the opposing armies, armed only with a sling. Goliath laughed when he saw the diminutive figure of David. He assured his young opponent that before nightfall, David's flesh would be picked at by the birds. But his laughter died on his breath when David picked a pebble and swung it with full force at the giant's head, right between his eyes. The lifeless body of Goliath thudded to the ground. The Philistine hordes were so shocked that they turned and fled the scene, leaving the Israelites in command of the field.

Caravaggio, "David with the Head of Goliath" (1607)

Saul, always a man of uneven character, immediately felt a pang of jealousy. A plot was hatched to kill David -- by stealth or in battle, if at all possible. David was forced to flee, finding refuge in the Philistine homelands along the coast. After Saul's forces were beaten in an epic battle with the Philistines near Mount Gilboa, the southern tribes rose and clamored for David. The young man was duly anointed king in the city of Hebron, home of the family tomb of Israel's patriarchs. David then massed his troops and thoroughly defeated the Philistines.

David then focused on nation-building. Israel had been a tribal society, where the role of the family and the clan was paramount. How to weld these fractious tribes into one unified kingdom? The answer was the cult of YAHWEH. By turning the worship of the supreme Lord, traditionally a tribal affair, into a national religion, David hoped to foster a new sense of identity that would cement his unified Kingdom for the centuries to come.

The Ark of the Covenant, from a 1st century carving in Capernaum

But where should the national temple to YAHWEH be located? So far, the Ark of the Covenant, which contained the tablets of God's compact with his people, had traveled with the tribes. It had briefly been captured by the Philistines, but duly returned.

David's eye then fell on the central shrine of a group of people known as the Jesubites, located on Mount Zion. What intrigued David was that the Jesubites had deferred the role of religious leader to their king, making him, in effect, both monarch and high priest. What's more, Mount Zion was well situated, with a commanding view of three surrounding valleys: the valley of Hinnom, the valley of Kidron and the Central valley. It also had its own source of water in the Spring of Gihon. Most importantly, the Jebusite stronghold was neutral territory. No tribe could accuse David of favoritism by making the Jesubite hill the location of national YAHWEH worship.

And so, as the Book of II Samuel tells us, the king and his men marched to Jerusalem against the Jesubites, took it, and named it "the City of David" (II Samuel 5: 6-9). Archaeologists have since excavated this Davidic compound in the Ophel area, located just south of Temple Mount in Jerusalem. Here, the Israeli archaeologist Yigal Shiloh laid bare the base of a massive fortress, built by the Canaanites in the 18th century B.C.E., and later incorporated into the city of David.

The site of the ancient Jesubite stronghold on Mount Zion

Some 100 yards below, is the Spring of Gihon that would supply the Israelites in Jerusalem during innumerable sieges to come.

Following Jesubite precedent, David then combined the role of king and high priest, making himself the living presence of God's special relationship with the Israelites. This implied that he now ruled by divine right -- a right that gave him unquestioned authority over all the tribes in his dominion. David became 'the anointed one,' the *Mashiach,* or "Messiah".

In the time span of a single generation, David had achieved what had been a dream since the days of Abraham. Israel's enemies had been repelled; the tribes had united into one nation; and all of Israel worshiped YAHWEH, the Lord of Moses, in their new capital of Jerusalem. Little wonder, then, that in the centuries to come, people would look back at this moment and think of it as the very apex in the Jewish experience. Particularly after the break-up of the kingdom and the decline of Israel into captivity, the hope for a new *Mashiach* who would once again restore Israel to its former glory became a key motif of intertestamental Judaism.

The Qur'an, too, praises David's great achievement. As God said to the prophet Muhammad: "Call to mind Our servant David, a man of great power, who constantly turned to Us.... We made his Kingdom strong, and bestowed upon him wisdom and decisive judgment" (Q. 38.16).

The Davidic Citadel, following excavations in the 1970s

David was succeeded by one of his younger sons, Solomon, in 970 B.C.E. Unlike his father, who rose to power from humble beginnings, Solomon was educated, sophisticated and urbane. Where David was earthy and effusive, Solomon was cool and dispassionate, and quite ruthless. The Bible tells us that at the beginning of his reign, Solomon turned to God for guidance. And God replied, 'Ask what I should give you.' And Solomon said, 'Give your Servant an understanding mind to govern your people, able to discern between good and evil' (1 Kings 3: 7-9). As the Qur'an tells us, "Solomon succeeded David and said, O people, we have been given all necessary knowledge. This is indeed the manifest grace of God" (Q 27.16).

Solomon re-organized the kingdom into twelve new districts so as to improve his control over local government and expedite the collection of taxes. He also recognized that the Greater Kingdom of Israel, bestowed upon him by David, now straddled almost all of the principal trade routes between Assyria and Egypt, including the "Way of the Philistines" along the coast, and the "King's Highway" that ran through Israel's interior. This most famous of all caravan routes led from the Gulf of Aqaba straight across Edom, Moab and Ammon to Damascus and the markets of Mesopotamia beyond.

Shipment of timber from Lebanon by boat, from a 7th century Assyrian panel

Some of the valuable commodities that passed through the Kingdom were horses from Cappadocia (today southern Turkey), on their way to Egypt, and in reverse, nimble wooden chariots from Egypt. The renowned timber from the cedar forests of Lebanon was prized above all, for which Egypt paid with artifacts such as statues, jewelry, papyrus or gold.

Solomon recognized that there was little point in serving as a mere tollbooth on the caravan route. He wanted to become a major trade broker himself: arranging for credit, providing transport, even offering Israel's growing agricultural surplus up for sale. The Book of Kings tells us that Solomon was able to finance his fledgling import/export business with the proceeds from the gold mines of Ophir, on the east coast of Africa. The Book tells us that in *just one year*, Solomon received gold revenues of "six hundred sixty-six talents", roughly the equivalent of 50,000 pounds of gold (1 Kings 10:14). "Jerusalem," said the Jewish historian Josephus some 900 years later, "had silver as plentiful as stones in the street."

With his new-found wealth, Solomon turned to construction; specifically, the design of an all-new sacred precinct for the Ark of the Covenant. His architects, steeped in Mesopotamian archetypes, designed a *megaron,* a rectangular shrine, preceded by a portal and flanked by naves, which ended in the inner sanctuary proper, known as the *debir.* In this Holy of Holies, covered throughout with gold, the Ark of the Covenant was placed. In front of the temple complex was a courtyard. Here Solomon placed a sacrificial altar and a bronze vessel called the "Sea of Bronze".

The Canaanite megaron of Hazor, which its excavator, Yigael Yadin, called "a prototype of the Temple of Solomon"

But all was not well in the kingdom. The northern tribes felt neglected, since much of the king's attention was focused on the southern tribe of Judah. They also didn't understand why David had chosen Jerusalem as the place of national worship when the North had ancient shrines like Shechem that went back to the days of the Patriarchs. In fact, none of the Northern tribes had ever accepted the idea of a *dynastic* monarchy that drew its kings *exclusively* from the tribe of Judah. All they had agreed to was to be recognized as an affiliated territory, not an integral 'province' of the Davidic Kingdom.

As soon as the reign of Solomon drew to a close, the Kingdom of Israel began to crumble. First, the region of Damascus revolted, broke away and set up an independent monarchy ruled by an Aramaean dynasty. Egypt then invaded and captured both Edom and Philistia, robbing Solomon of many of his most valuable ports.

Solomon's successor, his son Rohoboam, was wholly unequipped to deal with this threat. Sensing his weakness, the northern tribes broke their treaty with Jerusalem and anointed one of their own tribal leaders, Jeroboam, as king of a new state -- a *northern* state, henceforth to be known as "Israel". As a result, Rohoboam's kingdom shrunk to little more than the size of the tribe of Judah and Benjamin. It would be referred to as "Judah" from this time forward.

THE NARRATIVE OF THE next 900 years, from the split of Solomon's Kingdom to the conquest of Judaea by Rome, is the sad story of how Israel's flame of freedom flickered, sputtered and was ultimately extinguished. Until the 20th century, the principal sources for this story were the biblical Book of Kings (I and II), which offer a chronology from the death of David to the Babylonian captivity. But since the decipherment of cuneiform text in the early 1920's, a wealth of Assyrian and Babylonian literature has been made available to the modern historian as well. Naturally, the Mesopotamian and biblical texts often differ on details, and chronology is sometimes difficult to ascertain.

But it is unquestionable that these texts (and the rich legacy of Assyrian and Babylonian art) often provide an astonishing corroboration of the story as described in the Bible.

The reason for the decline of Israel is a topic of intense scholarly debate. For the Bible, however, the matter is quite clear. The very foundation of Israel, indeed its *raîson d'être*, was its covenant with YAHWEH. However, in the decades and centuries that followed the death of Solomon, the Israelites would consistently violate these terms. The Northern Kingdom, for example, broke away from Jerusalem and proceeded to set up rival shrines in the North. Both North and South would then succumb to the temptation of pagan gods and the false sense of security that they offered.

The Bible tells us that God then sent prophets, from Elijah to Jeremiah, to warn the headstrong rulers in both kingdoms that their faithlessness would provoke God's wrath; but with rare exceptions, these kings did not listen. The result was the ultimate destruction of their kingdoms: the North fell in 721 B.C.E., and the South ceased to exist in 587. As the final act of God's wrath, Jerusalem was destroyed, and all its inhabitants were led away into captivity.

The story of the fall of the Northern kingdom begins with the reign of a remarkably able ruler who rose to power in 885 B.C.E. His name was Omri, a general who had commanded the forces of the Northern Kingdom during one of its periodic campaigns against the Philistines. Omri sued for peace with the Southern Kingdom of Judah, and struck a pact with Tyre on the Phoenician coast, thus securing his eastern borders. He then sealed the treaty by marrying his son Ahab to Jezebel, daughter of Ethbaal, king of Sidon – with far-reaching consequences. Omri next marshaled his forces and rode out to reconquer the land of Moab, east of the Dead Sea, that once had been part of David's kingdom. In 1868, a missionary discovered a *stele* or marker of black basalt, carved with an inscription, near the town of Dhiban. The inscription reads:

> I am Mesha son of Chemosh ... king of Moab.
> Omri king of Israel had oppressed Moab for
> many days, as did his son...

The Moab stone, with a reference to king Omri, and 'vessels of 'Yahweh'

The stone thus provides a powerful confirmation of the narrative of the Bible. Moreover, the stone explicitly refers to the divine name *yhwh*: "(Mesha) took from there the vessels of Yahweh and dragged them before Chemosh."

His kingdom now expanded, Omri built a new capital for his Northern Kingdom -- one that could rival Jerusalem in the south. He settled on a hill in the mountains nearby, just northwest of Shechem, "and he called the name of the city which he built 'Samaria', after the name of Shemer, owner of the hill" (1 Kings 16:24). Thus rose Samaria, the capital of the Northern Kingdom of Israel. Upon Omri's death, his son Ahab continued work on the royal palace. Today, the remains of this palace are plainly visible, spread over a vast terrace buttressed by a thick, fortified wall that ranges 15 to 30 feet in width.

View of the Samaria palace complex, with Herodian additions in the foreground

Unfortunately, the Phoenician artisans who decorated the palace with ivory brought other things as well. They worshipped ancient Mesopotamian divinities we encountered earlier in Mesopotamia, such as Astarte and her consort, the fertility god Baal (known to the Phoenicians as *Asherah* and *Melkart*). King Ahab did little to deter this influx of heresy, for fear of insulting his wife Jezebel, the Phoenician princess. In fact, Jezebel was busy building a shrine to Baal of her own.

These pagan shrines infuriated a prophet known as Elijah. Even the Qur'an tells us, "Elijah admonished his people: Will you not be mindful of your duty to God? Do you call on Baal, and forsake the Best of creators, God, your Lord and the Lord of your forefathers of old?" (Q. 37:124-126). Even though Elijah won an important contest with Baal's priests, his pleas fell on deaf ears, and the prophet was forced to flee. His last prophecy was that all of Israel and Judah would be destroyed, except for those who remained faithful to YAHWEH -- "all the knees which have not bowed unto Baal, and every mouth which has not kissed him" (1 Kings 19:18). His prophecy was correct. Israel, the Northern Kingdom, would only last for two centuries; seven of its nineteen kings would die a violent death. Judah, the Southern Kingdom, only fared marginally better: it lasted for 350 years, ruled consistently by monarchs from the House of David. Then, it too descended into chaos.

THE INSTRUMENT OF GOD'S WRATH, as the Bible presents it, was Assyria. With its capital of Ashur, Assyria had formed part of the old Babylonian Empire in the days of Abraham. It was an autonomous region with strong Akkadian influences. By the 14th century, before the period of the Exodus, Assyria began to assert itself. It conquered large swaths of land in what is today Armenia and northern Syria. By the 9th century, Assyria encompassed the northern half of Mesopotamia, from the river Diyala to Carchemish and Haran, the place where Abraham's father had passed away. It thus controlled the trade up and down the Tigris and the Euphrates.

In 883 B.C.E., a new Assyrian king named Ashurnasirpal II rose to power. Ashurnasirpal felt the time had come for Assyria to make its presence felt on the world stage. His official aim was religious in nature: he wanted to convert foreign peoples to the enlightened faith of the Assyrian god Ashur. Of course, this privilege would come with a heavy tribute.

To realize his dream, Ashurnasirpal pushed the Assyrian border to the Persian Gulf and conquered all of Babylonia. The key to this conquests was Ashurnasirpal's ingenuous use of cavalry units to spearhead and screen the movement of infantry and chariot forces. He was also the first to develop the concept of a heavy battering ram, placed on wheels, to break through the walls of cities that were foolish enough to resist him.

Ashurnasirpal's son Shalmaneser III continued this policy of aggressive military expansion. Since most of Mesopotamia was already under the Assyrian boot, the only available territory lay northwest. The king's forces won the battles of Carchemish and Aleppo, but then ran into determined resistance from an alliance that had been hastily cobbled together. This alliance not only included Phoenicians, Syrians and Egyptians (including Arab Bedouins mounted on camels), but also the forces of Israel led by king Ahab. Before long, however, the alliance was defeated.

A remarkably vivid "snapshot" of this state of affairs has come to us in the form a large black obelisk, now in the British Museum. The obelisk shows Shalmaneser and the winged god Assur receiving tribute from a king with clearly defined Semitic features. The inscription reads: "Tribute of Jehu the Israelite."

The Shalmaneser Obelisk, with Ahab's tribute to the Assyrian king

The name is spelled *ia-ú-a mar hu-um-ri-i*, which literally means "Jehu son of Omri."

In 744 B.C.E., Tiglath-pileser III (referred to as 'Pul' in the Bible) ascended to the Assyrian throne, and continued his predecessors' policy of conquest. His vision was to create a vast empire that would stretch from the Euphrates to the Nile. Ten years later, he was close to realizing his goal. Tiglath-pileser's armies had moved down the coast of Palestine and taken all the ports up to Gaza, close to the borders of Egypt. Once again, the regional monarchs agreed that it was time to put regional quarrels aside, and form a defensive alliance. The monarch of the southern Jewish Kingdom, King Ahaz of Judah, was far from pleased by these developments. He interpreted this *Einkreisung* as an attempt by the North to, once again, isolate and ultimately overrun the South.

A desperate man, Ahaz made a pact with the devil. He appealed for help from Tiglath-pileser himself. The Assyrian king was only too happy to oblige. To demonstrate his good faith, king Ahaz made a big show of importing Assyrian gods. He even went as far as to place these pagan symbols in Solomon's Temple precinct proper -- much to the astonishment of devout worshippers.

Tiglath-pileser then moved against the Anti-Assyrian coalition and rolled up the states of Syria, Tyre and Ashkelon, followed by the Northern Kingdom of Israel. This kingdom was broken up into the separate Assyrian provinces of Dor, Megiddo and Gilead. When the dismemberment was complete, the last remaining pieces around the capital of Samaria were tossed to King Hoshea, to rule as a puppet king under Assyria.

Tiglath-pileser next indulged in wholesale deportation. Entire villages were deported to Assyria and servitude, while Assyrian settlers and army veterans moved in to take over their possessions. As the Bible mournfully notes, "Tiglath-pileser King of Assyria came and captured Ijon, Abel-Beth-Maacah... Hazor, Gilead and Galilee, and all the land of Naphtali; and he carried the people captive to Assyria" (2 Kings 15:29).

Attack on an enemy town by Assyrian infantry, archers and a siege-engine. From Nimrud, ca. 865

Hoshea was then toppled by a new Assyrian ruler named Sargon II (721-705 B.C.E.). All of the remaining population of Israel was force-marched to Syria, Western Iran and northern Mesopotamia. In his annals, Sargon proudly boasts of having uprooted no less than 27,000 Israelites. Their homes, their fields and their cattle were appropriated by Babylonian "settlers," many of whom hailed from Cuthah in Babylonia.

These Babylonian newcomers assimilated with the remaining inhabitants of Samaria, married, and had children. In time, many of these foreign settlers were persuaded to abandon their native pagan worship and embrace the worship of YAHWEH. Thus was born a new group of Israelites, called the 'Samaritans'.

Still, Babylonian blood continued to course through their veins. The Israelites in surrounding regions never forgave them. The inhabitants of Samaria became pariahs, treated as outcasts by fellow Jews. The Jewish historian Flavius Josephus, writing in the late 1st century C.E., scathingly called them 'Cuthaeans' (*Ant.*

XI.2) The *apartheid* policy against the 'Samaritans' continued into the time of Jesus, and even to this day.

Then it was Judah's turn. Judah was ruled at the time by king Hezekiah, who wanted to restore Judah's role as broker and toll-keeper in the prosperous trade between Egypt and the Assyrian empire. To do so, Hezekiah struck an alliance with the vassal king of Babylonia, named Merodach-baladan. The rapprochement alarmed the prophet Isaiah. He feared that Hezekiah would fall into the same trap that his predecessor Ahaz had fallen into. Isaiah confronted the king and said, "Behold, the days come, that all that is in your house, and that which your fathers have laid up in store until this day, shall be carried into Babylon: nothing shall be left, says the Lord" (2 Kings 20:17).

Hezekiah did not listen. In fact, he hatched an audacious plan: to launch a rebellion against Assyria with his new partner, Babylonia. Unfortunately, the Assyrian King Sennacherib (704-681 B.C.E.) was served by a highly efficient intelligence service. He found out about the plot well before the Babylonian emissaries returned home. Sennacherib met the forces of king Merodach-baladan, defeated them, and put a new puppet king on the Babylonian throne. He then turned his forces west, and systematically began to destroy all of Hezekiah's fortified cities. As the Book of Kings tells us, "in the fourteenth year of king Hezekiah did Sennacherib king of Assyria come up against all the fenced cities of Judah, and took them" (2 Kings 18:13). The biblical account is confirmed by Sennacherib's delicately carved clay prism (a block with six sides), which describes the Assyrian campaign in detail:

> As to Hezekiah (*ha-za-qi-a-u*), the Jew, he did not
> submit to my yoke, so I laid siege to 46 of his strong
> cities, walled forts and to the countless small villages in
> their vicinity, and conquered these by means of
> earth-ramps and battering rams, with an attack

by foot soldiers.

One of these 'strong cities' was the Judean city of Lachish. The grisly details of this battle would later inspire artists in Niniveh to produce four panels in bas-relief, which today can be seen in the British Museum in London. The panels feature the redoubtable Assyrian armored battering ram on wheels, the tank of antiquity. Another panel shows the male defenders being stripped and bound by Assyrian soldiers, before being forcibly impaled on stakes.

Prisoners of Lachish are impaled by their Assyrian conquerors. Nimrud, 700 B.C.E.

Jerusalem was next. But then, one day, the army of Sennacherib pulled up the pegs of its tents, loaded its wagons, and headed home. The Bible suggests the hand of God in all this. According to the Book of Kings, YAHWEH struck the army with the plague.

What does Sennacherib's prism stone say? Nothing, other than the tribute offered by Hezekiah. So what happened? Historians are not ready to discount the possibility of a sudden disease ravaging the ranks of the Assyrians; after all, they had been campaigning for quite some time, and the land of Judah was harsh terrain. Then again, we also know of another sudden uprising in the north, in Babylonia. Perhaps Sennacherib thought that the denuded and impoverished Jewish king was not worth the lives of his veteran soldiers. They were needed elsewhere, in the homelands of Assyria itself. Indeed, Sennacherib would spend the last twelve years of his life trying to suppress the ever-budding nationalist forces within his far-flung realm.

The 'Taylor Prism', which lists the military campaigns of Sennacherib. Niniveh, 691 B.C.E.

The last chapter of Judah was written by king Josiah, who was crowned in 641 by popular acclamation, even though he was only eight years old. Fortunately, Josiah was an excellent choice. During his reign, the flame of Judah's independence would flicker one last time before it was finally extinguished for centuries to come.

Josiah dared to dream of fulfilling Israel's destiny, and restore the glory of the Davidic Empire. Other Judean kings had had the same vision, and had come to regret it. But Josiah seemed to be guided by a divine hand. In short order, Josiah was able to reassert Jewish control over territories previously lost to Philistia, Ephraim and Assyria. In the span of twenty years, Josiah recovered all of Judah, Samaria and Gilead, as well as the Galilean hills. With all these territories under one crown, Josiah realized that mere conquest was not enough. In order to bind this greater Israel together, he needed a focal point to foster a sense of national identity, through the national worship of YAHWEH. The allusion to the Davidic precedent is obvious.

The Bible tells us that Josiah set about to restore the Temple and purge the land of pagan gods. He issued a decree against the worship of Baal or Astarte. The king also punished those who continued to practice the odious cult of child sacrifice, which continued to take place in the shrines to Moloch in the Valley of Hinnom (or *Gehenna*, a word that would become synonymous with 'hell').

But most of his people had forgotten about YAHWEH. Who indeed, still remembered the Mosaic Laws, let alone practiced them? Josiah recognized that the record of Jewish history, and the scope of the Mosaic Laws, needed to be written down and codified. Thus began the first organized attempt to record the Bible, by compiling the many (and often conflicting) fragments of oral and written history into one comprehensive volume of books, which would ultimately produce the Pentateuch and Deuteronomistic History that we have today.

Meanwhile, in 612 B.C.E., the Medean Kingdom had joined forces with the Babylonians and dealt a stunning defeat to Assyria. They even succeeded in sacking the capital of Niniveh. Assyria, thoroughly weakened, looked about for allies, and entered into an treaty with Egypt. This filled King Josiah with dread. He had little doubt about what would happen to Israel if Egypt and Assyria were able to reassert themselves. The king of Judah summoned his army and encamped near Megiddo, opposite the Mount Carmel passes through which the phalanx of Pharaoah was expected to march. Here, Josiah lay in ambush, and as soon as the Egyptians appeared, his forces fell upon them. Alas, the Egyptians had far more chariot forces and archers than he had expected. Josiah lay mortally wounded by an arrow. With him fell the last Jewish hope for independence.

The fortress of Megiddo, where king Josiah was killed

The new Babylonian king, Nebuchadnezzar, vowed he would punish Egypt's traitorous support of Assyria, and levied a heavy tribute on the new king of Judah, Jehoiakim. But to the astonishment of his officials, Jehoiakim began talking of a new anti-Babylonian Alliance. The prophet Jeremiah strenuously tried to discourage Jehoiakim from this course of action. Like Isaiah before him, Jeremiah had an accurate premonition of the fate that was in store for Judah if the King persisted with his ambitious folly. He was incensed Jehoiakim allowed Judah to slide back in its old ways of worshipping Baal and Moloch.

Jeremiah warned that God's revenge would be swift and merciless. "For 23 years, the word of the Lord has come to me, and I have spoken to you," Jeremah railed against the people of Jerusalem, "but you did not listen" (Jer 25:3). If Judah persisted in its evil ways, the prophet said, he would send "Nebuchadrezzar the king of Babylon, my servant, who would bring them against this land, and against the inhabitants thereof, and against all these nations round about, and will utterly destroy them" (Jer 25: 9-11).

Jeremiah's prediction was spot on. "In the ninth year of Zedekiah king of Judah," says the book of Jeremiah, "in the tenth month, came Nebuchadrezzar king of Babylon and all his army against Jerusalem, and they besieged it" (Jer 39:2). Tormented by the stultifying heat of August, 587, the exhausted city finally gave in. The invaders gave no quarter. Jerusalem and its Temple, built by Solomon, were systematically razed. Virtually all of its inhabitants were either slaughtered or carried off into captivity.

Nebuchadnezzar knew about Jeremiah and the prophet's prophesy that the city would be captured. The king left instructions that Jeremiah should be spared. The prophet was set free and given passage to Egypt, where he lived his final years.

LOOKING BACK, THEN, THE THREE hundred years since the days of David and Solomon seem a never-ending tale of strife, intrigue, war and wholesale slaughter. Why? Why did the Golden Age evaporate so quickly?

The Israelite prophets, according to the Bible's Deuteronomistic History, argued that it was the fault of the Hebrews themselves. Time and again, they had allowed themselves to be seduced by the lure of foreign gods and their exotic practices. Historians, however, believe that there were other factors at play.

Firstly, the unified kingdom of David and Solomon was in truth little more a chimera, a state based on wishful thinking rather than hard tribal support. The northern tribes had never submitted to the authority of Jerusalem; they had merely agreed to be "allied" with the king. These tribes resented the favoritism shown by David to the tribe of Judah, and thus chose to abandon the unified kingdom at the first available opportunity, in order to form their own "united tribes" of the North. Thus deprived of the revenues from the fertile northern valleys, cut off from the principal ports by the newly independent coastal states, Judah's economy was bound to falter. The ensuing cold war between the two Jewish kingdoms merely served to weaken their defenses when they should have been more concerned about the new superpower to the north, Assyria and its successor, Neo-Babylonia.

The saga of ancient Israel had the misfortune of unfolding during a time of political landslides that changed the landscape of the Middle East forever. For centuries, Egypt's power had served to stabilize the Fertile Crescent and thwart foreign aggression. But Egypt's power was on the decline, its economy exhausted by a royal funerary cult that consumed a disproportionate share of its gross national product. The result was an economic vacuum that caused the migration of thousands of disenfranchised people, and invited foreign intervention.

In the centuries to come, there would come moments when it appeared that a restoration was possible, particularly during the period of the Maccabean princes. But then another calamity would strike, or another foreign potentate would squash the hopes of Jewish independence.

And in the meantime, the Hebrew captives sighed and sang their forlorn hymns at the rivers of Babylon.

Chapter Ten

From Alexander to Herod the Great

The theater of Scythopolis (Beth She'an), one of several "Hellenized" cities in Palestine

With the advent of the 6th century B.C.E., the world entered into a new era. The first ruler to make his mark on the region's history during this period was Cyrus II, king of a vassal kingdom called Persia. He first defeated king Astyages of the Medes (550 B.C.E.) and the legendary King Croesus of the kingdom of Lydia (547 B.C.E.). He then conquered Babylonia, creating the new Persian Empire in the process.

The principal counterweight to Persian expansion was Greece, with Athens at the center of the Greek "sphere of influence". Athens would continue to dominate cultural activity in the Mediterranean basin long after the political control of Greece had ceased. Art, architecture, literature, rhetoric, drama, philosophy and statecraft were Greek exports that would be admired and imitated for centuries to come – particularly after the rise of one indomitable Greek conqueror, Alexander the Great. This pervasive cultural influence, which extended into the lands of the former kingdoms of Judah and Israel, is called "Hellenism" – after the Greek word *Hellas* or "Greece".

Fortunately for the Hebrew exiles in Babylon, Cyrus II was an enlightened ruler quite unlike the Assyrian and Babylonian kings that preceded him. The Persian king had a policy of trying to "win the hearts and minds" of his newly conquered territories. He promised to respect native gods and cults, appointed local governors, and generally left people to sort out their own affairs, provided they paid the annual tribute.

The Bible hails Cyrus as the king who released the Jews from their Babylonian captivity. He even granted the exiles safe passage back to Judah – which was now known as the sub-province of *Yehud*, part of the fifth Persian satrapy known as *'Abar nahara* ("Beyond the [Euphrates] River"), rather than a Babylonian province.

This is when we first hear of a Hebrew author/prophet who is not known by name. He speaks in the name of Isaiah, even though Isaiah has been dead for years. As a result, most sources call him 'Second Isaiah'. But his powers as an orator are beyond doubt. What's more, his God is a different God. This is no longer the YAHWEH of Old Testament *terribilità*, the War God who "smites" his enemies and torments the Hebrew nation with foreign invaders. This is a kinder and gentler God, a God of an era in which political ambition has become irrelevant:

> (Second) Isaiah
> Comfort, O comfort my people, says your God.
> Speak tenderly to Jerusalem, and cry unto her,
> that her term has been served.
> A voice cries out in the wilderness,
> Prepare the way of the LORD, make straight
> in the desert a highway for our God.

Every valley shall be exalted, and every mountain
and hill shall be made low: and the crooked shall
be made straight, and the rough places plain.
(Isa. 40:1-4)

"Every valley shall be exalted, and every mountain made low." It is a vision of utopia, a world far removed from the terror of Nebuchadnezzar, or the jaded indulgence of Babylon. What Second Isaiah is telling his people, is that God has been mollified; the penalty has been paid. From now on, God will "feed his flock like a shepherd: he shall gather the lambs with his arm, and carry them in his bosom, and shall gently lead those that are with young" (Isa. 40:11).

Slowly but surely, Jerusalem began to assume a Jewish identity once again. But what did it mean to be a Jew? Naturally, the old dream of restoring independence was out of the question. There was neither an army nor a treasure to pay for it. Besides, few Jews were willing to exchange the security of the *Pax Medea* for a return to the days of danger, siege and plunder.

As a result, the very idea of a Jewish identity began to shift. It moved from a political to a spiritual dimension. People began to realize that it was the worship of YAHWEH, rather than national statehood, that made the Jewish people special and unique. Observing the Mosaic rites of sacrifice and purity, retelling the stories of the escape from Egypt, or singing David's psalms could be as much a celebration of the Jewish consciousness as anything else.

As it happened, the priesthood had anticipated this need. During the Exile in Babylon, with little else to do, some priests had seized the opportunity to continue the work of organizing the Hebrew Scriptures that had begun during the time of king Josiah. Preserving these Jewish traditions had become a matter of some urgency, lest the Jewish exiles forget their national heritage – indeed their very identity as descendants of Moses. Thus, beginning with the Exile and continuing after their return in Jerusalem, the priests and their scribes set to work to "catalog" what would ultimately become the Hebrew Scriptures.

BLESSED BY CYRUS' PATRONAGE, the reconstruction of the Temple in Jerusalem – now known as the "Second Temple" – was duly completed in 515 B.C.E. However, despite the resumption of sacrifice and the ongoing work of "redacting" the Bible, few people actually practiced the Mosaic laws. Many of the recent arrivals from Babylonia had married with existing settlers, who were not Jews at all but resettled peoples from every corner of the Babylonian empire. The post-captivity land of Yehud threatened to become a melting pot in which the Jewish character was slowly disappearing.

Word of this filtered back to Ezra, who was greatly troubled. He appealed to the successor of Cyrus, Artaxerxes I, who had continued Cyrus' religious policies. Artaxerxes shared Ezra's concern, but for different reasons. He knew a mixed population of different racial and religious backgrounds would eventually reject the jurisdiction of the Jewish priesthood, and clamor for new legislation -- possibly even a new régime -- of their own. Artaxerxes thereupon authorized Ezra to return to Jerusalem and enforce a strict observance of the Jewish laws. It is interesting to note that the segment in the Book of Ezra that quotes this mandate of Artaxerxes is written in Aramaic, the *lingua franca* of the Persian Empire, instead of the customary Hebrew. It is possible that the author is paraphrasing directly from the official court document that charged Ezra with his mission, as the Bible suggests: "This is a copy of the letter that King Artaxerxes gave to the priest Ezra" (Ezra 7:11-14).

Ezra followed his instructions to the letter. He ordered everyone to adhere to a strict observance of the Mosaic laws and to obey the priesthood -- even to the point of divorcing any spouse who was not Jewish. For the next several decades, the people of Yehud were left in peace. But in the restless world of the Near East, great changes were once again afoot.

FOR SEVERAL CENTURIES, Greece and Persia had eyed each other warily across the Mediterranean. The Greek city-states were often embroiled in civil war, but when in 492 B.C.E. Persia appeared on the shores of the Aegean Sea, all rivalry was forgotten. Sparta, Athens and others joined forces to repel the Persian invader. A peace was signed in 449 B.C.E., but a cold war of clashing economic interests continued.

The seductive elegance of Greek culture continued to seep into the Persia and the Near East at large. Judah was no exception. By the 4th century, there was a large Greek colony in Akko and other coastal communities. Thus, the Hellenization of Judah was already under way well before a dynamic young warrior named Alexander the Great appeared on the scene. The son of Philip, King of Macedon, Alexander had updated the military concept first introduced by the Assyrians: the flying cavalry, working in tandem with *hoplites* or heavy infantry.

Alexander the Great, a posthumous portrait from the 2^{-} century B.C.E.

Alexander proceeded to create an empire at the expense of Greece's arch-enemy Persia. He dealt a crushing defeat to the Persian King Darius III in 333. Alexander continued his steamroller into the Persian realm. One after one, Tyre, Judah and Egypt fell prey to the young god from Macedon.

Ten years later, Alexander was killed in battle, and a power struggle ensued among his generals about control of the new Macedonian Empire. Ptolemy, one of Alexander's ablest generals, acquired the Persian satrapies of Egypt and Yehud. He went on to establish the Ptolemaic Dynasty, which would rule over the region until the advent of the Seleucid era.

The Ptolemies brought many changes to Yehud – or Judaea, as it now became known. Hellenistic "pagan" influence was no longer incidental; it became the coin of the realm. For the next 300 years, the Jews would fight this new cultural imperialism with varying degrees of success until the arrival of a new and far more brutal imperialism imposed by Rome.

At first, it appeared that Greek and Jewish cultural values could co-exist. Since Egypt and Judaea were now one political entity, a number of enterprising Jews settled in Alexandria, founded by Alexander the Great in 332 B.C.E. Under Ptolemy I, it became the new capital of Egypt. By the 3rd century B.C.E., Alexandria was the Athens of the Middle East. Here was an astronomical observatory, a zoo, a botanical garden, and above all, a magnificent library. Soon, this library would boast over 400,000 volumes – the greatest concentration of learning in Antiquity.

As the Jewish community in Alexandria grew, so too did its assimilation with the local population. Naturally, they were no longer able to sacrifice in the Temple in Jerusalem -- but worship they did. For this purpose, they built small community houses known as *synagogues*. Here, the congregation would come together on the Sabbath and read from the Hebrew Scriptures, now available in a canon thanks to the scribes and priests of the 6th and 5th centuries.

The only problem was its language. The sacred scrolls of the Torah were, naturally, written in Hebrew. But in Alexandria as in most of the Mediterranean, people spoke Greek. The obvious solution was to translate the Hebrew Bible into Greek. The result was a work known as the *Septuagint* - from the Latin word for 'seventy,' based on the legend that 72 Jewish scribes from Jerusalem were tasked to work on the translation. Most historians believe that the translation was actually carried out by scribes in the Alexandrian community itself, but that the hand print of Jerusalem scholars was added so as to lend greater authority to the work.

The tensions between Greek and Jewish culture worsened when in 198 B.C.E. king Ptolemy V was defeated in the battle of Paneion. The victor was Antiochus III, the Seleucid king of Syria, likewise a descendant of one of Alexander's generals. As a result, Judaea now became part of the satrapy of Syria and Phoenicia.

The Aphrodite of Cnidos, after the Greek original by Praxiteles, 350 B.C.E. Whilst much of the Mediterranean world embraced Greek art, observant Jews were horrified by its penchant for nude statuary

At first, Antiochus ruled as a benign despot. He expressly granted the Jews the freedom to live and worship according to their law and custom. But his successor, Antiochus IV, thought that his realm should become more thoroughly unified. He decreed a total and thorough embrace of Hellenistic values, rites and culture. Local customs and beliefs were forbidden -- including the Mosaic Laws and Temple sacrifice.

When the Jews strenuously resisted, Antiochus rounded up thousands of Jews and sold them into slavery. He forced others to participate in the drunken rites of Dionysius, the Greek god of wine. Worst of all, he planted an altar in the center of the Second Temple in Jerusalem, dedicated to none other than the Greek Upper God, Zeus. It was the final straw.

Horrified by this terror, a priest named Mattathias retaliated and killed one of Antiochus' officials. This dramatic act galvanized the resistance. Mattathias and three of his sons – Judas, Jonathan and Simon – launched a revolt that ultimately established the *Hasmonean* dynasty, named after Mattathias' great-grandfather, Asamonaios. When Mattathias was killed shortly thereafter, his son Judas, appropriately called *Maccabeus* ("The Hammer") took over the torch of the rebellion. Jewish able-bodied men throughout the region flocked to his call.

Surprisingly, the so-called 'Maccabean Revolt', a movement enshrined in the national pride of modern Israel, succeeded above all expectations. In 164 B.C.E., Judas was able to cleanse the temple and re-dedicate it to Jewish worship -- an event still celebrated to this day with the Jewish festival of Hanukkah. The war with Antiochus IV continued unabated, but Judas gave no quarter. In 161 B.C.E., he achieved a spectacular victory over the forces of the Syrian commander Nicanor and his elephant cavalry. When Judas himself was killed in the following year, his brother Jonathan took over the leadership of the revolt. Jonathan continued to pound the Seleucid armies until Antiochus' successor, Demetrius I, finally sued for peace.

Under the terms of the treaty of 152 B.C.E., Jonathan was invested as governor of the autonomous province of Judaea.

Two years later, when Demetrius was succeeded by king Alexander Balas, the Seleucid leadership went a step further: it also appointed Jonathan as the hereditary high priest of the Temple in Jerusalem -- combining the roles of Ruler and High Priest as in the days of King David. Jonathan was killed by Seleucid assassins, but his younger brother Simon succeeded him and continued the struggle for complete independence. That moment arrived five years later, in 142 B.C.E., some 445 years after the capture of Jerusalem by Nebuchadnezzar. Judaea was once again an independent kingdom. The Jews were free -- free to worship, free to sacrifice, free to live according to the laws promulgated by Moses.

Unfortunately, all was not well. The problem was the priesthood. For centuries now, the priests who ministered to the Temple were selected from an exclusive class that traced its lineage back to Zadok, the high priest of king David. Jonathan did not belong to that class. Hence, his assumption of the position of High Priest, regardless of his pivotal role in the struggle for Jewish independence, was invalid. This is why large portions of the Jewish population deeply resented the Hasmonean dynasty and their usurpation of priestly status.

The 'Intertestamental Writings' – books written by Jews in the era between the Hebrew Scriptures and the New Testament — are full of apocalyptic visions, a genre rarely seen in preceding centuries. Certainly, the presence of a 'false' priest-king spurred the Jewish desire for the return of a true Davidic King, a genuinely anointed ruler or *Messiah,* with greater urgency than ever before. One such book is the 'Psalms of Solomon', written (despite its title) in the first century B.C.E. "(God) shall judge peoples and nations in the wisdom of his righteousness," says its author; "and he shall have the heathen nations to serve him under his yoke" (Ps. of Sol. XVII: 31-32). Elsewhere, the author articulates his generation's desire for a 'cleansing' of the nation by the firm hand of a Messiah:

Psalms
May God cleanse Israel against the day of mercy and blessing, against the day of choice when He brings back His anointed. Blessed shall be they that live in those days, for they shall see the goodness of the Lord which He shall perform for the generation that is to come, under the chastening rod of the Lord's anointed.
(Ps. of Sol. XVIII: 6-8)

The dissatisfaction with the priestly community spread. 'Dissident' sects sprang up -- a new and ominous development in Judaism. One sect was so horrified by Jonathan's assumption of the role of High Priest that they broke away from urban culture altogether and fled into the desert. There, they reportedly formed a commune and lived an ascetic lifestyle that focused exclusively on the pursuit of the Mosaic Laws -- specifically, its rigorous rules of cleanliness. Much has been written about this sect, which was identified by the Jewish historian Josephus as the Essenes. These Jews dressed in simple robes, prayed at regular intervals, and worked long hours to till the desert soil. Like the author of the 'Psalms of Solomon', the Essenes longed for the arrival of a genuine Messiah, a king from the line of David, who would herald a new era of political freedom and strict observance of the Mosaic Laws.

It is possible that the Essenes were also scribes. A long debate has been raging in archaeological circles whether the remains of a 1st century community in Qumran, close to the Dead Sea, is in some way linked to the sect of Essenes described by Josephus. Recent scholars have suggested they may have been a faction that broke away from the Essenes.

The remains of the settlement at Qumran, believed to have been used by a sect responsible for creating the Dead Sea Scrolls

Whatever the case may be, the Qumran community copied almost all of the Hebrew Scriptures as they appeared in the first century. When not in use, these scrolls were placed for safekeeping in large clay jars. When in 70 C.E. ("Common Era" or 'AD') the Roman army moved closer to crush the Jewish revolt of 66-70, the Qumranites hastily gathered the jars and placed them in caves, high up in the mountains of the Judaean Desert. There they remained as the centuries rolled on, preserved in the dry air of the desert, until 1947 when a young Bedouin shepherd went looking for a lost sheep and stumbled upon them.

These 'Dead Sea Scrolls' are nearly a thousand years older than what was previously the oldest extant manuscript of the Bible, which dates from the 9th century. In all, the treasure trove near the Dead Sea contained over 400 manuscripts, including 100 works related to the Hebrew Scriptures.

One of the caves in which the Dead Sea Scrolls were found in 1947.

Meanwhile, trouble was brewing in the ruling Hasmonean House. Upon the death of Salome Alexandra in 67 B.C.E., her two sons Hyrcanus II and Aristobulus II both vied for the throne. At Hyrcanus' bidding, the Nabataean king Aretas III lay siege to Jerusalem, plunging the nation into civil war.

It so happened that the Roman General Pompey and his army were in the region to put an end to a war waged by Mithradates VI, the king of Pontus (the northern coastal region of modern Turkey). When news of the Hasmonean strife reached him, Pompey had already extended Roman rule from the Caucasus to Syria. The Roman general was delighted to hear of the Hasmonean conlfict. It gave him the perfect pretext to swing his armies around and extend the 'Pax Romana' into Judaea, to the very borders of Egypt -- Rome's strategic source of wheat. Thus, in 63 B.C.E., Pompey invaded the Jewish kingdom and extinguished the brief flame of Jewish independence.

Hyrcanus won his crown, but Judaea was now a vassal state, ruled by a puppet king under orders from Rome.

The maneuvering between Pompey and Hyrcanus was observed with keen interest by a young man named Herod. Herod's father, Antipater, was a wealthy Idumaean (the region of the Dead Sea) who had married the daughter of a nobleman from Nabataea. Thus, Arab blood flowed in Herod's veins, even though his family ostensibly practiced the Jewish faith, as all inhabitants of Idumaea were forced to do after the conquest of their territory by the Hasmoneans. Antipater had long pondered the rise of Roman power and decided that it would be wise to cultivate ties with Rome. When Pompey arrived, he rushed to pledge his support, in the hope that Pompey would look favorably on his family's ambitions. Before long, Antipater and his son Herod were welcomed in the circle of Julius Caesar. Here, Herod began a life-long friendship with Mark Antony.

In 47 B.C.E., Antipater's efforts paid off when he was duly named procurator of Judaea, a role akin to that of 'Prime Minister' under Hyrcanus, and given the extraordinary honor of Roman citizenship. Antipater wasted no time in appointing his own son Herod governor of Galilee. Seven years later, this happy state of affairs was thrown into disarray when the Parthians invaded Judaea, endangering not only the power of the Herodian family, but Roman sovereignty itself.

Herod fled to Rome and was invited to address the Roman Senate. He persuaded the senators that he, Herod, was Rome's best hope for restoring law and order in Judaea. The Senate agreed, and promised to make him king of Judaea if he succeeded. They also voted for a Roman army to accompany him. Thus Herod returned to Judaea in 37 B.C.E., brought the region under his control after a series of bloody clashes, and began a reign of 32 years, protected by the long arm of Rome.

Herod soon revealed himself as a shrewd operator with an uncanny talent for survival – as well as an almost pathological streak of cruelty. For the king was forced to to walk a fine line between placating his Jewish population and abetting his Roman protectors, so despised by his subjects.

To curry favor with both, Herod launched a vast building program. On the coast between Joppa and Haifa, he created a state-of-the-art harbor dedicated to Julius Caesar, named Caesarea. To buttress his unpopular rule, Herod threw a ring of defensive forts around his realm. The most famous fortifications were the massive Herodium in the Judaean desert, and the 'hanging palace' of the fortress of Masada, overlooking the Dead Sea.

In Jerusalem, Herod built a military complex, including an arsenal and troop barracks, known as the Antonia Fortress, in honor of Mark Antony. It bordered directly on the Temple precinct, for Herod knew that if trouble came, it would most likely occur in the forecourt of the Temple. From the Antonia, Roman soldiers could surround the Temple area in minutes -- as they would soon be called upon to do.

Undoubtedly, Herod's greatest achievement was the extension of the Second Temple into a magnificent sacred complex, built to the highest standards of Hellenistic architecture. Covering no less than one-sixth the area of the city, it featured a large central platform with running colonnades, accessible through staircases on two sides. Part of this staircase is still visible today.

The entire complex was supported by a huge wall. Josephus, who knew the Temple well, gives us an eyewitness account:

> "The temple had doors also at the entrance, and lintels over them, of the same height with the temple itself. They were adorned with embroidered veils, with their flowers of purple, and pillars interwoven; and over these, but under the crown-work, was spread out a golden vine, with its branches hanging down from a great height, the largeness and fine workmanship of which was a surprising sight to the spectators, to see what vast materials there were, and with

what great skill the workmanship was done." (Josephus, *Antiquities*, XV:11)

The recently excavated staircase in the Ophel archaeological park, which led to one of the entrances of the Herodian Temple complex

AS THE LAST DECADE BEFORE the beginning of the Common Era began, Herod could gaze upon a land that had changed beyond all recognition. In many places, dusty Jewish settlements were now splendid cities graced with sparkling colonnades, with palaces and fora, all trimmed with red tile and marble. New roads cut across the country, patrolled by Roman soldiers as well as Herod's militia to secure the safety of travelers. Great *trireme* ships plied the waters and nestled in the magnificent embrace of the port of Caesarea.

However, all this was on the surface. Beneath the veneer of Hellenistic gentility, unrest seethed throughout the country. Herod's boom economy had only paid dividends to the upper crust of society that was willing to collaborate with the Roman occupiers. The vast majority of Jews, if not pressed into work gangs on Herod's projects, remained disenfranchised.

Worse, all Jews had to register with the censor so that they could be taxed more effectively, and pay *both* the Roman Emperor *and* the court of Herod. This double taxation, which came on top of the 10% of harvest proceeds due to the priesthood, destroyed the social fabric of the nation, particularly in Galilee, where thousands lost their lands to forfeiture because of non-payment of taxes. The terrible socio-economic crisis wrought by Herod in Galilee, and the attendant specter of thousands of homeless and dispossessed farmers, would form the stage (if not the primary motive) for Jesus' ministry in the generation to come.

A new proletariat was emerging in Judaea. This was a silent mass of uneducated, marginalized Jews, the flotsam of a stagnant economy, with little hope of improving their lot.

This aqueduct formed part of Herod's vast new harbor complex in Caesarea, later the headquarters of the Roman prefect in Judaea

The third column of Jewish society, religious sects like the Sadducees, the Essenes and the Pharisees, were opposed to Herod as well. The Sadducees (or *Tzedoqim* in Hebrew) formed the priestly sect that had originally been charged with the maintenance of the Temple and supervision of the rites of sacrifice. Tradition suggests that they descended from the High Priest Zadok, who served under David and Solomon. With their privileged status, the Sadducees were truly the aristocracy of Jewish society. They were wealthy, arch-conservative, and generally well-disposed towards the Roman Occupation. Roman suzerainty guaranteed stability and peace, thus allowing Jews throughout the realm to come and sacrifice at the Temple as often as possible.

Because of their wealth and superior attitude, the Sadducees were heartily despised by the common man. Many Jews (including Jesus) felt that the Sadducees were hypocrites, outwardly more concerned with the minutiae of the Law than with piety for God. What's more, the Sadducees did not accept any scripture beyond the Pentateuch – the Five Books of Moses. All the subsequent writings of the Prophets, the Psalms and the Oral Law meant little to them.

Unlike their chief rivals, the Pharisees, Sadducees had real power. In a carefully negotiated deal, the Sadducees had agreed to relinquish their power over the appointment of the High Priest to the Romans, in return for gaining jurisdiction over all principal domestic matters through the agency of the Priestly Council (or *Sanhedrin*), in which they had a controlling vote. The Romans gained a free hand in appointing a High Priest who was most favorable to their interests. Candidates were usually chosen from a small group of politically reliable families. For example, no less than seven members of the family of the Sadducee Annas (including his son-in-law, Caiaphas) held the office of High Priest in succession.

By contrast, the Pharisees were a group of pious laymen who passionately believed in the validity of post-Mosaic Scripture as well as the growing corpus of the so-called Oral Law. This comprised a body of commentary developed by Jewish scholars and theologians over the preceding centuries. The Pharisees believed that while the Torah was the pre-eminent authority, it was, admittedly, written in a very different frame of time. The purpose of the Oral Law, then, was to record the application of the Written Law during subsequent generations of Jews, living in periods of great upheaval, each of which would deepen the understanding of the Law and prepare future generations for the challenges of their time. The Torah, for the Pharisees, was not a document frozen in time, but a living body of Divine wisdom that could lead to new solutions as the context of time warranted.

The Pharisees were therefore a progressive force in terms of biblical exegesis, and it is probably due to their efforts that the accumulated body of Oral Law would become enshrined in the *Mishnah* of the 3rd century C.E., as the first component of the Jewish Talmud.

The Pharisees also maintained a strict code of ritual observance, including rules of purity originally developed for the Temple, in their own homes. The sophistication of this Pharisaic lifestyle had a particular appeal to well-to-do urban Jews, who could afford their own bathing pools or *mikva'ot*, and had easy access to "living" (i.e., running, not stagnant) water. "To country folk, including villagers in Galilee, the Pharisees came across as effete," Prof. Bruce Chilton suggests. "They thought the Pharisees were overly concerned with outwardly appearances and with little regard for the practical demands of a working life. Therein lay the source of the tension between the Pharisees and one particular rural figure, named Jesus."

The Western Wall is a Herodian wall that once supported the vast Temple platform

As the years passed, Herod's reign became ever more repressive. His jails swelled with political prisoners. When Herod moved to suppress one particularly energetic revolt with a bloodbath of untold proportions, even Augustus had to acknowledge that the man was mad, and had become a liability.

According to the Gospel of Matthew, Herod was so enraged at the rumor that a new king had been born in the town of Bethlehem that he ordered all the newly born infants in that city put to death. While scholars doubt that this massacre actually took place, it was not difficult for Matthew's audience to imagine that Herod could actually revert to such horrific measures. He was a tyrant, and tyrants do unspeakable things.

Punishment for his sins was not long in coming. Wracked by illness, Herod spent his last years in debilitating pain. He finally died in 4 B.C.E., much to the relief of his subjects. The Herodian kingdom, created and enlarged at such enormous cost, was carved up between his three sons. Archelaus, the eldest surviving son, gained the principal share of Judaea, Idumaea and Samaria; Philip became Tetrarch of the Transjordan, and Herod Antipas became Tetrarch of Galilee and Peraea.

By that time, an infant born to a woman in Nazareth was just beginning to walk.

Chapter Eleven
A Child in Nazareth

The rolling hills of Lower Galilee.

Nazareth in Jesus' time was a rather small and insignificant hamlet -- so small, in fact, that it does not register in any of the books of the Hebrew Scriptures, nor in the writings of Josephus, who otherwise cites 204 such hamlets. Many of these villages clung tenaciously to their ancestral faith and customs, even as the world around them became first a Hellenistic and then a Roman preserve. This is why Talmudic literature makes a sharp distinction between a village (*kfr*), a township (*'yr*), and a city (*kerakh,* similar to the Greek word *polis*). Cities such as Sepphoris or Scythopolis (Beth She'an) could have a population of twenty thousand or more, usually a mixture of Jews and Gentiles. Townships, also mixed, numbered anywhere from two to five thousand inhabitants. But only the villages were predominantly Jewish, many not larger than eight to ten *dunams* (each *dunam* representing 10 families), living in huts and mud brick homes over an area of no more than two and a half acres.

This Galilean community of rural hamlets and villages thus formed a tight and devoutly Jewish enclave in an otherwise Hellenistic world. To the north and east was the Greek community of the "Ten Cities" or *Decapolis;* to the west, the thoroughly Hellenized cities of Ptolemais, Tyre and Sidon on the Mediterranean coast. The result was what the archaeologist Eric Meyer has called a rather mixed "cosmopolitan and multilingual atmosphere" in Lower Galilee that, for better or worse, reached its apex during the boom times of the reign of king Herod.

The rural context of Jesus' life is important for many reasons, one of which is that few, if any, Jewish villagers in Galilee could read, let alone write. The New Testament Book of 'Acts of the Apostles' specifies that the apostles were "uneducated and ordinary men" (Acts, 4:13). We must therefore assume that the followers of Jesus were illiterate. It is likely that Jesus could read, though not certain, since knowledge of the Scriptures was often taught by rote. But nowhere do we find any evidence that Jesus could also write. If we assume that there was no scribe in the immediate circle of Jesus, then the inevitable conclusion is that all information about him during his lifetime relied on oral transmission. The followers of Jesus saw, remembered, and passed their impressions on. This process continued until the ever expanding circle of Jesus followers encountered individuals with the requisite talent (or money) to commit these memories to paper.

Of course, each person's impression is different. What's more, the apostles were fishermen, not scholars trained in analysis and observation. As each person related his views of their great rabbi, each may have emphasized certain aspects of Jesus that he or she found particularly compelling. As a result, multiple strains of 'Jesus information' soon developed within the interval between Jesus' life and the writing of the Gospels.

The Sea of Galilee as seen from the western shore

We must also remember that Jesus' ministry was unbelievably short -- a span of not more than two years, by most accounts. That is astonishing in itself. Great prophets like Moses, Isaiah and Jeremiah had the luxury of a lifespan to reflect, analyze and articulate their divine inspirations. But Jesus' ministry was compressed to mere months, undertaken by a thirty year-old man who had only recently begun to grasp the divine source that spoke within him -- and was perhaps still struggling to make sense out of it. Most importantly, Jesus was not around long enough to see his *halakha*, his teachings, committed to paper. Unlike Moses, unlike Muhammad and countless other prophets, he did not leave an authorized, undisputed record of his revelations that would leave little doubt as to the ultimate purpose of his movement.

Why is this important? Because it helps to explain why after Jesus' untimely death, we initially witness a movement in disarray. We see a "School of Jesus" prone to multiple interpretations of who Jesus was and what his message was all about. This led to a number of different "oral traditions" which, many decades later, the evangelists would be hard-pressed to reconcile.

This is the reason why – as anyone who has read the Gospels can attest – the Gospel narratives do not agree with one another on many counts, and sometimes give conflicting reports about specific events and sayings by Jesus. If we agree with the majority opinion of scholars that the earliest Gospel -- that of Mark -- was not written until forty years after the crucifixion, and knowing the average lifespan of an adult male in Palestine (ca. 35-40 years), it is unlikely that the evangelists knew Jesus personally, or that they were eyewitnesses to the events that they wrote about. This is certainly true for Matthew, Luke and John, who probably wrote in the '80s and '90s -- that is, more than fifty years after the crucifixion. It follows, then, that they had to rely on a variety of (oral or written) sources that were then at least thirty or forty years old.

For many Christians, of course, the New Testament suffices as the definitive and final word on Jesus, in the same manner that many Jews believe that every word in the Torah is the word of God. Such belief commands respect, but in this book we are interested in tracing the development of the three faiths in their *historical* context. We want to learn about men and women who lived and breathed in the community of their times. It is their footprints, rather than their legends, that we are after.

Fortunately, the 'canonical' Gospels (meaning, the Gospels authorized by church fathers to be included in the New Testament) are not the only sources about Jesus. We also have other important sources from the 1st century C.E., including:

1. A collection of sayings tentatively identified as *Q*
2. A collection of sayings known as the *Gospel of Thomas*

3. Letters written by Paul and others in Paul's circle

'Q' is a recent product of biblical research. Scholars have known for some time that Luke and Matthew used the Gospel of Mark as a major source of information. Luke adapts no less that 350 verses from Mark's Gospel. Matthew goes even further and uses more than 600 verses. But it is clear that both evangelists also used *another* source, with material that does *not* appear in Mark at all. Since the 1980's, scholars have tried to piece together this mysterious document. The result is hypothetical collage of quotes, referred to as 'Q', based on the German word for 'source' or *Quelle*. Some scholars have even gone as far as translating 'Q' back to the original Aramaic as spoken by Jesus, with sometimes surprising results.

Another Christian source is the collection of so-called Gnostic Gospels, most of which were discovered by chance in a cave near the Egyptian city of Nag Hammadi in 1945. Many of these works date from the 2nd century C.E. and espouse the views of several dissident sects known collectively as 'Gnostic Christians'. The collection contained one particularly tantalizing gospel, known as the 'Gospel of Thomas'. This work appears to be based on a collection of sayings that can be traced back to the period immediately following Jesus' death. In fact, the Gospel of Thomas bears a strong resemblance to the artificially constructed document of 'Q'.

Last but not least, we have the letters of Paul of Tarsus, which are the earliest surviving documents about Jesus. Paul's *epistles* or letters were probably written in the early to mid-50's. The oldest and least disputed letters are those Paul wrote to Christian communities among the Galatians and the Thessalonians. However, Paul never met Jesus personally (a fact of which he was always painfully aware), which is perhaps the reason why there is little historical information about Jesus in Paul's letters, nor in those letters written by others under his name.

We may know little about the historical Jesus, but we have a wealth of information about the world in which he lived and moved. Indeed, it is Josephus, the Jewish historian whom we encountered earlier, who gives a most detailed account of Jesus' time. It is precisely because of a single reference to Jesus that his book, *Antiquities of the Jews*, has been faithfully copied and preserved throughout the centuries. Unfortunately, the monks and scribes responsible for its survival may have found it necessary to modify the text – in effect, to elaborate on certain themes that clearly were not obvious to Josephus himself. And so the original text is replete with additions -- the scholarly term is *interpolations* -- that belong to a later age. Several historians have tried to isolate these interpolations, which are marked below between brackets:

Josephus
Now there was about this time Jesus, a wise man
[if indeed one might call him a man;]
for he was a doer of wonderful works,
a teacher of such men as receive the truth with pleasure.
He drew over to him both many of the Jews
and many of the Gentiles. [*He was the Christ*].
And when Pilate, at the suggestion of the principal men
amongst us, had condemned him to the cross,
those that loved him at the first did not cease
to be attached to him [for he appeared to them alive
again the third day as the divine prophets had foretold
these and ten thousand other wonderful things
concerning him]. And the tribe of Christians,
so named from him, are not extinct at this day.
(Antiquities, 18.63-64)

Even without the awkward additions, there is no question that this paragraph in Book 18 of *The Antiquities* is a powerful attestation of the historical existence of Jesus. What Josephus tells us is that (1) Jesus was a wise man; (2) that he was a teacher, who did many wonderful works; (3) that he was executed by crucifixion during the term of Pilate as prefect of Judaea; and (4) that he had followers who remained faithful to him after his death.

As we have seen in the foregoing, the world in which Jesus was born was changing. This Judaea, this land with its 1000-year history of Jewish civilization, had become a deeply polarized society, unmoored from the very anchor that had held the Jewish community together: its Temple, its priesthood, and the centralized worship of YAHWEH. Now the priesthood had become compromised, tainted by political and financial ambition. What's more, Judaea was a captive land. It was ruled by a foreign power that had little patience for the spiritual and cultic sensitivities of the native population. As a result, many Jews were demoralized and bewildered. As in the case of the Essenes, a number of sects and 'prophets' sprang to their rescue, each offering an "alternative" way to worship and seek a remission of the "sins" of their time. Seen in this light, the ministry of Jesus may not have been as unprecedented as Christian tradition wants us to believe.

TRADITION HOLDS THAT *Yeshua ben Yoseph* (*Yeshua'* being a contraction of *Yehoshuah*, meaning 'God is salvation') was born in the year zero of our Common Era (or what is also referred to as 'AD' -- *Anno Domini*, the year of our Lord). We now know that this is an error. According to Matthew and Luke, Jesus was born when Herod the Great was still on his throne, which places the date *before* Herod's death in 4 B.C.E.

Luke also says that "in those days ... there went out a decree from Caesar Augustus, that all the world should be taxed" (Lk. 2:1-2). By "all the world" Luke meant the Roman Empire, and indeed, Roman governors occasionally did order a comprehensive census of subjects in their allotted territories.

Interior of the Church of the Nativity in Bethlehem, originally built by the Byzantine emperor Justinian in the 6th century C.E.

Such a census had one goal: to create a comprehensive inventory of tax-paying individuals and their property, so that an accurate forecast of the region's tax yields could be drawn up. A forecast was important, because the Roman occupation authorities did not collect the taxes themselves. They "outsourced" this activity to free agents known as tax collectors or publicans. By making a comprehensive assessment of projected tax revenues from a given territory, therefore, the Romans were able to give these publicans a well-informed benchmark that they were expected to meet or be suspected of cheating.

Luke tells us that this census was "the first registration" (i.e. since the beginning of the Roman conquest of Palestine) and that it was taken on orders of "Quirinius, governor of Syria" (Lk 2:2). At first glance, this appears to be accurate. Even in Herod's days, as we have seen, Judea formed part of the greater Roman province of Syria, so that Herod, in effect, "reported" to the governor based in the Syrian capital of Antioch. The problem, however, is that in Herod's time, the Syrian governor was not

Quirinius at all, but a man named Sentius Saturninus, who served in office from 9 to 6 B.C.E. He, in turn, was succeeded by Quintilius Varus, who ruled from 6 to 4 B.C.E., the year of Herod's death. There *was* a governor in Syria named Quirinius, but he did not enter office until 6 C.E., a full ten years *after* the death of Herod.

The link with Quirinius is not the only problem we have with Luke's dating system. Another, more substantial problem is the very mechanism of a Roman census. While Herod was still in power, it fell to Herod's government to collect the taxes in his realm, rather than to the Romans. It was only *after* Herod's death, and the subsequent dismissal of his son Archelaus as ruler of Judea in 6 C.E., that the Romans decided to take charge of the administrative control of this region themselves. Judea became, in effect, a Roman sub-province under the supervision of a Roman career diplomat, subordinate to the Roman governor in Syria, with the title of prefect.

This meant that the Romans now took direct responsibility for tax collecting in the area. Since they had no idea what Judea was worth in terms of projected tax revenues, the then-governor, quite possibly the same Quirinius referred to in Luke, ordered a census to be taken. However, this census pertained only to the sub-province of Judea and *not* to Galilee, for Galilee remained under the control of one of Herod's other sons, Herod Antipas. Therefore, the census would not have affected Joseph's or Mary's family in Nazareth any way.

Lastly, even if there had been such a census, and even if by some stretch of the imagination Joseph would have been compelled to register, he would not have traveled to Bethlehem at all, even if – as the Gospels tell us – Joseph's family originally hailed from that village. The whole purpose of a Roman census was to update the mechanism of *taxation*. Therefore, the Romans would have wanted people to appear in their current place of residence, where the taxman could find them, rather than in the place of their ancestral home, which in some cases could have been many miles away. And as Luke makes it eminently clear, Joseph and Mary resided in Nazareth, in Galilee.

View of the modern city of Nazareth, with the Church of the Annunciation in center

In Matthew's Gospel, three wise men (or "kings") are alerted to the birth of Jesus by the appearance of a bright star: "Where is he that is born King of the Jews? For we have seen his star in the east, and are come to worship him" (Mt 2:2). Some 1600 years later, on the evening of December 17, 1603, the astronomer Johannes Kepler pointed his rudimentary telescope to the night sky. His eye was soon drawn to a bright conjunction of the planets Jupiter and Saturn in the constellation of Pisces. Working his way backwards, he calculated that a very similar phenomenon must have occurred in 7 B.C.E. A devout Lutheran, Kepler immediately identified this phenomenon with the "star in the east" described by Matthew.

Babylonian astrologers would have agreed. In 1925, the German scholar P. Schnabel deciphered a cuneiform inscription from the ancient astrological archives of Babylon that contained an observation of Jupiter and Saturn. Their convergence in Pisces had been recorded over a period of five months in the year 7 B.C.E. - exactly the date postulated by Kepler.

What makes this observation even more intriguing is its echo in the 15th century writings of a rabbinical sage known as Abravanel (1437-1508), who prophesied that when Saturn and Jupiter conjoined in Pisces, the Messiah would come. This argument was based not on observation, but on ancient Jewish exegesis and astrology. In rabbinical writings, the House of Israel was sometimes identified with the constellation of Pisces as symbol of the Messiah. In this context, the planet Jupiter symbolized the royal star of the house of David, and Saturn was the protecting star of Israel.

There is no way of verifying whether the symbolic meaning of Pisces was already current in 1st century Palestine, whether Matthew was familiar with such symbolism, or whether, indeed, the "star in the east" is in any way related to the conjunction of Jupiter and Saturn, which could have easily been observed with the naked eye. However, one only has to travel into the Judean desert to get an idea of how impossibly clear the unpolluted night sky over 1st century Judea would have been, undimmed by the lights of today's urban centers. In such an environment, any planet, whether Venus, Jupiter, or Saturn, could easily have been taken for a "bright star."

An entirely different explanation for Matthew's "star from the east" comes from China, where Chinese astronomers during the Han Dynasty recorded their observation of what was probably a supernova in the year 5 B.C.E. This supernova, Chinese records show, was observed for at least "seventy days."

Clearly, it is impossible to date the birth of Jesus with any accuracy, based on the information contained in the Gospels. The one indication that most scholars do accept is, however, the death of Herod the Great. Josephus tells us that the death of the monarch was accompanied by an eclipse. Modern astronomers have ascertained that such an eclipse would indeed have occurred over Judea, specifically between Sunday, March 12, 4 B.C.E., and the Passover eve of Wednesday, April 11, 4 B.C.E.

In sum, if we assume that Matthew and Luke are correct and that Jesus was born in the waning days of Herod's reign, then it seems logical to assume his birth took place sometime between 7 and 4 B.C.E.

IF WE TAKE MARK – the earliest Gospel and therefore probably our closest 'witness' –the story of Jesus begins when he is a grown man. There is no reference to Jesus' birth, nor to Jesus' father or to the town in which Jesus grew up as a boy. In fact, Mark's Gospel begins with John the Baptist, a man who "did baptize in the wilderness, and preached the baptism of repentance for the remission of sins" (Mk 1:4). Jesus himself does not appear until verse 9: "and it came to pass in those days, that Jesus came from Nazareth of Galilee, and was baptized of John in Jordan."

Matthew and Luke, on the other hand, provide us with an extensive Nativity story, although the versions differ in details. In Matthew, the annunciation of Jesus' birth is given to Joseph. In Luke, on the other hand, it is Mary who receives the glad tidings. In fact, the Lucan Annunciation to Mary ranks as the finest of New Testament literature. What's more, it has close parallels with the Annunciation in the Qur'an, as follows:

> *Luke*
> And in the sixth month the angel
> Gabriel was sent from God unto a city of Galilee, named
> Nazareth, to a virgin espoused to a man whose name was
> Joseph, of the house of David; and the virgin's name was
> Mary. And the angel came in unto her, and said,
> (Lk. 1:26-28)

Qur'an
O Mary! Verily God has chosen thee above all the women
of the world. Truly, God gives you glad tidings of a
word from Him.
(Q. 3.42,45)

Luke
Behold, thou shalt conceive in thy womb, and
bring forth a son...
(Lk. 1: 31)

Qur'an
His name shall be the *Messiah*, Jesus the son
of Mary, and regarded in this world and the next
with those whose place is near to God.
(Q 3.45)

Luke
Then said Mary unto the angel, How can this be,
since I do not know a man? And the angel answered,
(Lk.1:34-35)

Qur'an
This is the Lord's will. Nothing is difficult for
Him. The Lord has said: 'He shall be a sign for
mankind and a blessing from Us.'
(Q. 19.16-21)

Luke
And Mary said, Behold the handmaid of the Lord;
be it unto me according to thy word.
(Lk. 1:38)

Despite the similarity of both narratives, however, each version has a different purpose. Luke's story of Mary's conception was meant to demonstrate the divine origin of Jesus. The version of the Qur'an, on the other hand, stresses the fact that Jesus was born without sin. "Indeed," says Prof. Peter Awn, "the idea that Mary was conceived without the stain of original sin, that very traditional Roman Catholic theological principle, is echoed in Islam."

Matthew and Luke are both at pains to place the birth of Jesus in the village of Bethlehem, lest his birth fail to meet the criterion, defined by the prophet Micah, that he "who is to rule in Israel" shall come from Bethlehem, the birth city of David (Micah 5:2). To make this happen, Matthew and Luke avail themselves of different scenarios. Matthew avoids any reference to Mary's and Joseph's place of residence, and obliquely implies that both were living in Bethlehem at the time of the birth. Luke, who is more concerned about historical authenticity throughout his Gospel, cannot bring himself to deny that Mary was a resident of Nazareth. But he still must find a way to get Joseph and Mary down to Judea, to the little town of Bethlehem, in time for her to give birth to Jesus. His account of the census decree from Augustus serves as the motive to do so. Today, many scholars tend to accept that Jesus was probably both in Nazareth, or in a nearby village known as 'Bethlehem-in-Galilee'.

Tradition holds that Joseph was a carpenter, and that therefore Jesus (as his first-born) would have been trained in his craft as well. But reading through the Gospels, we get a different impression. As countless parables testify, Jesus was intimately familiar with agriculture and the cultivation of the Galilean soil.

In the eloquent words of Luke, Jesus speaks of a "grain of mustard seed, which a man took, and cast into his garden; and it grew, and waxed a great tree; and the fowls of the air lodged in the branches of it" (Lk. 13:19).

The fecund fields of the Beth-Netopha Valley near Nazareth

Casting a practiced eye on a fig tree which has not born fruit for three years, Jesus counsels the owner to "let it alone this year also, till I shall dig about it, and dung it: And if it bear fruit, well: and if not, then after that you should cut it down" (Lk. 13:8-9). And to emphasize that the goodness of one's heart produces good, Jesus reminds his audience that it is not "for thorns that men gather figs, nor for bramble bush that they gather grapes" (Lk. 6:44).

Surely, this Jesus is a Galilean farmer's son, through and through, who grew up in the fields while helping with the harvest. This is not surprising if we remember what Josephus told us -- that virtually everyone in Galilee was in some way or form involved with farming the land. True, Joseph may have offered his services as a craftsman or woodworker to augment his income, as many farmers did in some way or form; but otherwise Joseph was most likely a tenant farmer, like his fellow Galileans.

But the baby Jesus was growing up under a cloud. As the Nativity cycles in Luke and Matthew tell us, Mary was pregnant with Jesus *before* she was married to Joseph. In the tight-knit community of Nazareth, the uncertainty of his paternity would have haunted Jesus and his parents. According to Deuteronomy, such a child was designated a *mamzer*, doomed to be ostracized from the congregation and social life. The Mishnah, too, castigates *mamzers* as children born of an illegitimate sexual union. The Talmud states that *mamzers* can have no voice in public congregations - they are supposed to be silent at all times.

It is difficult to imagine the impact of being stigmatized as a 'mamzer' in a small, gossip-ridden hamlet like Nazareth. Bruce Chilton believes that it would have had a profound psychological impact on the development of the young Jesus. The other children in the village would have been forbidden to play with him. If Jesus was allowed to participate in "synagogue" gatherings at all, he would have been prevented from speaking up. Quite possibly, he would not even have been able to attend.

As a social outcast, the young Jesus may have spent a lot of time in the open fields of Nazareth, cooled by breezes from the Sea of Galilee. Here, in solitude, he may have developed a very special, intimate relationship with God whom he called his *abba*, his *true* father.

One of the most exciting insights in the life of the young Jesus in recent decades are provided by the excavation of Sepphoris, located some five miles distant from Nazareth. As we have seen, Antipas was the son of Herod the Great who received a slice of Herod's Greater Kingdom after his death – namely, Galilee and Perea. Like his father before him, Antipas embarked on a building program to turn his capital from a provincial town into a fully Hellenized, modern city.

This ancient town has now come to light, following excavation campaigns by Duke and South Florida Universities. What has emerged from the sand is a typical Roman city. Antipas' Roman-trained architects used the familiar street grid, with one main avenue or *Cardo* running from north to south, bisected at right angles by another main axis known as the *decumanus*. Each main avenue was bordered by shops and offices, and led to the commercial and religious center of the forum. In addition, Antipater had indulged in the unheard-of expense of a 1,500-seat theater, similar to the famous amphitheater of Jerusalem built by his father.

The construction of Sepphoris took many years, which sucked all the manpower and treasure from the surrounding region. It is therefore hard to imagine that such a vast undertaking would have left the family of Jesus untouched. Several scholars, including Shirley Case of the University of Chicago, have suggested that Joseph and his eldest son worked on one of Antipas' construction projects for much of Jesus' teenage years and into early adulthood.

The theater of Sepphoris, begun by Herod Antipas in the early 1st century C.E. and expanded in the 3rd century C.E.

Some authors (including myself) have put forth the suggestion that Joseph died in the work pits, possibly as a result of a construction accident, since Joseph eventually fades from the Gospel accounts without a trace.

REGARDLESS OF HOW WE TRY to interpret the early years of Jesus' life, it is clear that the baptism by John marks a major point in Jesus' life. Jesus is marking a clean break with his past, including his career as a journeyman and farmer in Nazareth and vicinity. As Mark attests, Jesus had four brothers, including James, Joses, Juda and Simon – proper Jewish names from what was clearly an observant and pious home. In addition, there were sisters; Mark does not tell us how many (girls in Antiquity did not rate as highly as men), but the plural would indicate that there were at least two (Mk 6:3). Quite possibly, then, Jesus waited this long -- around 28 CE -- until his brothers would be old enough to take over Jesus' role as the principal provider for Mary and her family.

Why does Jesus choose to go to John? Why does he travel to the desert of the lower Jordan, in search of a hermit who eats locusts and dresses himself in a tunic made of camel's hair? The answer may be provided by Josephus: John was perhaps the most famous 'dissident' of this time. As Josephus tells us:

> John was a good man, who commanded the Jews
> to exercise virtue, both as to righteousness towards
> one another and piety towards God, and so come to
> baptism. (*Antiquities*, XVIII:5)

What made John so special? The answer is that people in Judaea felt lost and unmoored from their Jewish identity, not in the least since many tenant farmers and peasants had lost their ancestral fields, due to foreclosure. How should they worship to YAHWEH, if the Temple priesthood itself was siding with the hated Roman oppressor? How could they contest the lurid appeal of pagan Greco-Roman culture? Was YAHWEH stirred to anger? Was another frightful catastrophe on the horizon?

John had answers. Yes, he said, God's punishment was imminent. The End of Time, the apocalypse was near. Jews, said John, should make a total break with their sinful past, and do so with the symbolic act of an all-cleansing submersion in water.

By espousing these ideas, John tapped into a number of radical ideas that had gained currency that over the preceding century, including the Greek idea of an afterlife. Jewish theology had always rejected the concept. Traditionally, Jews believed that the dead would dwell in a dark and featureless underworld known as *Sheol*, but after the Exile people began to think seriously of the possibility of the immortality of the soul.

Though there are inklings of a hope of resurrection in Third Isaiah, it is the Book of Enoch that boldly sets forth the idea that on the day of God's final judgment, the just will receive the afterlife – as spirits rather than in bodily form -- while the wicked will be punished.

The Jordan River, close to the location traditionally associated with John the Baptist

The book of the Wisdom of Solomon, tentatively dated to the 1st century B.C.E., goes a step further, arguing that the soul of the righteous enter God's heavenly realm immediately after death. "The righteous live forever," says its anonymous author, "and their reward is with the Lord" (*Wisdom*, 3:15). Unlike their opponents, the Sadducees, the Pharisees wholeheartedly embraced this view. Josephus confirms that the Pharisees believed in the immortality of the soul, while later rabbinical writings suggest that righteous would be resurrected in *body* and welcomed in heaven.

John's message was unique, because it offered a clear remedy. Like the Essenes, he preached the message that God's retribution was imminent. Like them, he warned that nothing else but a radical *re-birth* could save the Jews from utter destruction. This act of re-birth was symbolized by complete immersion in the waters of the Jordan.

In due course, John's activity came to the attention of Herod Antipas, since Perea, the region where John centered his ministry, fell under his jurisdiction. Josephus tells us that Herod was afraid John's followers might stage a rebellion; certainly, John's uncompromising sermons, preserved in Luke, are strident in their militancy. That is why, says Josephus, Herod decided to put John the Baptist to death. The Gospels tell us that John's arrest was prompted by John's criticism of Herod's marriage to his half-brother's wife. This may have played a role as well.

Few scholars have remarked on the fact that Herod did *not* involve the Sanhedrin to legitimize John's execution, though this Priestly Council would later play a major role in the future "trial" of Jesus. Though the Sanhedrin was based in Jerusalem, in Judaean territory, it is believed that the Council had authority throughout Palestine in religious matters. This is even more surprising since John was a very popular spiritual leader, whose death might well incite the very insurrection that Herod was trying to prevent. Apparently, however, Herod felt secure enough to arrest and kill this charismatic figure without covering himself with Sanhedrin's mantle of authority. John was beheaded – the common form of execution in Judaea. Josephus even gives us the details: he was executed in the fortress of Macherus, one of a string of garrison redoubts built by Herod the Great.

Naturally, John's followers were shocked, bewildered, adrift. Where should they go? Were they themselves in any danger? Many scholars believe, reading between the lines of the Gospel of John, that a number of the Baptist's disciples went over to Jesus. He became the natural successor of John. Like the Baptist, Jesus was a man of charisma. He was intelligent, and spoke with a steady voice; surely, he would know what to do.

And Jesus did. First and foremost, he moved out of the danger zone, out of the Jordan valley. Several of John's disciples followed him. We know of three: Simon Peter, Andrew and Philip. All three were from Bethsaida. This has led some scholars to suggest that Bethsaida was the group's first destination, since Bethsaida was located east of the Jordan River, just inside the lower Gaulanitis, the territory of the Tetrarch Philip. I

In Bethsaida, therefore, Jesus and his small group of followers could consider themselves reasonably safe from Antipas' roving patrols, if they were still looking for John's followers.

☙

Chapter Twelve
A Rabbi Named Jesus

The remains of basalt dwellings in Capernaum

And so, Jesus and the other disciples of John arrived in Galilee. As Matthew tells us, "Jesus went about all Galilee, teaching in their synagogues, and preaching the gospel of the kingdom" (Mt. 4:23). Jesus did not set up camp in the fields or the mountains, as John would have done, but right in the heart of a city. By this decision, Jesus made it clear that he is an independent thinker, a man who will define his own path – one that will lead to the very heart of Jewish urban life. After all, it was in the towns, rather than the villages, that the sinners, the publicans and the Roman collaborators could be found. Like a physician, Jesus went straight to the place where he would find the sick, waiting to be cured.

The first city was Capernaum. One only has to walk along the shores of the Sea of Galilee to see why. Capernaum was centrally located on the Sea, connected by boat traffic to either the eastern shore and the Decapolis, or the western shore and the cities of lower Galilee. The city was at the heart of what would become Jesus' "mission triangle", the area between Bethsaida, Korazin and Capernaum where he focused much of his activity.

Capernaum, a contraction of *Kfar Nahum* or "Nahum's village," was also a prosperous town. Coins excavated on the site indicate that it was founded sometime in the 2nd century B.C.E. during the Hasmonean period. It owed its prosperity to its location, straddling the road from Damascus to Jerusalem, right on the border between Galilee and the Gaulanitis. It therefore had a toll booth as well as a military garrison, while its location on the Sea of Galilee made it a convenient jumping-off point for shipping traffic across the entire lake. Lastly, it was a city known for its basalt industry, which was found nearby; most of the town's residences were, in fact, built with basalt stone.

"And," says Luke, "he came down to Capernaum, a city of Galilee, and taught them on the sabbath days. And they were astonished at his doctrine: for his word was with power" (Lk 4:31-32).

During the first excavations in Capernaum in 1905, German archaeologists H. Kohl and C. Watzinger were gripped with excitement as they discovered a beautiful, basilica-shaped synagogue. The limestone building featured a central prayer hall, screened from the two flanking aisles by richly carved Corinthian columns. The world held its breath as the dust was slowly swept away. Was this the synagogue in which Jesus first preached?

Alas, it was not to be. As the excavations continued well into the 1960's, it became clear that the synagogue dated from the 3rd or 4th century C.E. But there was some consolation: further digging revealed that this synagogue was built on top of an older and very similar house of worship. This older building could very well date back to the time of Jesus. Walking between the elegant columns of limestone, the visitor is thus assured that he is treading on the same place where Jesus may have taught 2,000 years ago.

The synagogue of Capernaum, now dated to the late 3rd or early 4th century C.E.

For the next few months, Jesus would often find himself with his new fishermen-turned-apostles on the Sea of Galilee. The boats used by these men allowed him to quickly traverse the lake and travel from one place to another. Unlike John, Jesus did not wait for the people to come to him. In these early months of his ministry, he actively courted his emerging audience by visiting as many different villages as possible. A small ship was the fastest and most economical means to do so.

There are some twenty references in the Gospels to the vessel used by Jesus. Matthew tells us that when he "entered the ship, his followers followed him" (Mt 8:23). This implies that the boat used by Jesus was no mere rowboat; it must have been a vessel able to accommodate at least ten or perhaps thirteen men - Jesus and the twelve apostles. What this boat looked like, we don't know. Or at least, we *didn't* know until in 1986 a drought of such severity hit the area around the Sea of Galilee that the water level dropped to unprecedented levels. One day, some locals were walking along the shore when they spotted the outline of a large boat. The ship appeared to be in excellent condition, fully preserved in the mud – at a distance of no more than five miles from the ancient city of Capernaum.

As the water slowly began to rise again, archaeologist Shelley Wachsman launched a frantic effort to preserve the wooden boat and carry it to the safety of a nearby museum. Here, expert restorers used carbon-14 dating to try to assess the age of the boat. They were astonished to find that the vessel was built between 50 B.C.E. and 50 C.E. – precisely the period of Jesus' lifetime.

The "Galilee Boat", dated between 50 B.C.E. and 50 C.E.

This "Galilean Boat", now proudly displayed in the Yigal Allom Memorial Museum at the Kibbutz Ginosar, is an impressive example of ancient craftsmanship. It is twenty-six feet long and seven and a half feet wide – large enough to comfortably accommodate ten people as well as pieces of equipment, such as nets. The planks are carefully bonded together with joints and fastened with pegs – the construction method favored by Greek shipbuilders throughout the Mediterranean.

The Gospel of Mark tells us that the sons of Zebedee were sitting in just such a ship, quietly mending their nets, when Jesus peremptorily ordered them to follow him. "And, says the author, "they left their father Zebedee in the ship with the hired servants, and went after him."

The word *apostle* is a translation of *shaliach,* which does not mean 'disciple' but 'delegate.' It gives us a clue as to the unique role played by the apostles in the Gospels. A *shaliach* in 1st century Palestine was a man charged with preparing the visit of a high official to a village or town. Such delegates formed, in essence, an 'advance party' to ensure that all was ready to receive the noble guest. In the same manner, Jesus' apostles prepared the way for him and enabled him to shuttle from one village to the next, over land or water. Matthew in particular spells out the instructions that Jesus gave his 'delegates' (Mt 10:1-16):

1. Avoid the cities of the Gentiles.

2. Avoid the territory of the Samaritans (who were considered outcasts by observant Jews)

3. Focus on Jewish villages, the "lost sheep of Israel"

4. Proclaim, as you enter, the "New Kingdom of the Heavens is coming!"

5. Do not carry gold or silver, or luggage with a change of clothes.

6. Appeal to the charity of the villagers, and so determine the quality of their character and their faith.

7. Once inside the village, locate a prominent home and enter it; if it is worthy, your peace will be upon it

The apostles faithfully follow Jesus' instructions. They go from house to house, begging for bread, fruit or dates. On some days, as in Bethany, they are put up in private dwellings. Here they gratefully use the local cistern to wash themselves, and stretch out their rugs on the floor, safe from the elements. But at other times, they must spend the night in the fields, and take turns to guard the camp against wild animals – or thieves.

Their travels take them to Tabgha, where according to tradition, Jesus proclaims the essence of his New Kingdom teaching. Tabgha is located just a short walk from Capernaum, the "base camp" of the Jesus movement. He turns and begins to climb the gentle slope, up the grass-covered hill. Crowds have gathered to see him. Using the hill as his sounding board, Jesus turns to them and begins to speak. His words still move us to this day:

> Happy are the poor, for theirs is the kingdom of heaven
> Happy are the mourners, for they shall be comforted
> Happy are the hungry, for they shall be satisfied

True, there are more *beatitudes* in the gospel of Matthew. But according to 'Q', the hypothetical source of first-layer 'sayings', the original beatitudes may have been limited to just these three statements, suggesting that others were added by either the evangelists or later redactors. Still, these three proverbs speak volumes about what Jesus was after. Jesus, in effect, turns the proverb on its head by using another favorite formula in the ancient Near East, the *paradox*.

For example, *Happy are the hungry* is a typical phrase designed to jolt Jesus' audience. It is a contradiction in terms. After all, the misery of hunger is *not* a conduit to happiness.

And yet that is the case, says Jesus, because your suffering today will be your admission to happiness tomorrow.

Happy are the mourners. In Galilee of 28 C.E., there were plenty of reasons to mourn. Mortality rates were high. Often, people died young of disease; many children were malnourished. By now, it is clear what Jesus' "target audience" is. It is the poor, the marginalized, the *proletariat* who, as we have seen, made up the majority of Jewish society. *Happy are the poor,* Jesus says in the beginning, and we can almost see the look of incredulity on across their faces, and hear the murmur of voices: *What is he saying?* Jesus begins again: "Truly, I tell you: happy are the poor, *for yours is the kingdom of God."*

THE KINGDOM OF GOD – with these words, Jesus defined his message. It is the central theme of his preaching, and the core of his ministry. Mark puts it most clearly: "Jesus came into Galilee, preaching the gospel of the kingdom of God, and saying, The time is fulfilled, and the kingdom of God is at hand" (Mk 1: 14-15). Not only is this 'Kingdom' upheld as the principal reward in the beatitudes, it is found throughout the four gospels. It also figures prominently in the very prayer that Jesus taught his disciples. Christians are familiar with the 'Our Father'. But this prayer is even more striking in its original Aramaic form, as suggested by the original phraseology of 'Q':

Father,
hallowed be your name.
Your kingdom come.
Our daily bread give us today.
And forgive us our debts,
as we forgive our debtors.
And do not lead us to the test.

The structure of this prayer, says John Meier (who includes this version in the second volume of his *A Marginal Jew*), "is tight and laconic, perfectly suitable for memorization." But what does *The Kingdom of God* really mean? Many authors have attacked the problem, but every interpretation is different. One reason why it is so hard to grasp the meaning of *The Kingdom of God* is that the apostles themselves had trouble understanding what it meant. Repeatedly, they asked their Teacher to explain it. Every time, Jesus replied with a story, a *parable*, one more mysterious than the next. For example:

1. The Kingdom of God is like a mustard seed, the smallest of all the seeds on earth, that when sown, becomes the greatest of all shrubs (Mt 13:31)
2. The Kingdom of Heaven is like yeast that a woman took and mixed in three measures of flour, till all of it was leavened (Mt 13:33)
3. The Kingdom of God is like a seed that sprouts while the farmer is asleep; it grows into a stalk, the head, and finally the grain, which the farmer cuts with his sickle (Mk 4: 26-29)

This elegant early 20th century church marks the spot where, according to tradition, Jesus preached the Sermon on the Mount

My conclusion is that what we see in the Gospels is not a contradictory account of different interpretations, but the process by which Jesus is slowly weighing and developing the *manifesto* that will anchor his teaching. For this reason, it is unfortunate that the evangelists did not organize Jesus' 'biography' in chronological order, as we would do today.

Such notions were alien to the author of Antiquity. Events, sayings and anecdotes merely served to underscore the moral pitch of the story. The arrangement in time was of no consequence except to serve the greater purpose. Indeed, as early as the 2nd century C.E., Bishop Papias noted with some regret that "Mark wrote accurately what he remembered the Lord said and did, though not in order." Without a clear chronological timeline of Jesus' sayings across the four Gospels as well as 'Q', there is no way we can accurately reconstruct the journey of Jesus' mind. But we can attempt to *infer* what Jesus ultimately arrived at by excavating through the different 'layers' of the Gospel tradition.

As we saw before, the concept of an afterlife, a 'heavenly kingdom' had recently gained currency among 'progressive' Jews, particularly the Pharisees. The Persians also believed in a *paradeison* after death. Reading the Beatitudes, we cannot escape the notion that this is precisely what Jesus is driving at. You are poor now – but your reward will be great in heaven. You are hungry now – but there will be plenty of food at the banquet of paradise.

This, of course, is the concept of 'Kingdom' embraced by mainstream Christianity. The kingdom of God is the Kingdom of Heaven, the reward for a moral life. Is this what Jesus meant? The problem is that in several sayings, enshrined in 'Q', Jesus insists that the Kingdom *could* be ours *today*. What does this mean? Does Jesus imply that the Great Apocalypse is imminent? This is precisely what the early Christians believed. Paul himself was eagerly anticipating the day when he, too, would be "caught up in the clouds." So what of this human nirvana? When – and how – was it supposed to come about?

Perhaps the answer lies in Luke, specifically the chapter in which Jesus confronts the *bêtes noirs* of the Lucan story, the Pharisees. He turns to the Pharisees and says, "The Kingdom of God is not coming with things that can be observed; you can't say, 'Look, here it is!' or 'There it is!' For in fact, the kingdom of God *is among you*" (Luke 17:20-21).

My conclusion, then, is that in Jesus' view the Kingdom of God is *not* a political entity *nor* (or at least, not exclusively) a distant reward after the passage of death; the Kingdom of God is also a *state of grace*. It is a blueprint for a society based on justice, compassion and surrender to God. Or to quote Martin Buber's famous letter to Franz Werfel: "the Kingdom … is no other-worldly consolation, no vague heavenly bliss. It is the perfect life of man with man."

It is, in short, a compact for ethical living that extends the Covenant of Moses into a new and more intimate sphere of human relations, and closer spiritual communion with God.

Chapter Fourteen
The Passover Events of 30 CE

*A View of Temple Mount from the Mount of Olives,
where Jesus spent the evening of his arrest*

Today, one can enter the old city of Jerusalem through several gates. One is the Damuscus Gate or *Bab al-'Amud*. After crossing the busy intersection at Sultan Suleiman, the visitor will feel as if he has left the 21st century behind. Here is the *shoukh*, the old Ottoman bazaar of Jerusalem, replete with sights and smells that have changed little over the course of the last 1,000 years. Much of what we see in the Old City today was built in the so-called Mamluk period (1248-1516 CE) when Jerusalem was one of the foremost cities of the Islamic Empire. So lofty was its reputation that many high officials chose to retire here -- reason why residences are often over 500 years old.

In Roman times, the Damascus Gate was also one of the principal gateways into the city. Nearby was Jerusalem's version of the *Cardo*, the ancient Roman boulevard that was the center of commercial activity. Today, the Cardo has been replaced by the *Souq Khan al-Zeit* that separates the Muslim quarter (at left) from the Christian quarter (at right). Here also begins the journey by which the visitor can retrace the steps of Jesus in the last few hours of his life.

Partially restored remains of the Roman/Byzantine 'Cardo', East Jerusalem

Pilgrims refer to the route of Jesus' passion as the *Via Dolorosa*, Latin for 'Road of Sorrow'. According to the local tradition, it begins some 300 steps from St. Stephen's Gate near the Muslim building of *Madrasa al-Dawadarrya*, and continues through the warren of narrow streets to the Church of the Holy Sepulcher. Along the way are plaques commemorating the fourteen stations of the Cross, each marking the spot where the Gospels place a certain event in the Passion story.

The *Madrasa* or Islamic school is the site where archaeologists have tentatively identified the remains of the Roman Antonia fortress, scene of Jesus' trial, which overlooked Herod's vast Temple compound. Nearby is a lovely Franciscan monastery that contains the presumed location of the Flagellation. Further down the cobblestone pavement of the Lion Gate Street is a fragment of a Roman arch. This arch has long been associated with the moment when Jesus, bleeding from his scourging, is shown to the people by Pilate with the words *Ecce Homo* - "behold the man" (John 19:5). The arch can also be glimpsed in the nearby convent of the Sisters of Zion; part of this Roman structure runs right behind the altar of the chapel. However, archaeologists now believe the arch dates from the time of Hadrian around 135 CE -- over 100 years after the crucifixion of Jesus.

This 14th century chapel is traditionally associated with the Last Supper of Jesus and his apostles

Is the Via Dolorosa truly the route that Jesus walked from Antonia Fortress to the execution hill on Golgotha? Once again, scholars cannot agree. For one, Jerusalem no longer resembles the city of Jesus' time, because it was raised to the ground by Roman forces in 70 C.E. – and again, for good measure, in 135 C.E.

Its walls shifted as the Mamluk rulers built a whole new city on the remains of the 2nd century Roman settlement. If Jesus would return today, he would be utterly lost in the byzantine alleyways of the Turkish bazaar.

The Gospels offer a very detailed version of the Passover events of about 30 C.E., based on a putative "Cross Gospel" that no longer exists. Mark, as well as Matthew and Luke, place the blame for Jesus' death on the Sanhedrin, the council of priests that, as we have seen, was controlled by the collaborationist Sadducees, as well as the Pharisees. "Now the chief priests and the whole council," Mark says, "were looking for testimony against Jesus to put him to death" (Mk 14:55).

Writing near the end of the 1st century, the Gospel of John no longer bothers with such distinctions and places the collective blame on "the Jews." At the time of John's writing, the "Jesus movement" had petered out among religious Jews in Palestine. One reason was that in the years after the crucifixion, Jewish communities had openly turned against the followers of this Messiah and had banned them from their synagogues. A genuine persecution followed. James, the brother of Jesus and head of the church in Jerusalem, was thrown to his death in the Kidron Valley in 62 C.E. -- apparently at the instigation of that same institution, the Sanhedrin.

An entirely different situation was emerging outside of Palestine, as we will see in the next chapter. In sharp contrast to Palestine, Roman and Greek communities around the Mediterranean -- both Jewish and Gentile -- were quite receptive to the teachings of this esoteric 'Messiah'. A budding Christian church was even present in the very city where Mark was writing his great opus -- *Rome*.

The evangelists, who wrote for Diaspora Jews and Gentiles in the Greco-Roman world, clearly understood that it would not help their cause to have Roman authority exposed as the villain in the story. It would alienate the very followers who had showed a keen interest in what Jesus had to say. By contrast, there was no love lost between the Christian and non-Christian Jews, since the latter had already turned their backs on the great Jewish reformer.

What's more, the ultimate target of Mark's enmity, the *Sanhedrin*, was now only a memory. After the destruction of Jerusalem by Titus in 70 C.E., the Temple lay in ruins, and the priesthood, including the Sadducees, were no more. Jewish scholarship had been evicted from Jerusalem and was now trying to build a new Jewish center of learning in Yabneh. Consequently, the Sanhedrin – and specifically, the Sadducees – were a safe choice as the culprits of the Passion story.

A powerful attestation of the historical Pilate is provided by this inscription, excavated in Caesarea in the 1960's, which reads: Tiberieum (Pon)tius Pilatus (Praef)ectus Iudae(ae), or "(This) Tiberium (was built by) Pontius Pilate, Prefect of Judaea"

It exonerated the Romans. It put the blame on an institution that had instigated the persecution of Christians, but conveniently enough, was no longer in being, so it couldn't contest the Christian interpretation of events.

By contrast, the Gospels depict Pilate as a compassionate man who readily grasps the innocence of Jesus. In fact, the Romans are shown to be extremely reluctant to move against Jesus. But Josephus tells us that Pilate was a bitter and spiteful man whose response to any challenge was to *crush* it. Indeed, Pilate was removed from office by the emperor in 36 C.E. for his excessive cruelty. The Pilate of history is therefore far removed from the noble and merciful character that appears in the New Testament.

We also know that contrary to the account in the gospels, the Sanhedrin certainly had the power to sentence a man to death, as attested in great detail in the Mishnah. This right was posted in capital letters all around the Temple precinct. According to Josephus, large inscriptions in Hebrew, Greek and Roman proclaimed that any foreigner who tried to pass the boundary of the *soreg* and enter the inner courtyard of the Temple would summarily be put to death. Paul discovered this to his discomfort when he was accused of taking Gentiles past the *soreg* and only escaped execution by appealing to his right, as a Roman citizen, to a proper trial under Roman law. Josephus' account was further corroborated when in 1935, archaeologists uncovered just such an inscription in the Herodian wall located close to the Lion's Gate. The inscription, written in Greek, ends with *Thanathos* -- the Greek word for 'death'.

In short, if the Sanhedrin wanted to get rid of someone whom they believed had violated their religious laws, they didn't need the Romans to do it for them. They could go ahead and take care of the matter themselves. This simple fact is dramatically illustrated in *Acts of the Apostles*. In it, we read that Stephen, one of the disciples of the early church, was accused of blasphemy by the Sanhedrin. He was immediately taken out and stoned to death. Not a single Roman soldier was involved.

In sum, the historical evidence indicates that Jesus was tried, convicted and executed by the Romans. The charge was sedition: Jesus was accused of inciting the people to establish a new Jewish kingdom, thus challenging the authority of Rome and the majesty of Tiberius himself. The method of execution was crucifixion, the mandatory punishment for political rebels. What's more, Pilate never ignored an opportunity to instruct the masses. Crucifying Jesus in public, during the Passover festival, sent a clear signal not to challenge Roman law and order.

And so, Jesus is crucified. While a crowd of followers look on, the sun slowly tracks across the killing field. Suddenly Jesus cries out with all his might, "*Eloi, Eloi, lama sabachthani?*" Here, as in other places, the gospel of Mark may be using the original Aramaic of the Cross Gospel, the Passion tradition underlying his story. We can certainly imagine Jesus, at this supreme moment of agony, feeling utterly abandoned by his *Abba*. On the other hand, the cry *Lord, Lord, why have you forsaken me?* is a verbatim quote from Psalm 22 and may have been interpolated by the evangelist to underscore the idea that Scriptural prophecy has been fulfilled.

A few hours pass, and the Roman soldiers decide to call it a day. They cannot leave the victims on the crosses, however, as they would anywhere else in the Roman Empire. In Jerusalem, in deference to the Mosaic Laws, a "hanged man" must be taken down before sundown. And so they take the mallet and move from cross to cross, smashing the legs of each condemned man. The purpose is simple: once his legs are broken, the victim can no longer raise himself to breathe. One by one, the condemned men struggle, gulp for air, and suffocate in agony. Within a few minutes, all the victims are dead. One of the soldiers raises his mallet to break the legs of Jesus too; but then he wonders whether Jesus is already dead. The soldier takes his *pilum* and pierces Jesus' side. There is no reaction. Jesus has been dead for more than an hour (Jn 19:32,34).

In 1968, a sensational discovery was made in the cemetery of Giv'at ha-Mivtar near Jerusalem. In this ancient cemetery, archaeologists uncovered several ossuaries – stone containers of bones collected after the body has decomposed. One of these boxes held the skeleton of an adult Jewish male from the 1st century CE, identified in an inscription as *Jehohanan*. Forensic research revealed that Jehohanan had been crucified. His ankle bones were still held together by a single, seven-inch nail. But most astonishing was the condition of the condemned man's legs. As Dr. Nicu Haas reported, "the right tibia and the left calf bones were all broken at the same level .. suggesting a single, strong blow." This suggests that the breaking of the legs in the Gospels is an authentic detail.

ONE BY ONE, THE CORPSES are dumped in a pit nearby to serve as carrion for birds and wild dogs. It is the last humiliation of crucifixion – denying a man a proper burial in his family plot or tomb. In later years, the *Mishnah* and the *Talmud* will confirm that condemned men may not be buried in their family plots and only in designated graveyards.

Suddenly, a man rushes up to the centurion in charge of the cohort, breathlessly holding out a written order from Pilate. The order states that if the officer can confirm that Jesus is dead, he is to release the corpse to the bearer. The centurion is surprised, but not unduly so. The man in front of him is well dressed and has several servants in tow. No doubt, the man has paid Pilate a hefty bribe to save Jesus' body from disgrace. Matthew concurs: the man from Arimathea was a *rich* man (Mk 15:42-45; Mt 27:57-58).

Why did Joseph of Arimathea, a member of the Great Sanhedrin, bother to claim the body of Jesus? The reason is what we have suspected all along: there were several Pharisees who were sympathetic to Jesus' cause. Joseph may have genuinely felt that Jesus was a holy man and deserved a decent burial. To arrange for a burial plot on such short notice was out of the question. If the Mishnah is correct, it would also have been against Pharisaic custom. The solution, then, was to have the body of Jesus rushed to Joseph's *own* tomb – even if it was just a temporary measure. Here, Jesus could be cleansed, wrapped and perfumed in secrecy, away from prying eyes.

The burial party arrives at the tomb sometime between the 10th or 11th hour. Mary Magdalene and two other women follow, carrying pitchers of water, a sponge and washing cloth, and burial linen to wrap the body.

This 'Garden Tomb' was believed by some to be the place of Jesus' burial. It has since been found to date to the 2nd century B.C.E.

Very little time remains before sundown. But the body must be wrapped in fragrant spices, so as to cover the odors of decomposition. This is customary because, during the first three days after death, the bereaved are expected to visit the tomb to ascertain that its occupant is truly dead, not just in a deep coma.

A passage in the Semahot notes two occasions on which a man was found alive and lived to old age. The Midrash states that "for three days [after death] the soul hovers over the body, intending to re-enter it, but as soon as it sees its appearance change, it departs, as it is written."

Myrrh and frankincense are the two most popular perfuming agents, but these are far beyond the means of Jesus' traveling band of followers. The Gospel of John claims that another wealthy individual, a man called Nicodemus, comes to the rescue. His servants bring jars of myrrh and aloes "about a hundred pounds in weight," which is John's way of saying that there was ointment aplenty.

TRADITION HOLDS THAT THE PLACE of this tomb can today be found in the heart of the Church of the Holy Sepulcher, in the Christian section of the old City. There is little doubt that this is the actual place. The mother of Constantine the Great, the Empress Helena, was a devout Christian who traveled to Jerusalem in the early 4th century to identify the place of Jesus' execution and burial. This was known as *Golgotha*, the Aramaic name for 'Place of the Skull' (or *Calvaria* in Latin).

It so happens that a Christian community had continued to live in Jerusalem after the destruction of the temple, led by an uninterrupted line of bishops. So it was that in 326, Bishop Macarius took the Empress to a place where one of her son's predecessors, Emperor Hadrian, had erected a temple to Venus.

The Church of the Holy Sepulcher contains this area, believed to mark the location of Golgotha, the place of Jesus' crucifixion

Much of the original topography had changed in order to accommodate this pagan temple; but local pilgrims insisted that the actual place of Jesus' tomb had remained largely untouched. The Empress immediately ordered the temple to Venus to be razed so that a small aedicule could be built over the tomb. She then set out to build a vast basilica. As her architects excavated the site, workers discovered a pit deep in the hill. Inside were a number of crosses, which Roman soldiers had tossed over the hill after each crucifixion.

Helena's church rose as a large Roman basilica with five aisles, centered on a domed crossing with the tomb of Jesus in its center. This Constantinian structure was completed in 335 C.E. Three hundred years later, it was destroyed in the wake of the Persian invasion of 614, after which a second, more modest church was built. This structure abandoned the former plan of a five-aisled basilica, but added an extension so as to better integrate the hill of Golgotha proper.

The dome of the central crossing in the Church of the Holy Sepulcher

The 7th century church was still unfinished when Jerusalem was captured during the Islamic conquest. Caliph el-Hakim ordered much of the structure destroyed, after which the Crusaders resumed work on the building in the early 12th century. Given this tortured history – and the fact that the church is managed by no less than six competing religious denominations – it should not come as a surprise that the Church of the Holy Sepulcher is one of the most bizarre and confusing structures in all of Christendom.

THREE DAYS GO BY, during which Jews believe that "the soul hovers over the body." According to the reckoning of the Jewish calendar, the "first day" would have begun at sundown on Passover day – the day of execution. Sabbath is the second day. And so it is on Sunday, the third day, that Mary, Salome and Mary the mother of James rise just before sunup (Mk 16:1-2).

They would have delegated the task of grinding flour and baking bread to other women in the group. They dress quickly, then hoist the vessels of myrrh on their shoulders. There is no one to help them. Even now, the men are still in hiding, afraid to show themselves lest one of Pilate's roving patrols catch them in the city.

But in fact, the execution of the Galilean rabbi is already forgotten. The Passover celebrations have been brought to a close without any further public disturbance. Back in Herod's old palace, Pilate is already up. With most of the pilgrims now flooding out of the gates, he can order his *Tribunus laticlavius* to prepare for the journey home. If they move quickly, they can be on the road by the 4th hour and reach Caesarea by sundown.

Meanwhile, Mary and her companions make their way to Joseph's tomb. All during the journey, Mary is wondering how three women can move the heavy rolling stone that is barring the entrance to the grave. She hopes there will be a friendly farmer or servant who can lend them a hand.

And indeed, as she approaches the tomb, she sees a man sitting nearby. Perhaps it is the gardener. Mary knows that wealthy individuals like Joseph often use gardeners to maintain the grounds around their family tombs. This man looks like a young fellow for whom rolling a stone will be an easy task. But then she looks past him to the tomb and stops in her tracks. The vessel with the precious myrrh falls to the ground. Her hand flies to her mouth. The stone has already been rolled away.

Here the original version of the Gospel of Mark, and the story of the historical Jesus, comes to an end. From here on, the story of Christ takes over.

Chapter Fourteen
The Rise of Christianity

The Library of Celsus in Ephesus, a major base for Paul's missionary campaigns in Asia Minor

The issue of the Resurrection of Jesus falls outside of the scope of this book, for it cannot be corroborated by archaeological or historical evidence. There are, of course, numerous Gospel accounts of Jesus appearing to his disciples after his death, but the reports are not always consistent. At times, Jesus appears as a man of flesh and blood. He breaks bread with his companions (Lk 24:30) and invites the disbelieving Thomas to touch his wounds (Jn 20:27). At other moments, Jesus appears as a transcendent being who moves in and out of rooms without ever passing through a door, and must urge Mary Magdalene, *noli me tangere* – "do not to touch me," because "I have not yet ascended to the Father." Once again, we may see many different oral traditions at work.

Consequently, the issue of the Resurrection cannot be a subject for a scholarly debate. It is an act of faith. From a strictly historical point of view, however, what matters is that many followers of Jesus eventually came to believe in it. They clung to the idea that Jesus had risen. And, whether physically or spiritually, Jesus *had* risen. The spirit that had touched and inspired Jesus himself now appeared to be spreading among the apostles themselves.

Nevertheless, bereft of its charismatic leader, the 'Jesus Movement' inevitably branched out into several different sects. One group, led by James, the brother of Jesus, argued for a principal base in Jerusalem itself. Here was the Temple; here, in the Temple forecourt, Jesus himself had preached. Clearly, the message of Jesus was one destined for Jews, James argued; it therefore behooved the movement to stay at the center of Judaism and try to reform the faith from within.

The southwestern corner of the Herodian supporting walls underneath the Temple esplanade are today the best-preserved elements of the Second Temple during the 1st century C.E.

Another movement entirely was the one that eventually coalesced around Paul. Paul (originally named *Saul*) was born in Tarsus, the capital of Cilicia. Tarsus was located close to the Tarsus river, near the modern city of Gözlükule, which today is some 10 miles distant from the Mediterranean coast.

In 64 B.C.E., Tarsus had been conquered by Rome and subsequently made the leading city of the Roman province of Cilicia. The city accepted its fate with equanimity. In fact, Tarsus was so faithful in its tribute and allegiance to Rome (which included the provision of mercenary soldiers), that Augustus granted the capital the exceptional status of a 'free Roman city.' This decree turned most of its principal inhabitants into Roman citizens. It also endowed Tarsus with a certain degree of political autonomy.

Philosophers of every ilk flocked to the city in the hope of finding patronage. "The inhabitants of Tarsus have become so enthusiastic for philosophy and the area of education," wrote the 1st century Roman geographer Strabo, "that they have surpassed Athens, Alexandra and any other place." Even after Paul was educated in Jerusalem -- by a noted Pharisaic rabbi named Gamaliel -- he remained fond of the pure intellectual exercise of analysis and debate that was practiced on every street corner in his hometown.

It molded his character, too. Paul was an intellectual, born in one of the most sophisticated *milieus* of the Roman Empire. The fellow students with whom he matched his wits in the Greek schools of Tarsus were a world apart from the crowd of uneducated apostles he would encounter in Jerusalem. A doctrinarian at heart, Paul instinctively knew that he was superbly qualified to elevate this freewheeling cult into a proper religious movement.

Ironically, Paul was a late convert to Jesus. While making a living as a tent maker or a leather worker (the historical record is not clear on this), he was recruited by his Pharasaic peers into a Jewish para-military group. The mission of this band was to make life extremely difficult for members of the Jesus cult in Jerusalem. Among others, Paul was present at the execution of Stephen, and watched while the crowd pounced on the poor man until he died. Perhaps he even organized the stoning, for Acts tells us, after Stephen was pronounced dead the killers "laid down their garments at the feet of a young man named Saul" (Acts 7:58). As Acts tells us, "on that day a severe persecution began against the church in Jerusalem."

Somewhere along the way, around the year 38 C.E., Paul had a complete change of heart. Paul himself describes this event. Riding on the road to Damascus, he was tossed from his horse by a shaft of light, and blinded. He heard the voice of Jesus calling to him -- *Saul, why do you persecute me?* Shortly thereafter, Paul decided to join the very movement that he had fought so hard to destroy. He remained in Damascus and learned all he could about this new Jewish movement. What he found was that the group had no central direction, no doctrine, no scripture. Clearly, the movement needed all these things, which, Paul believed, was the reason for his conversion. Later, he would write that he "possessed the mind of Christ," and that his acts were like the acts of the great Teacher himself (1 Cor 2:16). And then Paul began to preach, at first in Nabataean Arabia.

His efforts were successful; so successful, in fact, that local Jewish leaders lodged a complaint with the Nabataean ethnarch. This man duly issued a warrant for his arrest. Paul escaped in a basket that was lowered over the city walls, and finally made his way to Judaea where James, the brother of Jesus, as well as Peter were the recognized leaders the church of Jerusalem.

The meeting between these principals was surprisingly brief. Paul was not invited to other communities in the Jerusalem area. After two weeks, he was gone, determined to undertake a missionary tour of communities in Asia Minor, on his own accord. Clearly, the Jerusalem Church and the intellectual from Tarsus did not have a meeting of the mind.

And so, Paul embarked on his first journey, beginning with Antioch or *Antiocheia Pisidias* in Greek, located in Phrygia (today's central Turkey). It was in this cosmopolitan city that a disciple named Barnabas reported a keen interest in Jesus among the locals. Some of these new converts were Jewish; but there were also some Gentiles who were willing to be converted.

Gentile followers of Jesus? This was something new. Up to this point, the apostles had always targeted their conversion efforts on Jews, since this had been Jesus' own policy. "Think not that I came to destroy the Law, or the prophets;" Jesus had told them; "I did not come to destroy, but to fulfill" (Mt 5:17). Throughout his trips through Galilee, Jesus had eschewed Gentile cities. For Jesus, the Gentiles were irrelevant, for they lived in a pagan sphere that was anathema to the concept of one God.

But Paul was a man who was actually born and raised in one of those "worldly" cities. What's more, Paul sensed an opportunity -- a chance to launch the Jesus movement in a world that truly knew no bounds. On the strength of a Gentile following, Paul could in effect *define* the Jesus movement far from the apostolic jurisdiction of the Jerusalem group. Herein lay the seeds of a future schism, but it is unclear if Paul was aware of it at the time.

FOR THE NEXT FOURTEEN YEARS, Paul concentrated on his missionary work among both Jews and Gentiles, using Antioch as his base. During his first journey with Barnabas, he traveled to Cyprus and then continued to Asia Minor, preaching in Perga and Pamphylia. From there on they traveled to Iconium and Lystra before heading back to Attalia and ultimately back to Antioch. In the process, Paul began to refine a theology that would be understandable and appealing to the audience he had in mind: the communities of Asia Minor.

The forum of Perga, a leading city in Roman Lycia on Asia Minor

But how was he to explain to this Greco-Roman audience that a holy man of God was executed by Rome like a common criminal? And then, Paul saw the answer. Jesus died on the cross because this was *precisely* what God had intended for him. Why? Because his crucifixion served as the *ultimate* Passover sacrifice. which erased the slate of mankind, and offered a new and fresh start. By offering himself as the *über*-paschal lamb, Jesus had made Temple sacrifice redundant and its corrupt priesthood irrelevant. The proof of this divine intent was the Resurrection: a divine imprimatur that marked a new covenant between God and Man.

The concept of Resurrection struck a chord in Paul. As we have seen, educated Pharisees like Paul had far more in common with early Christianity than we often realize. The Pharisees believed that the soul of the righteous would find eternal life, and that their bodies would rise on the Last Day.

The idea that Jesus was resurrected by God underscored the divine importance of his mission. In fact, it was living proof that the apocalyptic changes foretold by Jesus had finally begun. Like the 'Son of Man' in the Book of Daniel, Paul envisioned Jesus sitting on his heavenly throne, closely monitoring the implementation of God's kingdom. From there, it was but one small step to the conclusion that Jesus himself was divine.

Divine, in what way? That Jesus was divinely inspired? That Jesus was touched by the spirit of God, like the prophets of Israel before him? No, said Paul, God had resurrected Jesus so that the world would know that he, Jesus, was divine himself – not the Son of Man, but the Son of God.

While these concepts have become commonplace in Christian theology, it is important to realize how far Paul (if indeed he was the one who synthesized the Resurrection belief) was straying from Jewish faith and Scripture. The idea that Jesus' death had been a 'sacrifice' to expunge the sin and guilt of mankind presumed that God could be assuaged by, or even *condone,* a human sacrifice. As we have seen, the idea of a human life being offered to YAHWEH was anathema to the Jewish faith. This was anchored in the story of Abraham sacrificing his son Isaac.

What's more, the idea that an observant Jew like Jesus could be considered the physical son of God would have been equally reprehensible to most Jews. Observant Jews were (and still are) in such awe of God that they dare not even *speak* the name of YAHWEH. To suggest that this Supreme Being had a son who was also divine, threatened to plunge the Jewish faith back into the polytheistic aberrations of Mesopotamia and the Greco-Roman world.

But – as Paul must have known – for a Gentile audience the idea of Jesus' divinity was *eminently* plausible. Rome was a world in which prominent men (such as Julius Caesar) habitually claimed ancestry from a god, and in which virtually every emperor after Augustus was posthumously worshipped as a deity. It would have been very difficult for Paul to convince his Greco-Roman audience that a peasant from Galilee, crucified as a terrorist, could somehow be a herald of God's kingdom, if he, too, hadn't been divine.

The Hebrew Scriptures also called their kings "sons of God," but that appellation meant something very different to Romans than to Jews, as Paul well knew. Romans were Europeans, and Europeans are not comfortable with the ephemeral mysteries of the Near East. They want something tangible, something physical. For them, as for the Greeks, gods are anthropomorphic beings, whose physical perfection is proof positive of their divine status. This is why Greek and Roman gods are invariably depicted as young and beautiful men and women in the nude. The Jews of Palestine, by contrast, eschewed the representation of living beings and were horrified by the very thought of depicting YHWH.

Thus, for Paul's Gentile audience, Jesus became the tangible expression of a new monotheism: a physical manifestation of an unseen God.

THERE IS NO PROOF that it was Paul who first preached to the world that Jesus was the Son of God; but the fact is that his letters, arguably the first written record of Christianity, espouse this theology with vigor. Paul's theology -- if we may call it such -- propelled the Antioch church and its satellite communities to astonishing growth. Encouraged, Paul embarked on a second and far more ambitious voyage, one that would take him to the heart of the sybaritic Greek culture: Athens and Corinth.

Between 48 and 51 CE, he moved from Antioch to the heart of Anatolia and on to Troas (near today's Istanbul). From there he crossed the Aegean by ship and continued on the Via Egnatia, the main military highway built by Rome, which took him to Philippi. He traveled through the Greek mainland, visiting Thessalonica and Athens, and ended with an 18-month stay in Corinth.

The Theater of Ephesus, where Paul was set upon by angry souvenir sellers, concerned that Paul's preaching would discourage the pilgrimage traffic to the shrine of Artemis

He then journeyed back to Asia Minor, landing at Ephesus. All along the way, he established new communities dedicated to *Christos,* the Greek word for Messiah, the Son of God.

Some of these were Jewish; others were Gentile and Greek in origin. The Gentiles, however, were concerned over the more onerous precepts of Judaism – such as circumcision (not a pleasant experience for grown men in those days), as well as the dietary laws and the strict limitations of the Sabbath. So the question rose: if they converted to Christianity, were they also expected to behave as Jews and adhere to the Laws of Moses? More specifically, were they supposed to be circumcised as well?

Paul then made extraordinary decision. Gentile followers of Jesus, he decreed, did *not* need to be circumcised. Why? Because the act of circumcision, of *branding* one as a believer in God as Abraham had once done, was now replaced by the act of baptism. The immersion in the baptismal font 'cleansed' one's soul for the reception of the holy Spirit.

This, of course, was a very momentous development. Deep in his heart, Paul must have realized that by unmooring the 'Christ' theology from the precepts of Judaism, he was in effect creating a new religion: a movement distinct from the Jewish faith. But then, the minutiae of the Mosaic Laws had never been foremost in Jesus' teachings. Had Jesus not told his apostles that "the Sabbath was made for man, not man for the Sabbath?" "A person," Paul wrote to the Galatians, "is justified not by the works of the Law but through faith in Jesus Christ." It was one's faith in God that defined one as a 'follower' of *Christos*.

The St. Paul's Pillar in Paphos, Cyprus, where according to tradition, Paul was flogged before being able to convert the Roman governor to Christianity

NATURALLY, IT WAS ONLY A MATTER of time before word of Paul's extraordinary exploits among the Gentiles filtered back to Jerusalem. It was met with astonishment. The Book of Acts suggests that Paul and Barnabas were summoned back to Jerusalem around 48 C.E. to account for their activities. This was a time of famine in Palestine, and the author known as 'Luke' presents this visit as a mission of mercy, permitting Paul to bring desperately needed relief. In his letters, however, Paul mentions no such visit.

Regardless of whether Paul reported to James on his activities or not, the Jerusalem church was deeply concerned by Paul's conversion of the Gentiles, and not only on the question of circumcision. Another vexing issue was the problem of the *shared meal*. As in Palestine, the proto-Christian communities often met to remember their great rabbi and discuss his teachings. For Jewish followers, the venue was obvious: they simply continued to meet in their synagogue, or in their homes.

But Gentile followers did not have synagogues. Instead, these early 'Christians' met in their family homes, often inviting their Jewish brethren to join in. From there it was but a short step to the idea of a communal meal. The Jewish purity laws, however, forbade Jews to share a table with Gentiles, because neither the food nor the wine offered by Gentile host was *kosher*. In Jerusalem, the problem did not arise because the church of James and Peter was Jewish. But in Antioch, in Ephesus and in Corinth, no such fine distinctions were made. Jews mixed with Gentiles, and sat down to eat.

The group of James was dumbfounded. They knew that Paul was a man of strong convictions who liked to follow his own lead. But they could not comprehend why Paul could abolish these hallowed traditions so easily. Not having witnessed Paul in action, not having seen the enthusiasm of Paul's congregation with their own eyes, they wondered if Paul had perhaps lost his head.

And so, a meeting was called. Paul was summoned to Jerusalem to explain himself. Depending on what source we read - Luke's *Acts* or Paul's *Letter to the Galatians*, this momentous conference took place sometime after 51 C.E. With startling frankness, Paul tells us how he defiantly ...

> "... spelled it out before them .. the whole gospel that I had proclaimed among the Gentiles, to make sure that I was not running, or had not run, in vain."
> (Gal. 2:2)

Paul knew that in stark contrast to *his* missionary work, the Palestinian church of James was floundering. Jewish Christians were on the defensive throughout Judaea. James' flock was being persecuted. Paul knew this, of course, for he once had energetically participated in this campaign. So to reject Paul's theology and policies among the Gentiles was tantamount to condemning the movement to a slow death in a besieged Judaea; to approve of Paul's campaign was to drive an indelible wedge between Jewish and non-Jewish followers of Jesus. A vexing dilemma.

And so, in the end, the Jerusalem Conference ended in a stalemate. In effect, the two factions agreed to disagree. Paul could go and minister to the Gentiles, if he so pleased; but James would continue to work among circumcised Jews *only*.

And Paul did. In some communities where the Septuagint (the Greek translation of the Hebrew Bible) was available, Paul directed them to relevant passages in the Books of the Prophets, which foretold of Jesus' coming. For those who didn't, Paul supplied scriptural guidance of his own, in the form of a steady stream of *epistles* or letters. These missives reminded the early Christians what Jesus' message had been about, how men and women should live in the imitation of Christos, and what practical deeds were required to ensure that they would enter 'the Kingdom of God'.

Many times, Paul would find that the initial enthusiasm of a particular community had waned. This is why Paul's letters sometimes carry a strident tone, reproaching one community for its lack of faith, or for its return to the pleasurable activities of its former pagan orientation.

By mid-century, then, three different 'Jesus Movements' had begun to evolve. One was the continuing, though beleaguered, Jewish "chapel" led by James and centered in Jerusalem. The second was the Pauline movement, which later became known as the *catholic* (literally, 'world-embracing') school. This movement embraced the Resurrection doctrine, as enshrined in the New Testament canon.

A third movement, however, had begun to coalesce around a very different interpretation of Jesus. For lack of a better term, biblical scholarship has coined the term *Gnostics* for these "dissident" followers. Gnosticism - derived from the Greek word *Gnosis*, meaning *knowledge* – was influenced by the ancient, Platonic idea that complete immersion in the Divine ultimately led to a secret knowledge about the divine.

IN THE GNOSTIC INTERPRETATION, Jesus propagated his New Kingdom theology as the key to unlocking the secrets of divine manifestation within oneself. This is why Jesus always spoke in parables when trying to describe the New Kingdom; because true knowledge of God in oneself was a secret that was only open to those who proved themselves worthy.

What's more, it underscored the belief that the New Kingdom was not a celestial theocracy in the wake of some cataclysmic apocalypse, but a state of grace that could be attained by any dedicated believer, provided he was willing to permeate the many layers surrounding true *gnosis*, inner knowledge.

In the Gnostic *Gospel of Thomas,* for example, Jesus ridicules those who think of the Kingdom of God as a new political order, or a new physical realm.

The ancient forum of Alexandria, an important center of the Gnostic Christian movement

"If those who lead you say to you, 'See, the Kingdom is in the sky,' 'then the birds of the sky will precede you,'" he says derisively. Instead, the Jesus of Thomas says:

> The Kingdom is inside of you, and it is outside of you.
> When you come to know yourselves, then you will
> become known, and you will realize that it is you
> who are 'the sons of the living Father. But if
> you will not know yourselves, you dwell in poverty
> and it is you who are that poverty."
> (Thomas, 3).

The Gnostics rejected the Pauline idea that the Death and Resurrection cycle *defined* Jesus' message, his ministry, indeed his very *raison d'être*. These followers were not concerned with darkness and death, but with light and life -- specifically, the light of divine spirituality that Jesus had shown to exist in himself and every man and women who followed his path.

There are some elements in Gnosticism that would have appealed to modern Christians. For one, the Gnostic communities embraced both men and women as equals, whereas the Catholic Church would eventually move to marginalize women, and forbid them to speak up in church. Some Gnostic sects, by contrast, accepted Mary Magdalene as an apostle who could speak with great authority about Jesus. Another (though much later) Gnostic document, *The Gospel of Philip,* underscores the close relationship between Jesus and Mary Magdalene, who (according to Philip) "was called his companion:"

> "[Christ] loved [Mary Magdalene] more than all the
> disciples, and used to kiss her often on her mouth.
> The rest of the disciples [objected].
> They said to him "Why do you love her more than all of us?"
> The Savior answered and said to them,
> "Why do I not love you like her? When a blind man and
> one who sees are both together in darkness, they are no
> different from one another. When the light comes, then he
> who sees will see the light, and he who is blind will remain
> in darkness."

Above all, the Gnostic Christians stressed the validity of *individual* revelation. Any Christian who underwent the spiritual transformation to true *gnosis,* became in essence an apostle. In the years to come, this aspect of Gnosticism would be violently attacked by orthodox Christians, because it negated the hierarchical model of authority that the Catholic Church was trying to build. But before the conflict between Gnosticism and orthodoxy could truly come to a head, another enemy loomed for both movements: the wrath of Rome.

IN 64 C.E., A TERRIBLE FIRE swept through Rome. Whether it was set deliberately by Nero in order to create space for his grandiose new city plan, or whether it was a genuine accidental calamity will continue to be debated for many years to come. According to the Roman historian Tacitus, Nero put the blame squarely on the most convenient scapegoat, namely the Christians, or *Chrestians,* as Tacitus calls them (*Annals,* XV,44).

In the persecutions that followed, scores of Christians were burned as human torches, or devoured by wild beasts in what Tacitus refers to as "the Circus".

To this day, Roman guides at the Coliseum will solemnly point at the spot where Christians were thrown to the lions. Alas, the Coliseum (or more properly, the Flavian Amphitheater) was built some eight years *after* the fire -- not by Nero but by emperor Vespasian.

The Roman Coliseum. Contrary to popular belief, no Christians were executed here during Nero's persecutions

Tacitus, in fact, may be referring to the Circus Maximus, which could boast a track of some 550 yards and was a favorite venue for chariot racing. Built before the time of Caesar, it was Rome's most popular entertainment spot. It was also constantly enlarged and embellished by every emperor who wished to stay in the good graces of the *plebs*. If Nero had wanted to stage a public spectacle, therefore, there is no question he would have taken his horror show to the Maximus, so as to accommodate the largest possible crowd. Indeed, after the fire Nero would extend the race track by about 100 yards.

It was the misfortune of Peter, poor *Cephas* or "The Rock," to be caught up in this massive Roman *progrom*. As legend has it, Peter was one of those who, according to Tacitus, were crucified in great numbers. Peter, however, demanded that his cross be turned upside down, for he found himself unworthy to die in the same position as Jesus.

TWO YEARS LATER, AN EVEN MORE cataclysmic event erupted in Judaea. The new Roman prefect, Porcius Festus, suddenly died in 62 C.E. Orders went out for a replacement. In the interim, Palestine experienced a temporary power vacuum. According to Josephus, the high priest Ananus chose this moment to strike against the heresy of the Jesus movement.

Ananus won the Sanhedrin's backing to indict both "James, the brother of Jesus known as Christ, and several others on the charge of breaking the Law." James, the leader of the Jerusalem church, was thrown off the Temple parapet, and stoned to death. With both James and Peter dead, the "Jerusalem Movement" was, in effect, decapitated.

Four years later, during the tenure of Gessius Florus as Roman prefect, a militant group called the Zealots saw their chance and staged a *coup d'état* in Judaea. The Zealots were a political faction; they rejected any form of collaboration with the Roman oppressor, and strove for a full restoration of the Jewish state. The Zealots ousted Florus and established a "revolutionary government". Eventually, the Roman Senate prevailed on Nero to send one of his ablest generals, Vespasian, to Palestine at the head of the Tenth Legion. Vespasian landed his troops in northern Palestine in the Spring of 67 C.E. Two years later,

Vespasian's own legion pronounced him emperor. Vespasian's son, Titus, was charged with conquering Jerusalem.

Titus proceeded with typical Roman efficiency. In 70 C.E., he took Jerusalem, the last holdout of the Zealots, and staged a massacre. But the Romans did more than kill. They wiped out the temple precinct of Jerusalem, the center of Jewish worship and sacrifice since the days of King David. This act of revenge all but destroyed the priesthood; the Sadducees simply faded away.

The inner panel of the Arch of Titus in Rome, showing the looting of the Menorah from the Temple

Back in Rome, this victory was celebrated with relief. Titus himself succeeded his father Vespasian as emperor. After his death in 81 C.E., the Senate voted him honors as a god, and ordered a monument to be built to his triumph in Jerusalem. This famous Arch of Titus still stands in the Roman Forum, at the end of the Via Sacra; on one of the panels, we see the *menorah*, the seven-armed candelabra from the innermost shrine of the Temple itself, carried off by soldiers as a piece of ordinary loot.

With Jerusalem in ashes, the Pharisees moved north, to the relative safety of Galilee. There, they developed an alternative form of Jewish practice for which they themselves had laid the foundation for so many years. This became known as *Rabbinic Judaism*, in which the study of Scripture replaced worship and sacrifice at the Temple. By building rabbinic schools and synagogues, these Pharisaic rabbis were able to help Jews overcome the trauma of losing their national shrine and continue to exist as a distinct faith community. The work of the *Oral Law*, of collecting Torah commentary, was continued by Rabbi Akiba and his disciples, which ultimately led to the *Mishnah*, the first part of the Talmud, in the century to come.

For Jewish Christians, however, the fall of the Temple was no less cataclysmic. According to church tradition, Simeon son of Cleopas, Jesus' uncle, took control of the movement, but any immediate hope of creating a new Christian center of gravity in Palestine was lost.

IT IS NOT SURPRISING, THEN, that in the years after the great upheaval in Jerusalem, we witness the desire by the evangelists (or their sponsors) to commit the story of Jesus to paper. Just as Judaism sought succor in the reassuring certainty of Scripture, so too did the Jesus movement yearn for a 'scripture' of its own – a comprehensive codex of Jesus theology that could inspire and support the movement through this difficult time. Mark, Luke and Matthew all appear to have written in a span of twenty years following the date of Jerusalem's destruction. There may even be more 'Gospels' from this period that have been lost to time.

At the same time, Pauline Christianity continued to expand. The reason was the excellent network of roads and trade routes in the Roman world. Jewish and Gentile Christians carried the story of Jesus throughout the empire: into Europe, along the caravan routes eastwards into Syria, or westwards towards

Alexandria. Christianity spread like wildfire precisely because it was simple, noble, and democratic. Unlike the Roman religion, with its mockery of self-serving emperor-deities, the Christian God was pure and all-encompassing, a source of unselfish love and compassion. Unlike Judaism, Christianity was open to all, regardless of nationality or race. It attracted both free men and slaves with its alluring concept of a Kingdom after death in which all wrongs would be made right; and it offered consolation to the poor and marginalized of all backgrounds.

Rome itself was ambivalent about this latest religious import from Asia. Domitian (81-96) and Trajan (98-117) engaged in some anti-Christian policies, but when the younger Pliny proudly boasted of his persecutions to Trajan, the emperor urged moderation, suggesting that he surely had better things to do. Things were also relatively quiet during the reign of Emperor Hadrian (117-138) – the very man who quite literally erased Jerusalem after the Bar Kochba Uprising, and built a new city, *Aelia Capitolina,* in its place. There were sometimes violent disturbances against Christians in the provinces, but only Septimus Severus did honor to his name and pursued a policy of persecution with the utmost dedication and severity.

Meanwhile, Christianity itself continued to splinter into various sects. Many of these sought to blend Christology with prevailing Greek philosophy and rhetoric. In the works of the theologian Origen (185-254), for example, Christ was equated with the quintessential Platonic *Reason* that permeates all living things. A Christian priest from Alexandria named Arius (256-336) echoed Origen's beliefs, and his 'heresy' – Arianism – would penetrate as far as Northern Europe, converting large numbers of Goths. Thus, ironically, many of the Germanic invaders who threatened the Roman homeland from 221 onwards were Arianist Christians.

Rent by sparring from within, threatened by political persecution from without, Christianity stumbled into the 3rd century C.E. and found a whole new situation altogether. An increasingly enfeebled Rome became prey to a number of barbarian attacks, which prompted the Romans to rally to their gods. In this religious-nationalistic fervor, anyone who engaged in anti-Roman behavior (such as refusing military service) was immediately branded a traitor. Emperor Decius (249-251), for example, reinstated Christian progroms to bring the "draft evaders" to heel.

In 261 came a turning point. Emperor Gallienus had ruled jointly with his father, Valerian, from 253 until 260. More than one supreme commander was needed to defend Rome's borders against barbaric invasions. Valerian took responsibility for the empire's eastern flank, while Gallienus tried to repel the Goths in the north. Gallienus was able to defeat the Alemanni, who had pushed as far as Milan; but his father was not so lucky. Emperor Valerian was captured by the Persian king Shapur I -- a shocking event that is captured in a vast rock-face relief still visible today near Persepolis.

The capture of Valerian by Shapur I

This left Gallienus in sole charge of the realm, which by now had shrunk to little more than today's borders of Italy and the Balkans. Gallienus – and not Constantine, as is often thought – thereupon became the first Roman emperor to issue a decree of toleration, granting Christianity the status of a *religio licita*, an officially recognized religion. For the first time since the death of Jesus, Christians could go and practice their faith in full public view. Confiscated property was restored. By the end of the 3rd century, some 10% of all inhabitants of Asia Minor were Christian.

And then, in 303, the pendulum once again swung the other way. Shortly after Diocletian (284-305) had acceded to the throne, the pressure of invading hordes became so great that a vast reorganization of the Empire was necessary.

The highly stylized statues of the 'Four Emperors' in Venice, showing the decline of Roman art

A *tetrarchy* was established, whereby the supreme power of Emperor was divided between two rulers, each assisted by a subordinate Caesar as a quasi 'Vice-President'. These four rulers appear to this day in a remarkable red porphyry sculpture on the southwest corner of the San Marco in Venice, abutting the Doge's Palace. Frozen in the stylized gestures of a Roman art in decline, the four rulers seem to reach out to one another for support, as if facing a universally hostile world. And indeed, the Empire was in bad shape. Trade routes had been disrupted; markets had been lost to barbarian conquest; the Roman economy was close to collapse. The middle class, deprived of land, was threatened with extinction; thousands roamed the streets, hungry and out of work. The Romans needed someone to blame, and settled on the Christians.

Diocletian thereupon launched a renewed persecution of the Christians. Churches throughout the realm were vandalized or destroyed. All Christian worship was outlawed. Scores of bishops and church leaders were arrested, tortured and put to death in ways that would have put Nero to shame. In an ironic twist of fate, Diocletian, the ablest emperor since Hadrian, arguably saved the Empire from certain ruin, yet nearly succeeded in destroying Christianity as well. Fortunately, in 311, a new emperor named Galerius recognized that things had gotten out of control. He once again permitted Christians to worship in public, giving a badly needed respite to the body of the Church.

Throughout these years of persecution and oppression, the Roman Christians had bravely soldiered on. With the Jerusalem church gone, and with the tombs of Peter and Paul in their midst, the Roman "church" considered itself the natural center of the movement, although it took some time before other churches shared that view. By that time, these regional "churches" had begun to appoint priestly leaders or *presbyters* on the strength of their ability and faith. After 95 C.E., the title of 'bishop' emerged. By the 2nd century, these bishops met in periodic synods, so as to agree on a unified defense against the challenge of dissident theologies, as well as Roman persecution.

During the synod of Nicaea, a watershed event in the history of the church, the bishop of Rome was recognized as the leading authority, closely followed by the bishops of Antioch and Alexandria. The Roman bishop adopted the Latin name for supreme priest, which was *Pontifex Maximus* or 'Pope'. Rome, the location of the seat once held by Peter, now stood the center of catholic Christianity, well-positioned to lead the movement into the next and most decisive phase of growth.

It so happened that between 310 and 313, several different emperor-pretenders once again vied for the throne. By 313, only two were still standing: Maxentius and Constantine. On the eve before their decisive battle near the Mulvian Bridge, Constantine had a vision: a luminescent cross appeared in the sky above his camp, blazing with the words *en toutoi nika* -- in this conquer.

The colossal head of emperor Constantine on the Capitol in Rome

Constantine then rode out into battle, and defeated the army of Maxentius. Not long thereafter, he issued the Edict of Milan in 313, reaffirming Gallienus' Decree of Toleration and granting Christians unlimited freedom to worship.

THE REIGN OF CONSTANTINE represented a critical turning point in the fortunes of both Christianity and Judaism. The Roman state had finally embraced the cult of the peasant preacher from the East.

The Palazzo dei Conservatori on the *Campidoglio* in Rome has a striking portrait of Constantine that once formed part of a colossal statue. The eyes and nose are vastly exaggerated and out of proportion to the head itself. Part of this magnification was necessary in order to clearly show the emperor's features when seen from the ground. The emphasis on visual expression at the expense of realism, however, will become a hallmark of all Byzantine art. The large head is only the beginning of a trend that will lead to two-dimensional Byzantine mosaics, where form has become secondary. An ethereal, unearthly majesty replaces the tactile realism of the Roman secular world.

Perhaps Constantine most significant work is the church that he ordered built on the reputed site of the tomb of Simon Peter, near the *Ager Vaticanus*. Indeed, excavations under the current St. Peter's Basilica have uncovered an ancient necropolis, which predates the time of Constantine. Among the remains of various graves, some archaeologists believe to have identified the tomb of Peter himself.

Constantine's architects, however, faced a dilemma: what should a Roman temple dedicated to Christ look like? Up to this point, Christian shrines had been small and often haphazardly built, in secret. The archetype of the pagan temple – portico, worship hall and inner sanctum – was suitable for individual sacrifice, but not for mass assembly at a service like the Eucharist. Besides, Constantine may have felt uncomfortable using a pagan paradigm for a Christian church.

His architects decided to use the archetype of the basilica. The choice was perfect. The Roman basilica was a large, rectangular building designed for civic functions, the courts, and large assemblies. Because of its civic character it was, from a religious perspective, neutral. And it invariably ended in a monumental apse that usually accommodated a large statue of the reigning emperor; this now became the location of the Christian altar.

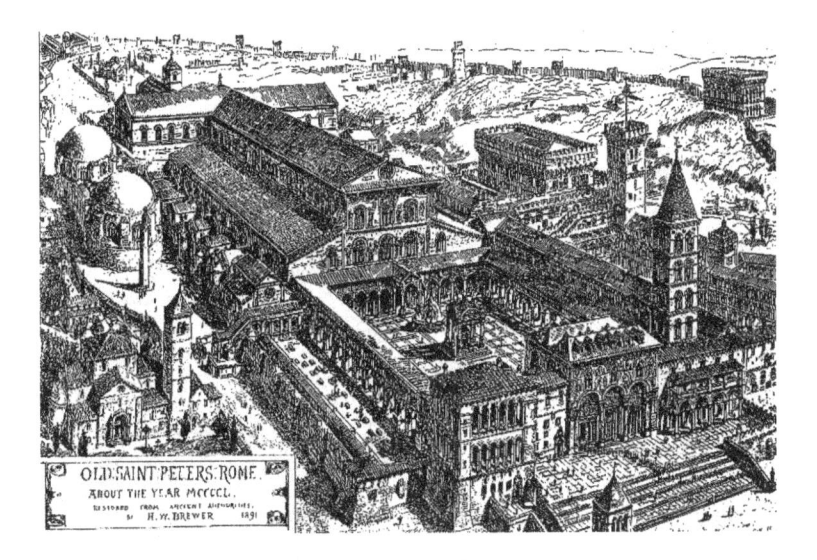

The original St. Peter's in Rome, based on the model of a Roman basilica

Even though the Constantine church no longer exists (it was replaced during the Renaissance by the current basilica, designed by Bramante and Michelangelo), it stood and functioned more than a thousand years after it was built.

Meanwhile, the emancipation of the Christian faith meant that wealthy Christian patrons could now avail themselves of the best sculptors to create their sarcophagi. These vast marble coffins became the favorite form of burial for the well-to-do, since Christianity expressly forbade cremation, as practiced by pagan Romans. In the early 20th century, archaeologists discovered a beautiful sarcophagus near the Villa Felice in Rome. Carved around 314, it shows scenes of St. Peter and Christ, including the entry of Jesus in Jerusalem, riding a donkey. Stylistically, the figures betray the Roman art of sculpture in decline; the details of folds, beards and hair are not sculpted but carved with a hard drill. Nevertheless, the detail of a horse grazing nearby, the child clinging to the folds of his father's tunic, or the man climbing a tree so as to better witness the entry, all suggest that the Roman artist continued to have a keen eye for detail.

Roman sarcophagus showing the entry of Christ in Jerusalem (ca. 314 C.E.)

Constantine attended to other matters as well. As a sign of the times, he resolved to move the imperial capital from Rome to a location closer to the East, to Byzantium. The emperor had concluded that Rome's destiny, economically and militarily, lay closer to Asia Minor. Perhaps Constantine harbored the hope of renewing lucrative trade routes to Arabia, Persia and India.

What's more, the population in Italy itself was on the decline. Many farms were abandoned; food production had plummeted; people had fewer children. Both Diocletian and Constantine tried to reverse the trend by instigating the Roman equivalent of a Five Year Plan, subjecting the economy to state planning. It failed to stem the decline and only succeeded in deterring entrepreneurial initiative. By contrast, population centers of Asia Minor were industrious and thriving.

Thus Constantine prepared to depart from Rome. He transferred his Lateran palace to the bishop of Rome; it would remain the official residence of the popes until 1308. He then charged the pope with civil authority, beginning the process that would ultimately invest the Church with political power in the new empire. And then he left.

This map illustrates the reach of Christianity in the 700 years following the death of Jesus

The new capital of the empire rose under the name of Constantinople or *Konstantinopolis* -- city of Constantine. And from this day forward, the Roman empire was known under a new name - Byzantium.

Under Constantine's successors, the "Byzantine emperors", Christianity grew rapidly. Monasteries and churches were built, while pagan temples were forcibly closed or destroyed. Emperor Julian the Apostate (the great-nephew of Constantine) tried to revert to pagan religion but was killed in the third year of his reign during a battle with the Persians.

Julian's successor, Emperor Theodosius, moved with a vengeance to reassert Christianity. In 380, he issued an astonishing imperial decree, making Christianity the *only* permitted religion in his realm. Twelve years later, the worship of pagan gods became a crime.

Encouraged by this bellicose stance, Christian monks throughout the Roman -- now Byzantine -- empire began to ransack the shuttered temples, destroying thousands of statues and making off with untold treasures of silver and gold. In Alexandria, Bishop Theophilus personally supervised the wholesale destruction of every pagan structure in the city, including the still-functioning Alexandrian Library and its affiliated Serapeum complex. Roman art, indeed Roman *culture*, had effectively come to an end.

The Western part of the empire, meanwhile, slowly succumbed to invading tribes from the North. In 410 CE, the Visigoths proceeded to sack Rome; the Vandals followed suit in 455. By the end of the 5th century, Theoderic the Ostrogoth had established his own kingdom on the Italian peninsula.

THESE DEVELOPMENTS WERE OBSERVED with interest by Persia, the superpower in the East that had long been Rome's nemesis. Persian might was experiencing a Renaissance of sorts. As we have seen, after the death of Alexander the Great the territory of Persia had become part of the Seleucid kingdom. In due course, this kingdom was overrun by nomadic people from the north called the Parthians. Their power was derived, to a great extent, from the import of silk from China and spices from India. Both were commodities that had always been in great demand in the patrician mansions of Rome. In its halcyon days, Rome had thought nothing of using its gold reserves to pay for these luxury goods. The flight of bullion to the East, even as the empire in the West began to crumble, would become a key factor in Rome's inability to stem its decline.

The Persians were the exclusive brokers of the Asian trade, since the trade routes ran across Persian territory. For this they charged a steep surcharge. The Romans found this difficult to stomach, but they had few alternatives. There were only two ways to circumvent the Persian Empire: one was the overland route through Eurasia, which was long and fraught with danger. The other was to cut through Arabia to Yemen, and from there by boat to India and beyond.

Rome then opted for the latter. From the 1st century C.E. onwards, Roman-sponsored trade expeditions increasingly used the cross-Arabian caravan route. The main terminus for this desert highway was the Nabataean city of Petra, today located in Jordan. Petra was blessed with two fortunes: it was a convenient jump-off point for caravans, and it had fresh-water wells. According to legend, this river was created when Moses had struck a rock with his staff; it is still known as *Wadi Musa* to this day. Petra was formally annexed by Trajan in 106, and the Nabataean kingdom, roughly equivalent to today's kingdom of Jordan, was made a Roman province named *Arabia Petraea*. The citizens of Petra hardly took notice; they were too busy making money.

The so-called 'Treasury' of Petra, a dramatic example of the city's cut-rock architecture

The principal by-products of the cross-Arabian trade were frankincense and myrrh, both found in southern Arabia (today's Oman). These substances were in high demand for use in temples throughout the Mediterranean world. In time, this trade activity stimulated the construction of caravan posts, which in turn led to settlements. Caravan settlements grew into villages, which in turn led to cities on the Greco-Roman model, so as to accommodate the growing merchant class. Some of these cities, like Palmyra on the rim between Syria and Arabia, or Gerasa in northern Jordan, were showcases of Greco-Roman urban splendor.

Wealth began to percolate throughout the Arabian peninsula. Urbanization encouraged local Arab and Bedouin tribes to coalesce into something resembling local fiefdoms. Eventually, the rulers of the territories of Saba and Himyar created a southern Arabian kingdom that, though short-lived, became the nucleus of a prosperity never seen before on the Arabian peninsula. These were the boom times, arguably the first time southern Arabia had experienced something approaching an indigenous civilization. Somewhat enviously, the Romans referred to southern desert region as *Arabia felix* - happy Arabia.

Meanwhile, the strength of Persia continued to grow. In 224, a Persian prince named Ardashir Papakan staged a coup and toppled the Parthian king Artabanus V, thus restoring Persian indigenous control of the empire. Ardashir then became the father of the Sasanid dynasty, which launched a campaign to expand Persia's borders, establishing Persian footholds in Bahrein and Mazun province (now Oman). The Sasanids even established their own silk weaving factories, further adding value to their silk routes.

The shores of Oman, source of the trade in frankincense and myrrh since the 2nd millennium B.C.E.

But the European market for these luxury products was fading. From the 3rd century onwards, the Roman Empire could no longer afford its expensive addiction to Asian luxury goods. Private capital shrank. The spice trade dried up. Excavations in India have failed to uncover any Roman coins after 250. The caravan trains became less frequent; some land routes were abandoned altogether. The great Roman global economy, running red-hot in the 2nd century, was disintegrating.

The bust had a severe effect on southern Arabia. The desert cities began to whither as people fled back to their ancestral tribes in the desert. Caravan traders became nomads. The great watering holes, placed strategically through the desert, were covered by sand and disappeared. Inevitably, Arabia sank back into its feudal past.

THROUGHOUT THESE UPHEAVALS, Jewish faith and practice remained remarkably resilient. The destruction of the Second Temple in 70 C.E. was a traumatic experience, but it did not jeopardize the survival of Jewish culture, for the simple reason that this culture was no longer confined to Judaea. The booming economies of the Persian, Alexandrian and Roman empires had prompted enterprising Jews to settle in the far corners of the realm. By the end of the first century C.E., there were flourishing Jewish communities throughout Asia Minor, Greece and the Italian peninsula, as well as in Egypt, Carthage and Spain.

The growing use of the synagogue as a center of prayer and scriptural study had prepared these communities for the day when the Temple in Jerusalem would no longer stand at the center of Jewish worship. Judaism had truly become an international phenomenon. Unshackled from its political dream of restoring the Kingdom of David, the Jewish faith now prospered on the strength of its laws, its prayer and, after 70 C.E., a growing focus on rabbinic study.

The Roman emperors realized that the industrious Jews held little threat to the State. On the contrary; their high moral standards and focus on family were a stabilizing force. Despite the lingering memories of the bitter Jewish War, discrimination against Jewish communities faded, particularly when Roman legions stationed abroad brought back a number of other Asian cults, including the cult of Mithras, Isis, Cybele, and Christianity. Simeon ben Gamaliel (135-175) was even able to secure Roman approval for the formation of a new Sanhedrin in 140 C.E. At the head of the Sanhedrin was the patriarch, a position that eventually became a hereditary office for those with a Davidic pedigree. Its authority approached that of the high priest during the Second Temple Period. Thus began the heyday of the Jewish patriarchate in Judea; over the next 200 years, its Jewish communities prospered, protected by special exemptions that acknowledged and respected the Mosaic Laws.

A synagogue in Tiberas, 2nd century C.E. Tiberias became an important center of Rabbinic Judaism, and seat of the Jewish Patriarchate

A cornerstone of rabbinic study was the *Mishnah*, a collection of civil and religious commentary that sought to adapt the Mosaic laws to the political and economic realities of the time. Most scholars accept that the Mishnah incorporates the corpus of "Oral Law" begun by the Pharisees. Compiled by Simeon ben Gamaliel (135 - 175) and Judah ha-Nasi (175 - 220), the Mishnah would inspire generations of *amoraim* or "interpreters" to devote their lives to biblical study. These subsequent rabbinical discussions (redacted in Aramaic as the *Gemara*) were recorded and, together with the Mishnah, included in a series of books known as the Talmud.

Talmudic scripture became an indispensable guide to Jews in the diaspora. It offered every Jew a uniform code of conduct that enabled him to remain faithful to Jewish cultic practice.

THE PEACEFUL CO-EXISTENCE BETWEEN international Judaism and the Roman Empire was shattered by Constantine's Edict of Milan in 313, and even more so by Theodosius' decree that Christianity was henceforth the *only* state religion. Suddenly, Palestine gained tremendous significance as the Holy Land, the very place where Christ had walked and preached.

This sudden "come-back" of the Jesus movement, in the form of a state religion sponsored by Rome, took the Jewish communities by surprise. Once again, they found themselves on the defensive against a religion that ostensibly traced its roots to Judaism itself. The Jewish Patriarchate in Tiberias watched with apprehension as their holy city, renamed *Aelia Capitolina* by Hadrian, reverted to "Jerusalem" – albeit in a thoroughly Christian mold. The newly arriving Christian prelates wasted no time to exploit their advantage. Motivated by the perceived anti-Jewish bias of the Gospels of Matthew and John, Roman sentiment swung against the recognition of Judaism's "special status". Privileges were suspended. In some parts of the empire, Christian communities adopted laws restricting the social and commercial freedom of Jews. The Visigoths, who despite their ferocity in combat were pious Christians, entertained such a loathing for Jews that they forbade the practice of the religion in all the territories they controlled, including Spain. The power of the Jewish patriarchate in Tiberias was thoroughly curtailed, while at the same time the office of the Christian bishop in Jerusalem was elevated to the status of Patriarch, placing Jerusalem on a par with Rome and Alexandria.

Subsequent Roman emperors singled out Jewish communities, including the Samaritans, for a 'penalty tax' that plunged many households into poverty. So odious was this tax that in 352, Jews and Samaritans rose in revolt. They were defeated, imprisoned and sold into slavery. Sepphoris, which had served as the first place of refuge for Pharasaic rabbis after the destruction of the Temple, was burned to the ground. So was the seat of the Jewish Patriarchate in Tiberias.

These discriminatory policies forced many Jewish families to emigrate from the Roman-Byzantine Empire. One destination of choice was Babylonia, where there had always been a thriving Jewish community since the days of the Captivity. The Sasanid rulers of Persia were not interested in proselytizing. Jewish communities were levied with a special tax, but it was much less onerous than the Roman penalty tax.

A similar tenacity was shown by Jewish communities throughout the Mediterranean. The Jews of Alexandra continued to be a sizable constituency, irrespective of the attitude of Greek Christians in the city. Other Jews had traveled along the coast of the Red Sea and settled in Ethiopia (or 'Abyssinia') and Yemen in search of new business opportunities.

In 532, a rash of disturbances known as the Nika riots led to the destruction of a Christian church in Constantinople. This church had been dedicated to God as the source of Holy Wisdom, or *Haghia Sophia*. The new emperor, Justinian, charged two of his finest architects, Anthenius of Tralles and Isidorus of Miletus, to build a new *Haghia Sophia* church that would surpass anything built in Christendom to date. To accomplish this feat, the architects had over 10,000 workers at their disposal; cost was of no consequence.

His architects immediately set to work, and under their hands rose a church that defies description. Its very plan is ambiguous: although conceived as a basilica, the emphasis rests on the central nave, shaped as an elliptical hall and anchored by four semicircular chapels.

Interior view of the Haghia Sophia, originally built by emperor Justinian in the 6th century B.C.E.

It is crowned by a dome, a stupendous creation that emphasizes the illusion of a centralized church. Some 180 feet high and 100 feet wide, this vast sphere seems to float effortlessly -- an impression that is reinforced by the string of windows at the very base of the dome. That this church is still standing, more or less, despite 1,500 years of neglect and plunder is amazing enough. Even more breathtaking was the interior in

Justinian's time, when its walls were covered with sparkling mosaics that reflected the sun streaming in through its myriad of windows. Most of these mosaics were destroyed in the 8th century by iconoclasts, after which new ones were made. These, in turn, were painted over by the Ottoman Turks, who converted the church to a mosque. These later mosaics were only discovered in the 1930's, when the Turkish leader Atatürk made the controversial decision to turn the Haghia Sophia into a national museum.

Today, as the visitor roams through this edifice and marvels at its cascade of niches and apses at every turn, he may be reminded of the famous phrase attributed to Justinian upon entering the church for the first time: *O Solomon, I have surpassed you!*

THROUGHOUT THIS PERIOD, PERSIA continued to outflank the Byzantine empire at every turn. The Sasanid kings knew that under Justinian, the economy of Asia Minor was experiencing a renaissance. Once again, caravans were dispatched to the East in search of silk and spices. Demand rose and markets throbbed, with the inevitable result that tensions between Byzantium and Persia escalated as well.

The recent revival of the international trace boosted the presence of Jewish communities all along the Red Sea down into Yemen. In 525, the king of the Himyarites in Yemen, Yusuf As'ar Yath'ar, took the extraordinary step of converting to Judaism. His decision created the first sovereign Jewish state since the fall of the Hasmoneans.

Naturally, Byzantium was not pleased by the conversion of the Himyar dynasty. It was well known that the Jews, piqued by Byzantium's discriminatory policies, were increasingly adopting a pro-Persian stance. A growing Jewish influence on the Red Sea and in southern Arabia was therefore a direct challenge to Byzantine attempts to regain control of the silk route.

Alabaster head of a man with laurel wreath, possibly the Himyar king Yusuf As'ar Yath'ar who converted to Judaism. Southern Arabia, 6 century C.E.

Constantinople responded with a military alliance with Christian Ethiopia, a major competitor of Yemen. Ethiopia had a major seaport, but Yemen's harbors were favored by the monsoon winds. The success of Yemeni trade had led to tributary routes and posts along the main Arabian caravan routes. One of these trading posts, known heretofore only to a handful of Arab tribes, was *Makkah* or Mecca. The Ethiopian ruler Abraha, encouraged by Byzantium, launched an invasion of Yemen, promising to kill all the Jews.

The result was a bitter and bloody war as Jew and Christian hacked at one another with abandon. Eventually, the war reached into the *Hijaz,* a region north of Yemen that comprised both Makkah and a city called Yathrib (later called Madinah or Medina). The bloodshed made a deep impression on the local tribes; their horror at the wanton murder, committed in the name of one God, still lingered in the critical decades to come. Meanwhile, Byzantium and Persia entered a state of all-out war.

The last years of Justinian's reign opened with a series of ominous signs. In 557, Constantinople was struck by an enormous earthquake. One year later, the great dome of the Haghia Sophia collapsed and had to be re-engineered from scratch. In 559, an army of Kutrigur Huns attacked the empire from the north and advanced up to the walls of Constantinople itself. In that same year, the merchants of Constantinople, pushed to the verge of bankruptcy by Justinian's reckless spending, tried to assassinate him.

In 565, the old emperor died at last, leaving an empty state coffer to his successor. Within months, his empire was once again under siege. And five years later, in Mecca, a young boy named Muhammad was born.

Chapter Fifteen
A Prophet in Mecca

Travelers in the Hijaz in today's Saudi Arabia.

As we have seen, the Roman province of *Arabia Petraea* formed only the tip of the Arabian peninsula, encompassing the old kingdom of Nabataea as well as Roman Syria, including the area around Philadelphia (today's Amman) and the city of Gerasa, once known to Jesus. It was made up of today's Sinai, Israel, Jordan and the northernmost corner of Saudi Arabia, with a slice of Syria and Lebanon thrown in. This was the edge of civilization as the Romans knew it; beyond this border the Arabian peninsula fell away to the southern region, controlled by a number of small fiefdoms and tribes.

The area of the *Hijaz*, in which the cities of Medina (then called Yathrib) and Makkah or Mecca were located, was far from the mainstream of Greco-Roman civilization. Until the Yemeni-Ethiopian War, this region was largely ignored by both Persia and Rome. In the Hijaz, the principal social, economic and political unit had always been the *tribe*. Ethnically, the Arabian tribes descended from two legendary ancestors, *'Adnan* in the north and *Qahtan* in the south. Though the descendants of Qahtan considered themselves the purer strain (also known as *al-'Arab al-'Aribah* or 'the true Arabs'), both 'Adnan and Qahtan traced their lineage back to Ishmael, son of Abraham.

Many of these tribes were either settlers (*al-hadar*) around oases or caravan posts, or Bedouin nomads (*al-badiyah*) who moved throughout the region with their sheep, camels and goats. These Bedouin were known to terrorize the settled tribes with sudden raids. The result was a deep antagonism between nomadic and settled tribes – an animosity that persisted well into the Islamic era.

Among the settled Arabs themselves, however, there was rarely peace. The tribes were highly class-conscious; pedigrees were jealously guarded and enforced. This prompted endless conflict over land, water rights or simply a lack of proper respect. Throughout this checkerboard of interlocking tribal fiefdoms ran the principal caravan routes. As we have seen, Petra was the main terminus of the caravan traffic, even though Bostra (today's Busrá ash-Sham, Syria) was at one point the nominal capital of Roman Arabia. To expedite transit times (and speed up military movements to potential trouble spots), the Romans built several roads connecting the principal cities in the northwest, including one that led all the way down to the Gulf of Aqaba.

Mecca is located in a valley that would have given travelers a welcome pause after the long and arduous journey through the Sirat mountains. The city is encircled by several impressive ridges: the 1,200 feet *Jebel Ajyad* and *Jebel Abu Qubays* in the east; the 1,400 foot peaks of the *Jebel Qu'ayqan* in the west; and the *Jebel an Nur* or *Jebel Hira* with an altitude of some 2,000 feet in the north. Arriving just after the rainy season in winter, caravan traders would be greeted with green foliage – *arta* shrubs, saltbushes, dry grass and even the occasional stalk of tarthuth, a Bedouin delicacy. What's more, Mecca had a year-round well called *Zamzam*.

Some scholars have argued that Mecca was too far from the main trade route to be of any major significance. A caravan moving from the Persian Gulf to Petra would have to make a significant detour to sample Mecca's delights, such as they were.

The modern city of Mecca (or Makkah) as seen from the Jebel an Nur

Perhaps, then, we should see Mecca more as a tributary of the trade routes leading from Yemen proper – certainly given the suggestion by some that Mecca was founded by Yemeni merchants to begin with.

Despite being hemmed in by three monotheistic faiths – Diaspora Judaism, Byzantine Christianity and Persian Zoroastrianism – the Arab tribes clung tenaciously to their pagan beliefs. This faith featured a panoply of local divinities, each tasked with a specific role – as had been the case in Canaan and Mesopotamia.

Despite their pagan gods, Arabs remained proud of their descendence from Ishmael and Abraham. According to the

Book of Jubilees, written in the late 2nd century B.C.E., the identification of Abraham's progeny with Arabia was still readily acknowledged. "And Ishmael and his sons," the book states, "settled between Paran to the borders of Babylon, in all the land that is toward the East, facing the desert. And these mingled with each other, and they were called Arabs and Ishmaelites" (Jubilees 20:11-13).

Even in Roman times, this 'legend' was well known. In his *Antiquities,* Josephus, citing from Genesis, provides a detailed Arab genealogy:

"(Ishmael) married a wife, by birth an Egyptian,
from whence the mother was herself derived originally.
Of this wife were born to Ismael twelve sons;
Nabaioth, Kedar, Abdeel, Mabsam, Idumas, Masmaos,
Masaos, Chodad, Theman, Jetur, Naphesus, Cadmas.
These inhabited all the country from Euphrates
to the Red Sea, and called it Nabatene.
They are an Arabian nation, and name their tribes
from these, both because of their own virtue, and
because of the dignity of Abraham their father."
(Antiquities, I:12)

What this literary trail suggests is that some five hundred years *before* the coming of Islam, there were a number of Arab tribes living in the Arabian peninsula who proudly considered themselves to be the descendants of the biblical Ishmael and his father Abraham.

But here is the vital question: does this mean that these ancient tribes continued to practice monotheism alongside their Jewish brethren in Palestine? Is it conceivable that some of these Arab communities remained faithful to the Abrahamaic faith as late as the late Roman and Byzantine period?

Scholars cannot answer the question with certainty, but it is possible that any such Abrahamaic worship of *El* (*Allah* in Arabic) was eventually overwhelmed by the influx of pagan idols, the inevitable by-product of the growing international trade in southern Arabia.

Islamic historians would agree. According to various *Hadith* traditions, Abraham's concubine, Hagar and her son Ishmael, settled in Mecca. Abraham came to visit them three times. During one visit, Abraham and Ishmael built a shrine to Allah, called the Ka'bah. In another *Hadith* associated with Ali Abi Talib (Muhammad's son-in-law and future caliph), the Ka'bah is actually an ancient shrine built in the time of Adam, prior to the Great Flood. Today, the Ka'bah it is the holiest shrine of Islam, located in Mecca.

The Kah'bah in Mecca today (Courtesy, Muhammad Mahdi Karim)

The Qur'an has several references to the Ka'bah as "a House a pilgrimage for men and a (place of) security." Here, believers will be able to "choose a place of prayer on the spot where Abraham once stood" (Q 2:125).

From a strictly archaeological point of view, the origins of the Kah'bah are difficult to ascertain. It is a cube-like structure, some 50 ft high and 40 ft wide, that appears to be aligned with the cardinal points of the compass. The shrine only has one windowless room. Today, this room is only entered once a year, for cleaning purposes. On the northwestern wall of the Ka'bah is a semicircular enclosure which, according to Muslim tradition, contains the graves of Hagar and Ishmael.

To Muslims, the almost primordial simplicity of the Ka'bah is evidence of its divinely inspired origin. "The builder knew that no beauty of architectural rhythm and no perfection of line, however great, could ever do justice to the idea of God," writes the Muslim author Muhammad Asad; "and so he confined himself to the simplest three-dimensional form imaginable—a cube of stone."

Was the Ka'bah originally associated with a monotheistic faith like Abraham's? Islamic sources confirm that Arab worship featured a supreme god. The name of this god was *Allah* (derived from *al-ilah*, 'the god'). He was, like the Egyptian Amun-Ra or Zeus in ancient Greece, the king of the gods, the Creator and Ruler of the heavens.

This is an important fact often overlooked by non-Muslims. *Allah* was a familiar figure to pre-Islamic Arabs, as the Qur'an itself makes patently clear. "If you ask [the pagans], 'Who created the heavens and the earth?' they would most certainly say: The Mighty, the Knowing One has created them" (Q 43:9). Hence, the concept of Allah as not only a Supreme Being but also the Creator of heaven and earth, conform the Judeo-Christian precedent, was established well before Muhammad received his first revelations. What Muhammad had to do, however, was to convince his audience that Allah was the *only* God, and that all other deities and idols were false. This explains the uncompromising attitude of the Qur'an vis-à-vis polytheism, why we so often hear nonbelievers described as *idolaters*.

Indeed, the Arabs of his time venerated many indigenous deities, like *Allat, Manat* and *al-'Uzza*, the daughters of Allah.

Allat was originally a Syrian moon goddess. *Al-'Uzza* was associated with the planet Venus and may have hailed from an ancient shrine in the Sinai. *Manat* is believed to be the goddess of fortune.

Above and beyond these pagan gods, the world of the Arab nomads was inhabited by countless evil spirits or *djinns*, which might shelter in wild animals, in certain trees or even a rock or a well. "Whereas the Jews and Christians culled their prophecies from Scripture," says one author of the early Islamic period, "the Arab soothsayers received their foreknowledge of most events from the djinns, spirits of the air who supposedly stole information by listening close to heaven."

Alabaster head of a female deity from southern Arabia, ca. 1st century C.E.

And so, at the beginning of the year 570, various religions co-existed across the peninsula. Arab tribes of the interior worshiped their local pagan gods. Arab communities on the frontiers of the Persia and Byzantium were mostly Christian. Yemen was Jewish. In addition, there were Jewish traders in posts along all the main trade routes of the Hijaz.

At that time, the idea of an Arab polity, a uniquely Arab state was as yet dormant. What little central authority existed in the fiefdoms of yesteryear had crumbled. For authority, security and justice, one looked towards one's family first; the clan, second; and the tribe, third. Beyond the perimeter of the tribe, there was nothing -- no law, no order, no moral code.

There was one exception: the Arab language. Arabs, whether settlers or nomads, loved their language and their poets, the way Greek civilization had worshipped poets like Homer. Each year, the tribes sent their most favored poets to quasi-national festivals in Mecca or Ukaz, where the clans could, for once, compete in bloodless fashion. Tradition claims that the most beautiful poems were written in gold on silk banners and hung over the black shrine of the Ka'bah -- hence their Arab name *Muallaqat*, which some believe means 'suspended'. Modern scholarship doubts this interpretation, but agrees that these fine poems certainly occupy an exalted place in Arab literature.

It is this fascination with elegantly composed, flowery Arabic that would set the stage for the text of the Qur'an – an instance of poetry that is to Arabs what the text of the King James Bible is to English-speaking Christians. In fact, Muslims believe that the very beauty of the Qur'an is vivid proof that its text was dictated, word for word, by God himself.

The tribes of Mecca also competed in the annual festivals. By far the most dominant tribe of Mecca was the Quraysh. Under their leadership, the city was slowly enjoying a revival in trade and the pilgrimage traffic to the shrine of the Ka'bah, when a boy named Muhammad was born.

WITH THE STORY OF MUHAMMAD, we face the same dilemma that we confronted with the life of Jesus: the biographical details are shrouded by the veil of legend. Most of what we know about

Muhammad was written down long after his death. What's more, there are very few archaeological remains that can tell us about the Hijaz of the 6th century. Thus, we are once again relegated to a literary archaeology of texts written in the centuries after Muhammad. The first and foremost of these texts is the Qur'an, the Holy Scripture of Islam which, Muslims believe, was revealed to Muhammad in stages by God.

The second most important collection of texts, and second only to the Qur'an in terms of theological authority, is Muslim commentary or *Tafsir* writings, distinguished in several classes of literature. The oral commentary of the highest authority is, of course, the body of statements that were reportedly made by the Prophet Muhammad himself, known as the *Hadith*. The problem is that these statements have come down to us via many different oral traditions. Since some of the Hadith appear to be contradictory, the oral provenance or "authenticity" of a Hadith is almost as important as the reported saying by the Prophet himself. It is the chain of narrators (*isnad* in Arabic) that ultimately traces the statement back to Muhammad, which establishes the authority of a Hadith.

Typically, this chain will include Companions and Followers. Companions (*Sahabah*) are contemporaries of Muhammad who not only followed his teachings, but were also in the Prophet's earshot at any given time during the years of his ministry. Some estimates have put the number of these potential eyewitnesses at 10,000, which underscores the importance of an authoritative provenance or *isnad*.

The Followers (*Tabi'un*) were the generation of believers that came *after* the Companions, and preserved the sayings of the prophet as communicated to them for later generations. A typical Hadith will therefore establish its *bona fides* by identifying both the Follower(s) and the original Companion to whom the reported saying by the Prophet is credited.

A secondary level of *Tafsir* commentary is exegesis that is traced back to the Companions or Followers themselves. While obviously such pronouncements do not have the authority of the Hadith (the words and deeds of the Prophet himself), lesser *Tafsir* commentary is nevertheless of great value for Muslim scholarship and for understanding the meaning of the Qur'an in general.

The third most important source, for our purposes, is a group of biographies written by Islamic historians, beginning with Muhammad Ibn Ishaq. Ibn Ishaq was born in Medina in the year after the *Hijra* AH 85, meaning around 707 CE. As in the case of the earliest biographical material of Jesus, Ibn Ishaq's original manuscript is no longer in existence, but his biography survives in a redacted version – with many interpolations – by the 9th century scholar Ibn Hisharn.

Lastly, there is a large body of Islamic commentary, not unlike the Jewish Talmud. Over the centuries Muslim scholars developed a unique form of exegesis known as *asbab al-nuzul* (occasions of the revelation), which aims to interpret the Quranic verses in their historical context. The goal of this scholarship is to assess the immediate historical circumstances of each revelation, so as to better understand the meaning and import of the verses. At the most basic level, suras are designated as belonging to either the Meccan or the Medinan period. A famous example is sura 4, which was reportedly received after the Battle of Uhud, when Muhammad suffered heavy losses among its ranks. This left many women among his followers widowed or orphaned, without any practical means of support. The verses of this sura revealed that Muslim men would be allowed to marry up to four wives.

Of course, with these texts we are somewhat limited by the fact that critical Muslim scholarship is still in its infancy. The Qur'an has rarely been subjected to the type of rigorous source or form criticism that has been used for "excavating" the underlying strata of the Hebrew Scriptures and the Gospels. The idea of a critical analysis of the Qur'an is difficult to accept for observant Muslims, since the idea that the Qur'an is the literal word of God is a firm article of faith. This is, of course, no different from the belief among conservative Jews and Christians that the Bible is the inviolable word of YAHWEH. The review of Islamic texts is, however, slowly changing as more scholars are drawn to the Qur'an as an instance of scripture, on a par with the Torah and the New Testament.

OUR STORY OF MUHAMMAD, then, begins as follows. According to Islamic tradition, a leading Quraysh chieftain named Qusayy had four sons. When he died, the oldest son named 'Abd ad-Dar took over as leader of the tribe; but his popularity was overshadowed by that of another son named 'Abd Mandaf. Slowly, a rift developed between the two. When 'Abd Mandaf's own son, Hashim, reached adulthood, matters came to a head. The tribe split into two. The larger group of people followed Hashim and would later be known as the 'Hashemites'.

Hashim married and had three sons, one of whom was 'Abd al-Muttalib; he, in turn, fathered a son named 'Abdullah. In 568 or 569, 'Abdullah decided to marry a beautiful young woman named Amina, whose family also traced its lineage back to the legendary Qusayy. Fatefully, 'Abdullah died shortly after the wedding during a visit to the town of Yathrib, and was buried there. The widow Amina then delivered a baby boy, and called him Muhammad.

Since the boy was without a father, he and his mother were taken in by their eldest relative, his grandfather 'Abd al-Muttalib. When Muhammad was six, his mother Amina took him to Yathrib to visit his father's grave. While there, Amina died suddenly as well, leaving Muhammad an orphan. He continued to live in the care of his grandfather, until he, too, passed away a short time thereafter.

It is not difficult to imagine how traumatic this string of tragedies would have been for a young boy like Muhammad. Later accounts would describe him as a quiet, introspective man. What's more, the theme of the 'orphan' would return time and again throughout Muhammad's later revelations. For him, the orphan became a quintessential symbol of the great social gap that existed in the merchant town of Mecca.

The young orphan Muhammad was now transferred to the household of an uncle named Abu Talib and put to work, tending the sheep in the sparse grazing areas around Makkah.

Arab trader with camels. Detail of a funerary moment from southern Arabia, dated to the 3rd century C.E.

From this point on, the story of Muhammad enters a period of darkness. As in the case of Jesus, Muhammad's years as a teenager and adolescent are lost to history. Pious legend later added stories to fill in the blanks. Some of these suggest that his uncle took him on a caravan journey to Bostra, the old capital of Roman Arabia.

In later years, we find Muhammad prospering as a successful merchant on the trade routes to Petra, Bostra and other caravan markets in Syria and the Near East. Some biographers have him travel as far as the Daba Market in Oman and the Hubashah Market in Yemen. Many of these cities were Christian, at a time when the strife between Byzantine orthodoxy and 'dissident' sects such as the Arianites, Monophysites and Nestorites was still raging. Many of these dissidents had settled in Arabia to practice their faith in the peace of the desert, undisturbed by the long reach of the Byzantine emperor.

It is quite possible that an inquisitive mind like Muhammad's would have been intrigued by this strange conflict between people who all claimed to be the followers of Christ. Christianity was not unknown to him, for there were Christians in both Mecca and Yathrib. By the same token, Muhammad would often have dealt with Jews, both as trading partners and as providers of letters of credit for long-haul cargo, in which Jewish merchant bankers excelled.

Orthodox Muslim scholarship is uncomfortable with this idea of Muhammad 'learning' about monotheism from Jews and Christians, lest it affects the integrity and inviolability of God's word in the Qur'an. But it certainly seems plausible when we remember that the many revelations featuring Jewish and Christian prophets in the Qur'an would have made no sense to Muhammad unless he had been exposed to these faiths, including their narratives and their practices.

I would even go as far as to suggest that Muhammad may have imagined how different Arabia would be, if its people could rally around one national religion, as the Jews, Christians and even the Persians had done. It would not only provide the Arabs with a social and ethical foundation, but also unify the country in a new body politic. Indeed, says Montgomery Watt in *Muhammad in Mecca*, "given the religious situation of Arabia, and particularly of Mecca as it was at the end of the sixth century, there must have been many serious-minded men who were aware of a vacuum and eager to find something to satisfy their deepest needs."

At age twenty-five, Muhammad caught the eye of a successful businesswoman named Khadija, of the clan of Asad. Khadija was a beautiful widow, reportedly forty years old, who was looking for a manager to attend to her various business interests. She offered the job to Muhammad, who accepted. In time, the two fell in love, and she proposed to him. They were duly married.

A camel market in Jeddah. Camels remain an important mode of transportation in Saudi Arabia, as it was in the days of the Prophet Muhammad

For the next twenty-six years, Khadija was Muhammad's sole and constant companion. By all accounts, it was a good and affectionate marriage; indeed, Muhammad remained monogamous until after her death. Khadija already had several children from her first marriage; she now bore Muhammad six or seven children, including at least two sons. Some scholars have argued that she therefore must have been considerably younger at the time of her marriage to Muhammad than tradition wants us to believe.

Sadly, all but one of the children died; only Muhammad's daughter Fatimah survived. Later, she would marry Muhammad's cousin 'Ali, whom the Shi'ah branch of Islam considers the true heir of Muhammad.

As Muhammad grew older and more prosperous, we are told, he grew restless and increasingly uncomfortable with the primitive idolatry and rituals of his tribe. He remembered that his grandfather had a habit of retiring to a lonely cave for reflection. He retraced his grandfather's steps to the spot on Mount Hira, which was located in the hills of *Jebel-an-Nur*. Here he would sit and meditate, fast and pray, often for days at end. And then, one day in the year 610 C.E., Muhammad had his first revelation. He heard the voice of God, which as his biographer describes it, was communicated through the persona of Gabriel, the same angel who had delivered the Annunciation to Mary:

> He came while I was asleep, with a cloth of brocade
> whereon there was writing, and he said, 'Read.'
> I replied, 'I cannot read it.' Then he pressed the cloth
> on me till I thought I was dying; he released his hold
> and said, 'Read.' I replied, 'I cannot read it'.....
> Then he said, 'Recite in the name of the Lord your
> creator; who created man from a drop of blood.
> Recite, your Lord is the most bountiful, who
> taught by means of the pen, taught man what
> he knew not.'

The same account can be found in the Qur'an, in the chapter entitled *Al-'Alaq* or 'The Clot:'

Qur'an
Recite in the name of your Lord Who created. He created

man from a clot. Recite, for your Lord is Most Honorable, who taught (to write) with the pen; taught man that which he knew not. (Q 96.1-5)

A later revelation was even more specific: "Go and declare the goodness of your Lord; recite what has come to you from God, and declare His bounty and grace in your mission."

This, in essence, is the principal message of the Qur'an. The word *Qur'an*, derived from the verb *qara'a*, means "that which is recited and rehearsed". The meaning is twofold. Since reportedly Muhammad could not write, the angel Gabriel made him repeat and memorize each revelation, so that it could be shared with his followers and ultimately written down by a scribe. But the Qur'an is also meant to be *declaimed*, to be recited out loud. Among Muhammad's followers or Companions, there were many who were able to recite the entire book by heart. Even today, there are several scholars and imams who can recite the text from start to finish.

We are told that these revelations took place over a span of twenty-two years. At first, the text was hastily jotted down on anything that was available, such as leather hides or palm leaves. Some of these transcripts were then copied by people in Muhammad's community, including his wife A'isha. In later years, it is said that the intervention by the angel Gabriel was no longer necessary; Muhammad's role as a *rasul* or 'messenger' had matured to a point where God's word was received by way of divine inspiration. As the revelations continued, Muhammad began to understand that together the texts could become a book of scripture. This combined record would ultimate produce the Qur'an.

Unlike the Hebrew Scriptures, therefore, or indeed the Gospels, the Qur'an is not a narrative in the biblical mold. It is not concerned with chronology, because its Scripture is not a cohesive epic, told from start to finish. It is quite literally a collection of divine sermons, often spoken by God in the first person, and each devoted to a particular topic.

This Qur'an from the 9th century, now in the Alexandrian Library, is one of the oldest extant manuscripts

Each of these chapters or *suras* contain either prophecies, admonitions or instructions, often using the examples of biblical prophets or Jesus to illustrate a particular point.

The Qur'an contains 114 revelations, though some scholars have argued that a few chapters, particularly the longer ones received near the end of Muhammad's life (some of which are as long as the Gospel of Mark), may in fact combine more than one revelation. By contrast, the earliest revelations, received while Muhammad was still in Mecca, are short, sometimes not more than 50 words long. These suras appear to deliberately use poetic devices such as rhythm and rhyme to facilitate memorization.

After Muhammad and his followers moved from Mecca to Yathrib (later known as Medina), the revelations became longer. They lost their imprint of lyrical poetry and instead assumed a more legalistic tone. Islamic scholars suggest that this made sense, for in Mecca Muhammad and his followers had formed an isolated community largely shunned by the rest of the town. In Medina, on the other hand, Muhammad became a statesman, preoccupied with managing the practical needs and aspirations of a large city.

The Qur'an is, however, organized by the *length* of the suras, starting with the most extensive revelations. That is why the most recent chapters are at the very beginning of the Qur'an, whereas the oldest revelations dating back to the days in Mecca are found near the end.

The principal focus of the Qur'an is to instruct the believer on the just path as desired by God, and to stress that God is the *only* God of the universe. This is the cardinal meaning of Islam, for the word *Islâm* itself means 'obedience to the will of God.' The word *Muslim* is derived from the same root and means "he who has submitted himself to God."

The Qur'an holds that it is divinely revealed scripture, but not the only one. In fact, the Qur'an argues that God has made his will known throughout the history of mankind, beginning with Adam. Just as Christians see the "New Testament" as the outcome of the Hebrew Scriptures (the "Old" Testament), so too does the Qur'an see itself as the logical conclusion of what God as revealed to Jews and Christians in the past. Muhammad is thus seen as the last in a long line of prophets. This is why the Qur'an accepts the Hebrew Scriptures and the New Testament as authentic revelations by God, and calls Jews and Christians the "People of the Book":

Qur'an
Indeed We have given to Abraham's children
the Book and the wisdom, and We have given
them a grand kingdom. (Q. 4: 54)

However, the Qur'an also argues that Jews and Christians often misinterpreted these revelations and allowed their faiths to be led astray. For example, the Qur'an treats Jesus as a leading *rasul* or prophet – with Moses, the most important individual after Muhammad – and accepts that Jesus' birth was divinely ordained. But the Qur'an cannot accept the notion that Jesus is divine. Sura 5, 'The Dinner Table,' tells us:

Qur'an
The Messiah, son of Mary is but an apostle;
apostles before him have indeed passed away;
and his mother was a truthful woman.
(Q. 5:75)

For Muslims, the idea that Jesus was the Son of God is anathema to the concept of monotheism. "The Christian texts, Muslims will argue, are quite authentic," says Peter Awn; "but it is the Christian interpretation of these texts that, for Muslims, has so distorted who Jesus is. So, he is a great messenger, a prophet, a man of great holiness, but, they would say, don't turn him into a Hellenistic divinity." But the Qur'an is more than a scripture of monotheism. Like the Hebrew Bible, it is a passionate appeal to its people, in this case the Arab tribes of the 7th century, to embrace their manifest destiny. And like Davidic Judaism, Islam would become a clarion call for political emancipation, for a great *ummah* of believers that would reach far beyond the borders of Islam and ultimately become an empire all of its own.

THE PROSPECT OF CREATING SUCH an empire, however, was still far in the future when Muhammad first shared his revelations with his people. Though his wife was supportive, Muhammad's clan was dismayed by his claim that he had suddenly become a *rasul Allah*, a messenger of an all-mighty God. Muhammad found only a handful of people in his immediate family who accepted his revelations, including his friend Abu Bakr.

The tribal elders were astonished as well. They interrogated him, wondering what had suddenly come over him. Did Muhammad not understand the confusion he was sowing among his tribe? Did he, a businessman, not grasp the impact that his new so-called faith would have on the pilgrimage traffic to the Ka'bah – so critical to the economic health of the city?

Muhammad persisted. He gathered a group of people who were prepared to accept him as a *nabi*, a bona fide prophet; one of them was a young man named al-Arqam who opened his house for worship. What form this worship should take, Muhammad told his followers, had been shown to him in successive stages by the angle Gabriel. It involved deep prostrations to the floor, symbolizing man's complete submission to God. Muhammad also introduced a ritual ablution for his followers so that they could purify themselves prior to prayer. Then the angel led him through the prayer cycle that would become the *salâh*: prayers at dawn, at noon (when the sun passed its zenith); in the afternoon when a man's body was as long as his shadow; at sunset when the sun had all but disappeared; and before retiring at night.

Meanwhile, the tribal nobles began to organize a formal opposition against Muhammad. They accused him of sorcery, of soothsaying, of pursuing a naked ambition for wealth and power. His followers were jeered, denounced and sometimes physically abused; their efforts to engage in trade were actively sabotaged. Tragically, the opposition to Muhammad was led by the clan of Abu Lahab -- Muhammad's own uncle.

Finally, the situation became so dire that Muhammad was forced to evacuate some eighty families to Christian Ethiopia, in the hope that they might be allowed to form an early Muslim community there. And in fact, they were. When the outraged Quraysh sent a deputation to the Ethiopian king Ashabah, demanding their forcible repatriation, the king patently refused. As a result, the first independent Muslim community was created not on Arabian, but Ethiopian soil.

Muhammad himself did not flee Mecca, for he enjoyed a measure of protection under the wing of his uncle and adoptive father, Abu Talib. The high social standing and wealth of Khadijah offered a sense of security as well. But this changed in the year 619, when both Khadiija and Abu Talib died in short order. Increasingly desperate, Muhammad cast about for a place where he and his followers could live and worship in peace. He chose a new wife named A'isha, who was the daughter of his close friend Abu Bakr. In some way, Abu Bakr was to Muhammad what Peter had been to Jesus: a solid, dependable right-hand-man. Later, he would serve as the first of the four 'Rightly Guided Caliphs'.

Arguably, this is the moment when the indigenous monotheistic movement of Arabia may have withered on the vine. But then fate intervened. Elsewhere in the Hijaz was a city in desperate social and political straits. That city was none other than Yathrib, the place where both Muhammad's father and mother had died and were buried. For several years now, the various settlements around Yathrib's oasis had lived in a state of war - another example of the inter-tribal rivalry that would vex Islam for many years to come. The chieftains put their heads together and resolved that they needed one man – an outsider without ties to any of the Yathrib clans – who could restore law and order, and return prosperity to the city. They resolved to ask Muhammad to mediate between the tribes in the hope of saving their city.

Yathrib had a large Jewish community. It is possible that the idea of a monotheistic preacher, who by all accounts was a forthright and honest man, would have appealed to a community in which Jews exerted a strong influence. And so it was that in 622, Muhammad and his community of followers found sanctuary in the city that had figured so prominently in the earlier tragedies of his life. It was a watershed event for the future of Islam; indeed, the Islamic lunar calendar marks this journey from Mecca to Yathrib, known as the *Hijrah*, as its point of origin. The year 622 of our Common Era therefore equals Year 1 AH (or *Anno Hegirae*) in the Muslim calendar.

MUHAMMAD WAS DULY INSTALLED as Yathrib's mediator. It was an exceptional opportunity. As head of this fragmented community, in a way a microcosm of Arabia itself, Muhammad could demonstrate his ability to dissolve internecine rivalry and mold the fiercely independent natives into a unified community, an *ummah* of believers.

He succeeded. Using a cadre of designated lieutenants known as *Ansar* (literally, 'helpers'), Muhammad not only negotiated a truce of sorts between the warring tribes, but also converted large segments of its population to the new faith of Islam.

Immediately before his journey to Yathrib, Islamic history tells us that Muhammad had an almost surreal experience that would seal his stature as the last in the line of God's prophets. He was, we are told, taken on an otherworldly visit by the angel Gabriel. First, he was whisked away to Jerusalem, to the very place on Temple Mount (or the Abrahamaic Mount Moriah) where Herod's Second Temple once stood.

Here, Muhammad was introduced to Abraham, Moses and Jesus, whom he engaged in animated conversation. According to Arabic tradition, refreshments were brought: a vessel filled with wine, and another filled with milk. Muhammad availed himself of a cup of milk and drank it, but did not touch the wine. This met with approval from the angel Gabriel, who said that 'wine is prohibited' to the followers of the 'true religion'. From that day forward, observant Muslims have abstained from wine or any other form of alcohol.

The Qubbet es-Sakhra or "Dome of the Rock" on the Haram al-Sharif in Jerusalem, which the Jews call Temple Mount, is the reputed place from where Muhammad briefly ascended into heaven

Next, a ladder appeared from heaven, the very ladder "which the dead may mount on the day of Last Judgment." Using Temple Mount as a platform, Muhammad ascended into heaven, passing through seven layers until he met Ishmael himself. Today, pious Muslim guides in Jerusalem will point to an impression resembling a sandaled foot in a stone in the Dome of the Rock, as the place where Muhammad set off on his celestial journey.

The account of Muhammad's *al miraj* or brief heavenly ascension is important for many reasons. It indicates that Muhammad was still keen to be recognized by both Judaism and Christianity as a sister religion of equal validity and authority. In fact, Muhammad hoped to convert the Jews and Christians of the Hijaz to "his" version of monotheism; at the very least, he coveted their respect and support. "Jews are one community with the Believers," he is reported to have said; "but they have their own religion as the Believers have theirs." Indeed, at this stage the *qibla* or orientation of the Muslim prostration during prayer was still in the direction of Jerusalem, the acknowledged place of origin for all three faiths. Muhammad also observed the *Ashura* fast on the tenth day of the Jewish month of Tishri, traditionally associated with the day on which Moses fastened in thanksgiving for receiving the *Torah* (the Law) on Mount Sinai.

Some Jews were intrigued with Muhammad's new interpretation of YAHWEH, but the majority of Yathrib Jews rebuffed him. These Jews had their revelation and their chief *rasul*, and his name was Moses. The laws that he had brought back from Mount Sinai would stand for all time.

This rejection came as a blow to Muhammad. He had always harbored a deep respect for Judaism as mankind's earliest revelation of God, and he greatly desired their friendship. Instead, the Jewish community of Yathrib turned their backs on Muhammad and forbade him to preach in their midst.

This was a turning point in the early gestation of Islam. Already, the new religion had adopted many features of Judaism: the daily cycle or prayer; the dietary laws demanding abstention of pork and other 'unclean' foodstuffs; and possibly, the proscription against 'graven images' and idolatry. But following the break with Yathrib's Jews, Muhammad young faith became more thoroughly 'Arabicized,' more consciously an indigenous religion. As part of his new policy, Muhammad decreed that the Ka'bah, despoiled by pagan idols though it may be, was Islam's holiest shrine. Consequently, the orientation of prayer was now directed towards Mecca. It also compelled Muhammad to find a way to go back to Mecca, take the city by force if need be, and restore the Ka'bah to the worship of the one and true God.

First, he raised a militia that could prey on caravans destined for Mecca – a prelude to the intense battles that were to follow. At the same time, Muhammad reached past Christianity and Judaism to an older, more pristine and "authentic" source. This is when early Islam begins to develop a highly proprietary attitude towards Abraham as the "original" and "pure" prophet of monotheism, in which Muhammad is cast as a direct descendant from the patriarch. At least one Hadith reports that Muhammad once called Abraham "his father," the first true Arab prophet. In another, Muhammad is quoted as saying that he prayed for his grandsons al-Husayn and al-Hasan as Abraham once prayed to God for his sons Ishmael and Isaac.

The idea that Islam is modeled on the more pristine faith of Abraham, an *Urglauben* predating both Judaism and Christianity, is argued with some vehemence by sura 3. "People of the Book!" the Qur'an asks sternly, "Why do you dispute concerning Abraham? The Torah and the Gospel were not sent down until after him." It is easy to question Islam's appropriation of Abraham' role, but we should remember that the Gospels, too, freely use passages in the Hebrew Scriptures to advance their theological vision.

THE YEARS IN YATHRIB – now known as *Medinat-un-Nabawi*, the 'City of the Prophet' or simply Medina – turned Muhammad from a preacher and prophet into a statesman. He drafted laws, dispensed justice, negotiated treaties and trade pacts, and settled legal disputes. As we have seen, the revelations of this period turn to decidedly secular and sometimes prosaic matters, including the issue of how a Muslim woman should dress. This, of course, is a highly controversial matter in our modern society, both in the United States and in Europe. However, the institution of the *hijab* or *burka* did not originate in the Qur'an, but in later Islamic writings. The Qur'an merely states that the women should be modest in manner and dress, including a veil across their bosom:

Qur'an
And say to the believing women that they cast down
their looks and guard their modesty, and do not
display their ornaments except what is (naturally) visible;

and let them wear their head-scarfs over their bosoms, and not display their ornaments except to their husbands or their fathers... (Q. 24.31)

Muslim women in Nigeria. The Qur'an decrees that women "guard their modesty .. and .. wear their head-scarfs over their bosoms"

This is the moment when a group of infiltrators from Mecca, aided and abetted by a local Jewish clan known as the Qurayzah, decided to undermine Muhammad in the city of Medina. Enraged, Muhammad denounced the Jewish community. He ordered their immediate eviction from the city. Later on, when the war between Medina and Mecca escalated, Muhammad's soldiers vented their ire on the remaining Jewish community. It is a stain on the early history of Islam that the male heads of these Jewish families were put to the sword, while their women and children were sold into slavery. Some historians have tried to explain this vengeful act by suggesting that many of these Jews formed a type of 'fifth column' that sought to subvert Muhammad's movement.

Mecca and medina then began an escalating war of attrition. Eventually, the conflict led to major battles as each side began to build an army in defense of its interests.

The first great battle of Badr in 624 was an astonishing success. Muhammad crushed the army of Mecca, even though it was far more powerful than the troops he himself was able to field. Alas, one year later the warriors of Mecca returned and dealt Muhammad's troops a stinging defeat near Mount Uhud. Many of Medina's soldiers were killed. By this time, Muhammad had remarried several times; one of his wives was a fifty-year old widow named Sawda. But the sudden loss of so many married men may have compelled him to take some of the widows as his wives as well.

Polygamy was, of course, a fact of life in ancient Arabia; for the community of Muslims in Medina, denuded of husbands and fathers, it may have been an issue of survival. Muhammad's generous attitude towards marriage may also have had strictly political reasons. As we have seen, A'isha was the daughter of his close friend (and wealthy merchant) Abu Bakr. Another wife was the daughter of 'Umar ibn al-Khattab, who ultimately would become the second caliph after Muhammad, and Umm Salâmah, who as a member of the Quraysh provided him with a back channel to sympathizers in Mecca. In all, there were ten or eleven wives after the death of his beloved Khadija; many of these were sent out by Muhammad to do charity work in the community, rather than spend the day in idleness at his home.

"The wives would lead other women in the *ummah,* who were quite an active group of social workers," says Ed Hotaling in his book *Islam without Illusions*, "fortified by the fact that they shared equal rights with men in many spheres."

Muhammad's ascendancy made a deep impression on members of Mecca's Quraysh tribe. His sudden rise in stature made many Hashimites – as well as other clans – rather proud. Defections began to occur as families switched sides, confident in the expectation that Muhammad would ultimately prevail.

When the armies of both cities met again at the Battle of the Trench, the outcome was decided in Muhammad's favor. The princes of Mecca were exhausted by years of warfare and the loss of their trade. An armistice was agreed upon, which led to the Treaty of al-Hudaybiyyah of 628. The terms of this accord provided for an armistice lasting ten years, during which Muhammad's followers would be permitted to make a pilgrimage journey, a *hajj*, to the Ka'bah in Makkah. This pilgrimage took place in 629, but the truce was short lived.

A centuries-old hostel in Jeddah, Saudi Arabia, the principal entry point for pilgrims joining the annual hajj

In 630, Muhammad marched down to Mecca with a vast new army. This time, he entered the city unopposed. Mecca was his; at long last, Islam had taken possession of its holy city. Muhammad immediately ordered all pagan idols to be thrown out of the Ka'bah precinct, and solemnly re-dedicated the shrine to Allah as the *sole* God of all creation. But many of the rites of worship remained. The traditional circumambulation around the Ka'bah, for example, which had been a time-honored pilgrim practice in pagan times, was maintained and absorbed in the *hajj*, the annual pilgrimage to Mecca.

As undisputed head of Mecca – and indeed the Hijaz – Muhammad began to consolidate his position as the leader of a new national faith for all Arabs. "Muhammad became both prophet and statesman," says Francis Peters, "since politics and religion have always been part of two sides of the same Islamic coin, from the beginning down to the present day." In this capacity, Muhammad sent emissaries to all major Arabian cities, inviting them to come to Mecca and pledge their allegiance to Islam. Such was his renown that many did submit themselves to the new faith and Muhammad's leadership. Buoyed by his growing support on the peninsula, Muhammad made overtures to both Persia and Byzantium. His was a bold suggestion: since Islam was the most recent manifestation of the one God that both emperors believed in, was it not time to unify the world in one global faith? A faith, moreover, that had absorbed all of the foregoing scripture, yet was the purest form of divine revelation yet?

Both emperor Heraclius of Constantinople and King Khosrow of Persia politely declined the offer. Then again, the timing of the offer was poor, for Persia and Byzantium were once again embroiled in war – and this time, the battleground was the Holy Land itself.

Chapter Sixteen
A Unified Arabia

In 610, the year of Muhammad's first revelation on Mount Hira, the Persian armies invaded Byzantine Anatolia. The thriving Christian city of Antioch was invested in 611. So were Armenia, Syria and the Caucasus kingdom of Lazica. In 614, the Persian general Shahrbaraz entered Palestine, looting and burning his way towards Jerusalem.

Over the past 300 years of Christian control, the Holy City had changed considerably. Roman temples and shrines had been destroyed; their columns, capitals and other useful *spolia* were recycled for use in the construction of Christian churches. The center of the city had shifted from Temple Mount, where the Second Temple had once stood, to the Church of the Holy Sepulcher, the presumed site of Golgotha.

The upper level of the Church of the Holy Sepulcher in Jerusalem, restored after the Persian sack of the city in 614

The city's walls had been rebuilt as well – a vast undertaking that had been initiated by Valentinian and ultimately completed by the Empress Eudoxia, the widow of Theodosius II, in 450 C.E. Streets that were once filled with Jewish worshippers during festivals were now crammed with monks, prelates and pilgrims from all parts of the Byzantine Empire.

When the Persian armies suddenly appeared at Jerusalem's gates, panic erupted among the Christians. The Jewish population, however, was ecstatic; according to the 'Chronicon Paschale', Khosrow's armies received the enthusiastic support of tens of thousands of Palestinian Jews. This is very likely an inflated number, but it may indicate the level of desperation among Jews living under the Byzantine yoke in Jerusalem.

Faced with the sheer might of Persia, Patriarch Zacharias of Jerusalem decided to surrender the city in order to save the city's churches, since the Persians had burned all Christian shrines they encountered on their way to Jerusalem. But Zacharias was overruled by militant Christians who, like the Jewish Zealots before them, were convinced that God would intervene to save his city. The Persian general Shahrbaraz then proceeded to systematically destroy every single Christian structure on the hills surrounding the city, including the Mount of Olives. After only three weeks, the city fell.

According to a monk named Antiochus Strategos, the Persians "slaughtered tender infants on the ground, and then with loud yelps called their parents... They destroyed persons of every age, massacred them like animals, cut them into pieces, mowed sundry of them down like cabbages, so that all alike had severally to drain the cup full of bitterness."

Once again, the streets of Jerusalem were running with blood. More than 65,000 Christians were killed. Those that survived were rounded up and, in a replay of the Babylonian captivity, dispatched into exile. Most churches were burned to the ground. The "True Cross" identified by Queen Helena was carried back to Persia in triumph.

In gratitude for their efforts on his behalf, Shahrbaraz handed control of Jerusalem back to the Jewish patriarchate. The Jewish community rejoiced; for the second time in their history, a Persian king had delivered them from a foreign oppressor. Jewish rabbis immediately began talking about the possibility of rebuilding the Temple. Worship on Temple Mount resumed. But it was not to be. In 616, the Persians rescinded their promise for Jewish autonomy. Palestine was incorporated in the local Persian satrapy.

The Byzantine Empire was facing enemies on all fronts, but it did not have the financial resources to raise armies and repel them. What the empire did have, however, was land. Emperor Heraclius thus came up with the idea to raise new legions by promising them parcels of land in the districts (or *themes*) in which they were based. This process took twelve years, but by 622 Heraclius had enough legions to resume the war with Persia.

Heraclius, an accomplished military strategist, steadily plowed through Asia Minor and succeeded in restoring the region to Byzantine sovereignty. He then plunged into Mesopotamia proper and dealt the Persian King Khosrow a stinging defeat at the Battle of Niniveh in 627, the same year that Muhammad won a decisive victory over Mecca at the Battle of the Trench. Khosrow was then toppled by his own son, who rushed to make peace with the Byzantine emperor.

It was an astonishing comeback. Not since Trajan had Roman forces moved so far East, or had its archenemy Persia been so thoroughly defeated. The triumph was complete when in 630, Heraclius solemnly returned the True Cross to Jerusalem. Christian control of the Holy Land was restored – or so it seemed. But less than four years after Heraclius' triumphant entry through the gates of Jerusalem, the Byzantine army would once again be at war.

MUHAMMAD, MEANWHILE, HAD STEADILY enlarged his following, to the point that much of eastern Arabia was now under Islam. Even the Persian governor of Yemen, the viceroy

Badhan, was a convert. Under Muhammad's rule, the cities of Medina and Mecca became preeminent Islamic centers.

Muhammad instituted the *adhan* or 'call to prayer', perhaps inspired by the Christian habit of summoning the faithful with church bells, or the Jewish custom of blowing the *shofar*, the horn of a ram. This led to the position of the *muezzin* (a title derived from the Arabic *mu'adhdhin*, which means 'he who delivers the *adhan*').

A recently excavated Byzantine dwelling in Jerusalem, 6th century C.E. Note the simple but elegant mosaic on the floor

We do not know what the first mosque looked like (the word 'mosque' is derived from the word *masjid*, the place in which one prostrates for prayer). One reference in the Hadith, reported by Anas bin Malik, suggests that Muhammad used to pray where the moment found him, often in a stable or courtyard "in the fold of goats and sheep". However, the Prophet was also wont to lead his community in prayer, and recognized that a permanent place of communal worship was needed. He settled on a piece of land that included a pagan cemetery, sheltered by trees.

Consequently, the first mosque was actually an open courtyard, about 800 square yards in size, surrounded by a perimeter of clay walls. Around the wall ran a colonnade of sorts, covered by a roof of palm stems and leaves, which offered some shade when the sun was high. On the eastern side of this courtyard, a simple dwelling was built to house the Prophet and his family.

The 9th century Mosque of Ibn Tulun in Cairo, Egypt, one of the oldest mosques still in use, follows the original Meccan precedent closely, with a sabil (ablution fountain) in its center

The rather humble features of this first mosque underscore the fact that Muhammad did not consider a mosque the dwelling place of God, as in the Christian tradition. Like a Jewish synagogue, it was merely a location for communal prayer, as well as other, civic functions. Muslims could conduct their prayers where they liked, provided the place was clean and they were facing the direction of Mecca; it was however considered more dignified, more 'worthy' to pray together in a common enclosure.

As the group of converts grew, the courtyard was eventually expanded to some 6,000 square feet. In time, this mosque area also became a center of Muhammad's administration, with offices for political meetings, the dispensing of justice, the shelter of pilgrims and the storage of arms. One hundred years later, in the early 8th century, the mosque of Medina had grown into a vast complex, including a hospice and charitable facilities like dining halls for dispensing meals.

The Umayyad Caliph al-Walid decided to add a tower or *manara* to each of the four corners of this complex. These 80 ft towers were not, as yet, intended for use by the *muezzin*, since mosques of this period accommodated the criers in a small pulpit-like structure on the roof, accessible from a staircase within the mosque. In fact, one Islamic tradition suggests that the *muezzin* were restrained from using high places because of fears that they might be able to peer into people's homes, thus violating their privacy. 'Ali ibn Abi Talib, the cousin of the Prophet and eventually the fourth Caliph, ruled that the call to prayer should not be issued from any place higher than the roof of the mosque. Archaeologists therefore conclude that the first minarets were simply an ornamental feature – a device to give a mosque the stature of a landmark, reminiscent of the bell towers of Christian churches.

Only in the 9th century, under the rule of the Abbasid caliphate, did the mosque reach the paradigm that we recognize today – a large courtyard surrounded by multi-purpose dwellings with a single tower, now used exclusively for the *adhan*. The tower would invariably be placed opposite the wall containing the *mihrab* – the prayer niche indicating the direction of prayer towards Mecca. This paradigm of courtyard, hall, and minaret would become the dominating *motif* of

Arabian mosques that, in various forms, were built throughout Africa, the Middle East and even China.

AS THE SPRING OF 632 DAWNED, Muhammad could look back on his work with satisfaction. Driven by God's revelations, he had forged a religion that was innately Arab yet followed in the footsteps of two of the world's most succesful religions: Christianity and Judaism. Whether through divine inspiration or through his own discerning mind (or perhaps a little of both), Islam had sought to include the "best" features of both monotheistic religions while eschewing its flaws.

The minaret of the Ibn Tulun Mosque has a helical outer staircase, a rare feature inspired by the minaret of Samarra, Iraq

As we have seen, the Prophet had adopted many of the Jewish laws, including its laws of physical and moral purity, the separation of men and women during prayer, the ban against depictions of living nature, the daily cycle of prayer, and its dietary laws, restricting Muslims to the consumption of *halal* foods and banning others, such as pork and blood. Christianity may have inspired Muhammad to care for the poor by virtue of an alms tax, and to propagate social justice in every layer of Arab society. Lastly, Muhammad had also retained some local features, including the pilgrimage to Mecca and the circumambulation around the Ka'bah.

But in other aspects, Muhammad had been careful to avoid what the Qur'an often terms the misguided ways of the 'People of the Book'. Unlike Jesus, Muhammad had the good fortune of a long life, enabling him to personally lead and nurture his movement into maturity, and to anchor the key tenets of his doctrine by virtue of scripture. For Muhammad, there would be no endless theological debates about the relationship between God and Man that continued to vex the Christian Church of his time.

In addition, Muhammad did not create a hierarchy of patriarchs, bishops, priests and prelates. In early Islam, there was no priestly hierarchy. In its stead came the legions of *imams*, roughly comparable to rabbinic scholars in Diaspora Judaism, who as theological experts would serve to enrich Islam with interpretations of the Qur'an, and dispense advice to the faithful.

Like Moses, Muhammad had been privileged to carry the tablets of law to his own people; but unlike Moses, he was able to see these laws implemented in a political state – first in Yathrib, then in Mecca, and finally in much of Arabia proper. Moses had died before setting foot in the Promised Land, but Muhammad lived to see his vision come true.

Like Davidic Judaism, and quite unlike Pauline Christianity, early Islam was as much a secular as a religious movement. It pursued the idea of an Arab nation, a theocratic political entity that would supersede tribal boundaries through the unifying authority of the Qur'an. Muhammad suspected, however, that a newly unified Arabia was bound to attract the attention of the Persian and the Byzantine empires. As a defensive maneuver, he ordered troops to be stationed along the northern border. There they stood in readiness, in the event that emperor Heraclius, flushed by his recent victory over the Persians, might want to strike. But in the end, it was the Muslim army that struck first.

The Mosque of the Prophet in Medina, Saudi Arabia, is the resting place of the Prophet Muhammad and the second holiest site in Islam

Muhammad had bequeathed his people a religion and a Promised Land. In 631, he made one last pilgrimage from Medina to the Ka'bah in Mecca, tracing the route of the *hajj* that millions of Muslims would follow to this day. But he was already stricken with fever. He died on June 8, 632 at age sixty-three, with A'isha by his side. He was buried in a simple grave in his home, which today is covered by the green dome of the Prophet's Mosque in Medina.

Muhammad died believing that his Islamic movement was secure, and that he had done everything to avoid political or theological schisms. But in this, he was mistaken. For Muhammad had neglected one thing. He had not designated a line of succession.

Chapter Eighteen
The Rise of the Islamic Empire

The 12th century Hassan Tower, part of an unfinished mosque in Rabat, Morocco, was intended to be the tallest minaret in the world

What followed in the years after the death of Muhammad was unprecedented in the history of Antiquity, indeed in all of human memory since the days of the first civilization of Mesopotamia. In an astonishingly short period of time, Islam would capture and amass a territory larger than any empire that had ever existed – larger than the Roman Empire, larger than the realm of Alexander the Great. At the apex of the Umayyad conquest, the Islamic Empire stretched from Toulouse in France to the borders of Persia and India; from the southern tip of Yemen to Tarsus, the birth city of Paul. Despite this stunning success (or perhaps because of it), the unity of this empire soon disintegrated along the fault lines of tribal fealty, pressured by the age-old rivalry among Arabs, rather than the friction between conqueror and conquered.

At its core lay the fact that Muhammad had never stipulated a clear, unambiguous line of succession. This is surprising, given that the Prophet had so carefully attended to other matters critical to Islam's future. Perhaps, like so many other great leaders before and after him, Muhammad never expected to die so soon, simply because there was still so much to be done.

And so it was that upon the death of Muhammad, a dispute arose over who would succeed him as spiritual leader and head of the Islamic Arab nation. There were two principal factions. On the one hand were the original 'charter members' of the movement, the Meccans who had emigrated to Medina during the Hijrah of 622. They were opposed by the Medina faction – the *ansar* or 'helpers' – who had been recruited in Medina itself.

Many felt, with some justification, that Abu Bakr should be the one to succeed Muhammad. After all, he had been Muhammad's trusted second-in-command ever since the earliest days of the revelations. He had been appointed by Muhammad to lead the faithful in prayer at the mosque enclosure in Medina. What's more, he was the father of A'isha, Muhammad's most beloved wife after Khadija. One tradition has it that upon Muhammad's death, A'isha ran to her father so that Abu Bakr could announce the terrible news to the *ummah*.

But another tradition insists that during Muhammad's last *hajj* from Medina to Mecca, he had pulled his cousin 'Ali to his side. As we will recall, 'Ali had married Muhammad's daughter Fatimah. Muhammad gazed upon his son-in-law and spoke the mysterious words "To all for whom I am a patron, 'Ali is their patron also."

What did this mean? Many thought that it meant that 'Ali should succeed Muhammad. After all, tribal leadership usually passed from father to son, as we have seen throughout the history of the three faiths. Since all of Muhammad's own sons had died in infancy, 'Ali was arguably the closest Muhammad ever came to having a male heir.

Eventually, 'Ali *did* succeed his father-in-law – but not before Abu Bakr had served as Islam's leader or *khalifa*. *Khalifa* or 'caliph' was an honorific meaning 'representative'. The official title of Muhammad's successors was 'Commander of the Faithful', but the term *khalifa* stuck. Indeed, the first four leaders after the Prophet would be known as the 'Four Rightly Guided Caliphs.'

Abu Bakr's election was fortunate, for he had fought in nearly all of Islam's early battles and was thus a man of considerable military experience. And a commander is what the movement needed, for with the death of the charismatic Muhammad, many tribal leaders felt they were absolved from their pledge of loyalty – as well as from paying taxes (*zakat*) to maintain the new religion in Mecca. Perhaps we can see a parallel in the early Israelite monarchy, when the death of King David prompted the tribal chieftains of the North to re-think their allegiance to Jerusalem. As we have seen, family, clan and tribe superseded everything else in Arabia; without Muhammad, there seemed to be little point in continuing the myth of political unity. Worse, the death of Muhammad prompted the appearance of a number of false 'prophets' who each claimed to have had revelations from God as well.

Abu Bakr thus saw himself thrust in the role of forcibly maintaining the fragile integrity of the Islamic *ummah* that Muhammad had fought so hard to create. For much of his two years as first caliph, he was wholly absorbed in suppressing tribal revolts throughout the Hijaz and southern Arabia. But then he pushed eastwards, into territory that had never belonged to Muhammad, ultimately unifying all of the Arabian peninsula under the banner of Islam.

Abu Bakr died in 634. Before his death, he had designated 'Umar bin al-Khattab as his successor, once again passing over 'Ali. This was a fateful choice, for it was 'Umar who decided to move beyond the natural borders of the peninsula and take the

Islamic conquest into the Byzantine and Persian realm. Already, a border war of sorts had been raging for quite some time on both sides of the frontier. In 634 'Umar plunged into Syria and Palestine, and dealt a stunning blow to the aging emperor Heraclius – who, as we have seen, thought the Holy Land secure from Persian aggression. If Heraclius had once again ridden at the head of his armies, as during the triumphant march of half a decade ago, things might have been different. As it was, the emperor stayed in Constantinople, delegating the conduct of war to his generals. The two great armies, Byzantine and Muslim, met in the battle of Yarmuk in 636. The Islamic forces proved victorious, partly because several Byzantine units (including the tribe of Ghassan and other groups sympathetic to the Arab cause) defected to 'Umar.

The battlefield in Yarmuk, where Muslim forces dealt a stinging defeat to the Byzantine armies

Now, 'Umar's armies poured into Palestine. They were enthusiastically received by Jews, who hoped that a Muslim victory over their Byzantine overlord would bring an end to discrimination and crippling taxes. Dissident Christian sects like the Arianites and Monophysites, who had also suffered from persecution, welcomed the arrival of the Muslims as well.

In 637, Heraclius' agents were able to retrieve the True Cross in the nick of time, before the Muslim armies laid siege to Jerusalem. For seven months, the Byzantine defenders held out under the leadership of Patriarch Sophronius. Then, in February of 638, the city was compelled to desist.

Sophronius beseeched 'Umar to spare everyone in the city. This was a remarkable request – none of Jerusalem's previous conquerors, including the Assyrians, Babylonians, Seleucids, Romans and Persians, had ever let her stubborn defenders get away without punishment. But 'Umar agreed.

'Umar was an unusual man. Later reports would often stress his simple lifestyle in imitation of Muhammad. He wore a threadbare tunic, and preferred to eat a simple diet of barley bread and dates in the company of his soldiers – quite unlike the ostentatious lifestyle of the future Umayyad caliphate. When Sophronius rode out to meet him, 'Umar refused to dress for the occasion. He simply got off his white camel and walked through the gates. Thus, Jerusalem became a Muslim city.

LEGEND TELLS US THAT SOPHRONIUS then took 'Umar on a tour of the city. The caliph was keen to visit the Temple Mount, since it was the reputed location of Muhammad's brief ascension into Heaven. As we have seen, the Jews had hoped to rebuild the Temple here during the brief period of Persian occupation. In revenge, the Christians had turned the site into a garbage dump following the reconquest by Heraclius. 'Umar was stunned when he saw the pitiful state of this holy ground. According to a Muslim historian, he unfurled his cloak and filled it with debris. Those with him did likewise. They then disposed of it and returned, again and again, until the whole area was cleared.

Thus cleansed, the thirty-five acres of the Temple Mount would become the Muslim *al-Haram al-Sharif*, the Noble Sanctuary of Muhammad's heavenly visit, as well as the traditional location of Abraham's sacrifice. 'Umar immediately ordered the construction of a vast mosque, built of wood, which reportedly could hold three thousand worshippers. He also promised the Christian population of Jerusalem ".. safety for their persons, their goods, churches, crosses ... No constraint shall be imposed upon them in matters of religion and no one among them shall be harmed."

The tolerant attitude towards the Christians and Jews in the new Islamic empire was not accidental. The Muslim administrators treated the 'People of the Book' with a circumspection befitting their status as believers in God's revelation, albeit a revelation that was not as perfect and complete as Islam's. Patriarch Eutychius of Alexandria (a Christian Arab also known as Sa'id ibn Batriq), further adds to the legend by telling us the story of 'Umar's visit to the Church of the Holy Sepulcher.

During the lengthy visit, the hour struck for 'Umar and his followers to pray. Patriarch Sophronius suggested that 'Umar pray in the Church. The Caliph politely thanked him, but went outside on the stairway to pray. Sophronius asked him why. With remarkable forbearance, Omar replied, 'If I had prayed inside the church, it would have been lost to you and would have slipped from your power; for after my death the Muslims would take it away from you, together saying, 'Omar prayed here'.

'UMAR THEN RESUMED HIS military campaign, capturing additional Persian and Byzantine territory. He dealt the Sasanid army of the Persians a crushing blow at the battle of Qadisiyya. In 637, the capital of Ctesiphon fell to the Arab invaders. Today, the magnificent brick arch of the Sasanid palace of Ctesiphon, located near Baghdad, still bears the marks of its destruction by

'Umar's forces. Meanwhile, Islamic generals plunged into Egypt and conquered Alexandria in 642.

The great brick arch of the Sasanid Palace of Ctesiphon still bears the damage of the Muslim conquest (Courtesy, James Dale)

In 649, Cyprus was taken. As the Arabs swept across the island, a devout and wealthy Christian family hastily buried their treasure, which consisted of eleven splendid dishes with scenes from the Old Testament. This hoard was discovered in 1902 near Karavas, a small city close to the Cyprus port of Lapithos. Known as the Karavas Treasure, it is now divided over museums in Cyprus, London and New York. The silver works are masterpieces of 7th century Byzantine art. One set depicts the story of David and Goliath, including a scene in which David is outfitted in Hellenistic armor, and a plate in which the young warrior defeats the Philistine giant. The figures are convincingly raised from the silver and betray a strong influence of Greek and Roman models. Quite possibly, the Cypriot artisan was inspired by Greek and Roman reliefs on sarcophagi that could be found in abundance throughout the island.

David and Goliath, from the 7th century Karavas Treasure, found in Cyprus

A SCANT TWENTY YEARS after the death of Muhammad, his Islamic state ranged from North Africa to Iran. This begs the question: why did these caliphs embark on a policy of territorial conquest, and why was their campaign such a dramatic success? The notion that Abu Bakr and 'Umar were out to convert the world to Islam has now been convincingly disproved by modern scholars. It was never the goal of the caliphs to forcibly convert their subject peoples. Like Persian Zoroastrianism, early Islam was unthinkable without the Arab culture, tradition, and above all the Arab language. The Islamic conquerors did not compel the Christians, Zoroastrians and Jews in their new domain to convert to Islam, but neither did they forbid it.

The real reason for the dramatic expansion of Islamic power is, quite simply, a search for living space. The population of the Arabian Peninsula had grown to a point where it could no longer be sustained by the desert. The irrigation systems, developed during the economic boom of the 4th century, had fallen in disrepair, and crop yields had steadily dropped. Territorial conquest was simply a matter of survival, for the limited water sources and agriculture that did exist on the dry central plateau were insufficient to support the indigenous population.

As a newly integrated people under the banner of Islam, the Arab Bedouins – always warriors of fierce renown – became a military force without parallel. Trained in desert combat, mounted on camels that could travel for two weeks without replenishment, the Islamic armies were perfectly suited for warfare on the plains of North Africa or the interior of Iran.

Second, the timing of the Islamic conquest was fortuitous. The two superpowers of Persia and Byzantium had just ended a prolonged period of attrition that left both sides exhausted and weary of war. The Persian King Khosrow II had died in 628, just before the beginning of the conquest; he was succeeded by a string of weak and inept rulers who neither had the will nor the treasure to mount a successful defense against the Arab armies.

Byzantium fared no better. As we have seen, Heraclius had triumphed over Persia, but his was a Pyrrhic victory. The treasury was depleted and the army was once again dispersed along its European frontiers to try to stem barbarian tribes. Physically broken, nursing wounds from countless battles, the Byzantine emperor lacked the will to marshall his realm once again for total war.

Lastly, the Muslim victories were abetted and welcomed by all those who had suffered from Byzantine persecution, including Jews and Christian dissident sects. Many segments of the Persian population embraced the Muslim conquerors as well. The last Sasanid king of Persia, Yazdegerd III, fled to the northern city of Merv and was betrayed by his own governor,

Mahuyeh. Shortly thereafter, the king was mugged and killed for his wallet. Islam, in sum, surged through the Middle East just when the dominant powers in the region were most vulnerable – and the caliphs made good use of the opportunity.

Except in Persia, where the new Islamic conquerors initiated a persecution of Zoroastrian followers (though later revoked), the inhabitants of the new empire were left to live, work and worship as they saw fit. As we have seen, Muhammad had always respected Christians and Jews, but for 'Umar the decision to 'live and let live' was also a matter of necessity. The Arab armies were simply overwhelmed by their military successes. Stretched thin all over the Middle East, 'Umar and his successors had no choice but govern by proxy, leaving local governments largely in place.

Property that had been abandoned by those who had fled – the ruling élites, in most cases – was readily confiscated, but otherwise the Arabs respected the land divisions in place. All this would change in the centuries to come; but for now, the Arab occupation was tolerant and mild.

One burden that all subject people did have to bear was the occupation tax, the *jizya*, which supported the new Arab government and its armies. Christians, Jews and other non-Muslims were levied at a higher rate than those who converted to Islam.

"Nevertheless," says Francis Peters, "there was a perception among some Christians and Jewish communities that Islam was a more straightforward, a more *enlightened* form of monotheism. A faith, in short, that was unencumbered by the theological dilemmas of Christianity nor the vast body of Mosaic legislation in Judaism."

As TIME WORE ON, a new class developed across the empire – an *Überschicht* of Arab overlords and bureaucrats who lived in ostentatious luxury. This was bound to create friction between Arab and non-Arab Muslims. Worse, the division of the spoils –

including lucrative appointments to key positions in the empire – led to heated arguments between the Arab occupiers themselves. Old tribal rivalries resurfaced.

These cracks in Arab solidarity first appeared under the third caliph. 'Umar was killed in 644 by a Persian slave in his retinue. Six prominent leaders in Mecca then selected a new ruler, named 'Uthman ibn Affan. Unlike Abu Bakr and 'Umar, who like Muhammad were members of Mecca's Hashimite middle class, 'Uthman was a nobleman from the Umayyad clan. His selection infuriated the faction from Medina, who remained steadfast in their support of Muhammad's young cousin (and son-in-law) 'Ali.

Hisham's Palace in Jericho, one of the oldest surviving examples of Muslim Umayyad architecture, ca 730-740 CE

As an aristocrat, 'Uthman was far removed from the egalitarian attitude and lifestyle of his predecessors. Imperious and autocratic, 'Uthman continued 'Umar's conquests but showed an alarming predisposition towards filling key positions with members of his own clan. Indeed, 'Uthman's ascension was a boon for the Umayyads, who had been marginalized in preceding years and now saw an opportunity to re-assert their former position as Arab noblemen.

'Uthman is known today as the caliph who authorized a complete written 'canon' of the Qur'an. In reality, however, his predeccesors had already laid the foundation. Abu Bakr was the first to try to collect the various revelations. This was continued by 'Umar as well his daughter Hafsa, who happened to be one of Muhammad's widows. 'Umar's concern for the preservation of the Qur'an was partly motivated by the large number of casualties resulting from the Battle of Yamama in 633, which decimated the ranks of those who knew the Qur'an by heart. It is unclear, however, whether he was able to collate the by now numerous and sometimes conflicting traditions into a comprehensive corpus.

'Uthman thereupon charged a team of scribes to create the official canon of the Qur'an. This is believed to be the version we have today, though some scholars continue to question some passages in the Uthmanic version, based on extant fragments that suggest various discrepancies. Others have levied the accusation that 'Uthman was highly selective in culling the various oral traditions, and that many legitimate (though differing) texts were withheld from the scribes, and burned at his instigation. Another complicating factor is the fact that the Uthmanic text was recorded in a consonantal script without vowels, which leaves many open questions about the meaning of some of the words and phrases. Fully vocalized versions would not appear for many centuries later.

As such, the ultimate collation of the Qur'an was a process not unlike that which attended the composition of the New Testament, when church scholars carefully sifted through different Christian gospels and writings before deciding which should be accepted as divinely inspired Scripture. In Arabia, too, many different oral traditions had to be culled and investigated before the material could be accepted as God's spoken word.

This is when Islamic scholars decided to arrange the chapters by their individual *length*, starting with the longest revelations. Since, as we have seen, these more extensive chapters originated near the end of the twenty-two year period, the Qur'an is actually read backwards, in a chronological sense, with the most recent chapters at the beginning, and the oldest revelations from the days in Mecca near the end.

Even then, the Qur'an never quite lost its oral character, compared to the very literary quality of the Hebrew Scriptures. "Certainly We have made the Qur'an easy for remembrance," says sura 54; "is there anyone who would mind?" Or as Francis Peters puts it, "Among the Jews the effort was to preserve a properly written text, whereas the Muslims have been more concerned with a properly remembered text."

This 8th century Umayyad Palace in Amman, Jordan, is an exquisite example of Umayyad domed architecture

Meanwhile, 'Uthman continued to expand the Islamic Empire by completing the conquest of the former empire of

Persia, and by pushing the Arab armies into Libya. However, his arbitrary appointment policy (and growing resentment over uneven distribution of the spoils of conquest) spurred a resurgence of tribal enmity at home. In 656, riots broke out in Medina. In the mêlee, 'Uthman himself was assassinated, though there are conflicting accounts about which faction was responsible for this deed.

The majority in Mecca immediately clamored for a return of a caliph drawn from the middle class, like Abu Bakr and 'Umar, rather than the ranks of nobility. Later, they would become known as *al-sunnah wa-l-jamaa,* followers of the traditions (*sunnah*) of the Prophet. Arrayed against them was the continuing faction in Medina who were supportes of 'Ali or *shi'at Ali.* Here lay the seeds of the first great schism in Islam – that between Sunnis and Shi'ites.

In the end, the *shi'at Ali* prevailed and 'Ali was chosen as the fourth caliph since the death of Muhammad. But his appointment brought no peace. The Umayyad nobility, which saw itself sidelined by both groups, demanded that 'Ali bring the assassins of 'Uthman to justice. 'Ali was reluctant to do so; perhaps he felt that a trial of those who were responsible for the murder would inflame tribal passions beyond his control. 'Ali's refusal disappointed many, including Muhammad's widow A'isha. According to some accounts, it was she who then organized an armed revolt against 'Ali. For the first time since the death of Muhammad, Arab blood was once again shed by Arabs on Arabian soil.

The rebellion was suppressed, but 'Ali's position was substantially weakened. One of the Umayyad viceroys appointed by 'Uthman, the governor of Syria and Iraq named Mu'awiya, saw his opportunity. He rallied his troops and met the forces of 'Ali near Siffin in 657. While the battle itself was inconclusive, support for 'Ali's caliphate began to evaporate. Mu'awiya then consolidated his position by taking control of Egypt. For four more years, both leaders engaged in civil war, until 'Ali was assassinated in 661.

Thus ended the period of the 'Four Rightly Guided Caliphs' who had gained power through an election. From this point forward, the Islamic empire would be ruled by a dynasty of Umayyad aristocrats. These Umayyads moved the capital of the new empire from quarrelsome Mecca to the city of Damascus, where their power was unchallenged.

THE UMAYYAD DYNASTY INTRODUCED a great flowering of Arab culture throughout the Islamic Empire. Muhammad had always maintained that the religion of Islam was a worldly religion. To pursue science, to investigate the beauty of the natural world, was to admire and appreciate the magnificent creation of God himself. This was the main impetus for a "second Islamic conquest", namely the acquisition and preservation of countless scholarly works of Antiquity that otherwise would have been lost to humankind. Islamic scholars pursued every field of science, from medicine to astronomy, from agriculture to algebra. For example, Islamic astronomy produced, in great quantity, an instrument known as the *astrolabe*, which enabled the user to fix the position of the time as well as the position of the sun and stars. The astrolabe was not only of scholarly interest. For the devout Muslim who might find himself in unfamiliar surroundings, it was the only way to establish the proper time of prayer, as well as the direction of Mecca.

At the same time, Islam developed an artistic style that found expression throughout its empire. Since Islam forbade the reproduction of living creatures, its art was rather constrained in its iconography. In fact, the Qur'an had never made such an injunction; but the Hadith include a verse as follows: "Allah, Most High said: 'And who is more unjust than those who try to create the likeness of My creation?'" Imams interpreted this statement to mean that any human attempt to imitate God's unparalleled creation was "weak" and meaningless. Since only

God can create life, any artistic imitation of nature was deemed to be interfering with God's greater plan.

An astrolabe from Iran, dated the year 1215 AH and signed by the artisan 'Abd al-A'imma

This interpretation was endorsed by A'isha, who reportedly stated that "those who will be punished most severely on the Day of Resurrection will be they who try to make the like of Allah's creation." As we have seen, the Jewish laws had said much the same thing; even the Byzantine Empire experienced a period of iconoclasm in the 8th and 9th centuries.

As a consequence, Islamic artists were forbidden to represent 'living things' such as animals and human beings (although in several regions of the empire, notably Persia, this proscription was roundly ignored). In its stead, artists developed a decorative virtuoso style that sought inspiration from the calligraphy of the Qur'an, combined with non-figurative geometric patterns known as *arabesques*. This calligraphy served not only to espouse the word of the Qur'an, but also to perpetuate Arabic as the *lingua franca* of the Islamic empire, pervading every aspect of government, science and artistic endeavor. In fact, the Arabic language would prove to be a lasting legacy of the Islamic conquest, for while the empire would soon disintegrate into separate Muslim political systems, its language endures in most of these territories to this day.

Glazed tiles decorated with arabesques and quotes from the Qur'an adorn the exterior of the Dome of the Rock, Jerusalem

Arabesques were inspired by the intricate interlacing of floral motifs, including foilage and fruits. With their beguiling curvilinear patterns that in some instances predate abstract art of the 20th century, arabesques were eminently suited for the decoration of curved objects such as vessels, plates and lamps.

Indeed, it is in pottery that we see the first flowering of a distinct Islamic culture. A key center of early Islamic pottery was the Carthage region, with centers like Sejenane, Moknine, Kairouan and particularly Nabeul, in today's Tunisia. Here, artisans developed geometric designs inspired by floral patterns, and drawn in vivid cobalt blue, that would become a hallmark of decorative tiles throughout North Africa. Elsewhere, Islamic artisans adopted the Persian technique of color glazing to develop *lustreware*, pottery covered by a metallic and iridescent veneer that creates luscious rainbow-colored effects.

Cup with hunters and game, 12th century, from Iran

Textiles, copper and precious metals also proved to be a popular canvas for Islamic artisans. Damascus became a center of fire-hardened and beautifully decorated ornamental swords and helmets. This soon attracted Persian craftsmen, bringing with them the rich tradition of Sasanid ornamental swords with which Persian kings had enforced their authority. Persia itself, meanwhile, became known for delicately knotted carpets – a tradition that endures to this day.

But perhaps the greatest achievement of early Islamic art was the building that still stands in the center of Temple Mount in Jerusalem – the shrine referred to as the "Dome of the Rock" (and known as *Qubbet es-Sakhra* to Muslims).

It was the fifth Umayyad caliph, Abd el-Malik, who decreed shortly after his accession in 685 that the Temple Mount, associated with Abraham's sacrifice should be covered with a domed structure of unprecedented magnificence. His architects designed an ingenious structure that weaves three central elements into one unit: a ring of piers supporting a dome and embraced by an ambulatory in the form of an octagon, which in turn is surrounded by a larger exterior octagon. Each of these has a symbolic significance: the outer ring represents the world, the ambulatory is the intermediate sphere between earth and the divine, and the inner space evokes the spiritual perfection of heaven itself.

The sheer simplicity of the architectural plan produced a work of enduring beauty. In fact, scholars have determined that the proportions of the building all correspond to interlocking elements of the same square unit – a superb example of the mathematical genius that would become one of the hallmarks of Islamic science.

Underneath the dome is the bare rock known as *Es-Sakhra* or Holy Rock, which as we noted earlier, was the point from where Muhammad reportedly ascended into heaven. Below is a cave called *Bir el-Arwah* or 'Well of Souls', where Muslims believe the souls of the dead will gather in anticipation of the Last Judgment. Here are two altars where according to tradition, David, Solomon, Elijah and Muhammad prayed to God. Muhammad is also symbolically present in the ambulatory; a reliquary reportedly contains some hairs from Muhammad's beard.

The Qubbet es-Sakhra or Dome of the Rock on the Haram al-Sharif (or Temple Mount) in Jerusalem

Stepping outside, the visitor sees a large trapezoidal platform supporting the Dome, which is aligned with the presumed location of Herod's Second Temple. In 1958, the dome was covered with gilded aluminum plates. This magnificent work was only completed in 1964, three years before the Six Day War in which Israeli forces took control of the East Jerusalem.

Nearby on the *Haram al-Sharif* is the El-Aqsa mosque (or *Masjid el-Aqsa*), which unlike the Dome of the Rock is a functioning mosque, not a shrine.

The El-Aqsa Mosque in Jerusalem. Crusaders, arriving in 1099, believed it was the Temple of Solomon

As we have seen, 'Umar was reputed to have built the first mosque on this spot after the capture of Jerusalem in 638; some archaeologists believe that he may have used the foundations of an earlier Byzantine basilica, dedicated to Mary. The Umayyad caliph El-Walid I replaced this wooden building with a vast, seven-aisled building culminating in a silver dome. So magnificent was this structure that the Crusaders, arriving in 1099, believed it was the Temple of Solomon.

Chapter Eighteen
The Golden Age of the Three Faiths

The palace of Umayyad Caliph Hisham in Jericho. Hisham sent Islamic forces in a bid to conquer France, which ultimately failed.

Is the Dome of the Rock rose on the platform where the Second Temple had once stood, the Islamic armies continued their advance, now under the command of Umayyad caliphs. After meeting fierce resistance from the Berbers of Northern Africa, these tribes were persuaded to convert to Islam.

The Muslim viceroy of North Africa, Musa ibn Nusayr, then suggested to the Berber general Tariq ibn Zayad that he undertake a daring raid across the Strait of Gibraltar – and onto Spanish soil. Tariq accepted the challenge. As soon as his troops landed in southern Spain, he set fire to his ships so that there would be no turning back. But he may not have bothered, for the army of the Visigoth king of Spain was no match for his Berber warriors. This feat is immortalized in the name of Gibraltar itself, for it is derived from the Arabic *Jebal Tariq* or 'Mountain of Tariq'.

The former Roman capital of Córdoba was taken in 711, followed by Toledo. Buoyed by this unexpected success, Musa ibn Nusayr now sent an even larger force with the full backing of the caliphate in Damascus. Musa may have hoped to carry the Islamic banner throughout Spain and into the heartland of Europe. At first, this appeared to be a real possibility, since many Spanish inhabitants welcomed the change from the arbitrary rule by the Visigoths, the nominal allies of Constantinople. But then quarrels broke out between the Arab and Berber factions. This strife may have contributed to the ultimate check on Islamic expansion, for in 732 Charles Martel was able to defeat the Islamic army at the Battle of Poitiers. The Muslims tried again and got as far as Arles and Avignon, but Pepin the Short finally evicted them out of France in 759. The line from Saragossa to the river Ebro became the nominal boundary between the Islamic and Christian spheres in Europe.

By then, the Umayyads themselves were coming under siege. The favoritism shown by the Umayyad aristocracy had riled the lower ranks of the Arab tribes throughout the empire. The Umayyads built lavish palaces and surrounded themselves with a luxury and wealth that was a far cry from the apostolic simplicity of Muhammad and Abu Bakr. The tribes of Mecca were not the only ones who felt resentment. Non-Arab Muslims, or *mawalis*, continued to be discriminated against by native Arabs throughout the Islamic Empire. These Muslim "New Men" objected to the old tribal cabals, which they felt were wholly inconsistent with Islam's new role as a cosmopolitan power. And so it was that the resistance against the Umayyad empire did not originate from along the newly conquered, but from within the Muslim administration itself. Descendants of the original Hashimite clan of Muhammad clamored for a return to power. So did the Shi'as and other minorities who were repelled by the sybaritic lifestyle of the Umayyads. During the reign of the Umayyad caliph Marwan II (744-750 CE), a huge earthquake struck Palestine and destroyed many of the buildings under construction in Jerusalem. It was seen as an omen of great changes to come.

The resistance against the Umayyads coalesced around the figure of Abu al-'Abbas, who claimed to be a descendant of Muhammad's Hashimite uncle al-'Abbas ibn Abd al-Muttalib. Centered in Persia, this movement steadily gained momentum and ultimately produced civil war between the Arab factions. This culminated in the Battle of Zab, where tribal blood flowed copiously in the Syrian plains. The army of Marwan II was routed, and virtually all of the Umayyads were killed in battle or executed afterwards. This marked the beginning of the dynasty established by al-'Abbas, known as the Abbasids.

Under Umayyad rule, however, the "People of the Book" had continued to be respected as *dhimmis*, a religious minority under the protection of Islam. The caliphs heeded the command of the Qur'an, which had stated that

Qur'an
Surely those who believe, those who are Jews .. and
the Christians; whoever believes in God and the last day
and does good-- they shall have no fear, nor shall they
grieve. (Q. 5:69)

This privilege came at a price, of course. As we have seen, the tax levied on Christians and Jews was higher than those Muslims were required to pay, and this may have been a powerful incentive for many former Byzantine Christians to convert. What's more, conversion was a prerequisite for a career in the ever-growing Islamic administration.

The Alcazaba Palace in Málaga, Spain, which once formed part of the Muslim region of Al-Andalus

Nevertheless, for a short period of time, the three Abrahamaic faiths proved that they could co-exist in relative peace – and nowhere more so than in the region known as *Al-Andalus*, today's Andalusia in southern Spain. The flowering of the 'Golden Era' of the *Convivencia* was due in no small measure to an Umayyad who had escaped from the massacre at Zab, namely 'Abd er-Rahman, grandson of caliph Hisham. Rahman fled to Córdoba. From there, he took control of Al Andalus by rallying the support of Muslim élites who were concerned that the Abbasids would nullify their titles and properties so recently bestowed by the Umayyad caliphs.

Religious tolerance was a novelty for the Spaniards, who had only known the fanatical Arianist brand of Christianity espoused by the Visigoths. It did not come easy, for Spain was still rent by many different sects, stoked by the rivalry between Toledo, Seville and Córdoba. Abd-al-Rahman III (912-961) put an end to the turmoil and began the period that is rightly called the first Renaissance on European soil since Antiquity. He suppressed the power of the feuding aristocrats, established peace and justice, and initiated a patronage of the arts that would be continued by many successors to come.

The flowering of the Islamic arts in Spain is exemplified by a round ivory box, carved from a single elephant tusk. Dated around 968 and known as the Mughira pyxis, this exquisite box is today in the collection of the Louvre in Paris. It depicts two mounted noblemen facing a tree with rich hanging fruit, surrounded by scenes of the hunt, including riders, musicians, horses and eagles. An inscription in Arabic running along the top rim of the box indicates that it was carved for the son of 'Abd al-Rahman III. Perhaps it is an idyllic representation of the good life in bountiful Spain, but it is also additional evidence that the Umayyad princes were not greatly troubled by the Islamic ban on depictions of living beings.

The Mughira Pyxis, Spain, carved from the tusk of an elephant and dedicated to the son of 'Abd al-Rahman III

At the same time, the city of Córdoba became an unprecedented center of learning. Its library was renowned around the world. The patronage of Islamic arts and letters was continued by Rahman's son, al-Hakam II (961-976), to whom the Mughira pyxis is dedicated. His University of Córdoba would soon become the leading academic center of the 10th century. The library ultimately grew to 400,000 volumes, including works by Plato, Aristotle, Archimedes and other Greek philosophers and scholars that otherwise would have been lost to civilization. More than 5,000 calligraphists were employed in copying the works.

Indeed, the Islamic effort to preserve the leading texts of Antiquity, encouraged by a faith that deemed all scholarly pursuits to be a manifestation of God's divine wisdom, laid the foundation for the literary revival of 14th and 15th century Europe, which in turn produced the Italian Renaissance.

Al-Hakam himself was too absorbed into scholarly pursuits to tend to matters of state, so he delegated much of his authority to his minister, a physician named Hasdai ibn Shaprut, who happened to be a Jew. Hasdai thereupon encouraged many Jewish scholars to come to Moorish Spain and partake in its great scientific revival. They settled in the *Judería*, the Jewish quarter of Córdoba. Here, Muslim artisans would later build a synagogue for Córdoba's Jewish population, decorated with their trademark *Mudéjar* stucco ornamentation. This synagogue is the only Jewish house of worship that survived the forced expulsion of the Jews after the Christian reconquest of Spain in 1492, and has now been lovingly restored.

Córdoba's mosque or *Mezquita* is perhaps the most visible symbol of the evolution of the three faiths in Moorish Spain. The mosque was built on the site of a Christian church, the Visigoth basilica of San Vicente, upon orders of Abd al-Rahman I. In fact, the Caliph first 'leased' the church from the Christian congregation of San Vicente, so that it could be used as a mosque. When the basilica could not longer contain the ever-growing Muslim congregation, Abd al-Rahman bought the property from the Christian parish, and tore it down. In its stead rose one of the most magnificent works ever built by Islam. The Mezquita's interior is a vast space of endless red-and-white, horseshoe-shaped arches that are supported by 850 columns of onyx, granite and marble. These arches, in turn, support a second arcade, using the weight distribution technique that Muslim architects copied from Roman aquaducts. In fact, many of the columns and capitals are *spolia* of the countless Roman ruins that could be found throughout the countryside.

The Mezquita or Mosque of Córdoba, built by the Umayyads

The Mezquita, with its sea of undulating rows of Moorish arches, is so vast that it dwarfs the baroque cathedral built by Charles V in its center. The king was properly appalled by the result. Upon visiting the cathedral he exclaimed that "had I known how it would turn out to be, I would have never allowed it," scolding his architects for having "destroyed something that was unique."

The *Convivencia* was not without its challenges. Jews, Christians and Muslims lived in separate quarters, as elsewhere in *Al-Andalus*. There was little social contact outside the spheres of science, government and commerce. Tempers rose when some Muslim *imams* ordered the bell towers of churches torn down – or at least cut in height – so that they would not rise higher than the minarets of the city's mosques. The Christian theologian Eulogius wrote that devout Christians – including his own grandfather – would hold their hands over their ears whenever the cry of the *muezzin* rose over the city. But otherwise, the three faiths co-existed with a remarkable degree of tolerance.

This tolerance came to an end when new wave of Berber armies entered Córdoba and the Abbasids began to assert their control over all of Islam. One Berber sect known as the Almohads (derived from the Arab name *al-Muwahhidun* or 'Unitarians') introduced a strict observance of Quranic precepts, ending the worldly pursuits that had made Córdoba the center of human civilization. At the same time, the political unity of *Al-Andalus* disintegrated into separate fiefdoms, known as *taifas* (based on the Arab word *ta'ifah* or 'faction'). Public worship by Jews and Christians was curtailed; many families were forced to flee to Toledo and other, more tolerant cities in the province or beyond.

But even in the final stages of the Golden Age, scholars of all faiths were able to make their impact. The Córdoban native Maimonides (1135-1204), nicknamed *Rambam* in Hebrew (an abbreviation of his Jewish name *Rabbi Moses ben Maimon*, Rabbi Moses son of Maimon), was only thirteen when the Almohads entered the city. His family continued to live in Córdoba for a decade longer, practicing their faith in the privacy of their homes while outwardly appearing as Muslims. Finally, the life in hiding became too much, and Maimon took his family to Fez, and ultimately Egypt. There, Maimonides studied medicine and found a position as the court physician to the Ayyubid Sultan Saladin, ruler of Egypt, Palestine and Syria.

While in the Sultan's employ, Maimonides was allowed to openly practice his faith, and to revitalize the Jewish community of Cairo. He wrote an extensive commentary on the Mishnah, written in Arabic, and an in-depth review of Jewish Law in Hebrew, entitled *The Torah Reviewed*. Reflecting on the Qur'an and the Torah, Maimonides wrote that "these are two manifestations of the same truth; there are only contradictions when one is too close to the literal meaning of scripture to overlook its essential meaning."

Arguably, Maimonides' Muslim counterpart (and contemporary) was an Arab physician and philosopher named Abu 'l-Walid Muhammad ibn Rushd, better known as Averroës (1126-1198). Averroës tried to reconcile the Greek concepts of reason with the Islamic faith in a single God, as countless Christian theologians had tried to do before him. Though his mentor was the Almohad caliph Abu Ya'qub Yusuf, Averroës wrote treatises on Plato and Aristotle that would exert great influence on Jewish and Christian thought in the Middle Ages. In the Muslim world, Averroës is principally known for his work on *fiqh* or Islamic jurisprudence, as both he and his father served as judges in Córdoba. But others also know him as the author of the *Compedium of Philosophy*, which encompasses subjects in physics, geography, meteorology and metaphysics. His medical encyclopedia, *Kitab al-kulliyat fil-Tibb,* covers everything from anatomy to diagnosis, health and diet.

Two hundred years later, when Chaucer wanted to describe the breadth of knowledge of one of his protagonists, a "Docteur of Phisik", he provided the following list:

Chaucer
Wel knew he the olde Esculapius,
And Deyscorides and eek Rufus,
Olde Ypocras, Haly, and Galyen,
Serapioun, Razis, and Avycen,
Averrois, Damascien, and Constantyn

(The Canterbury Tales - Prologue, l. 435)

Chaucer's compliment underscores the enduring renown of this Arab scholar throughout the Christian territories of Europe, long after the *Convivencia* was but a memory.

THE AGE OF THE CONVIVENCIA was short-lived, but it remains an unprecedented beacon of interfaith tolerance, certainly given the centuries of religious warfare that would follow.

In 1099, Pope Urban convoked the Council of Clermont where, as an afterthought, he noted that those who would come to the aid of the Christians in the Holy Land would be granted an immediate remission of all sins. The Pope's motives were not clear, though some recent research suggests that growing Muslim harassment of Christian pilgrims traveling in Palestine was partly to blame.

The response to the Pope's declaration, however, was beyond anything he could have imagined. Within months, the first Crusade was on its way, pausing to conduct wholesale massacres of *Jewish* communities throughout Eastern Europe, propelled by the battle cry *Deus Volt* ('God wills it.') On July 15, the Crusaders captured Jerusalem. Unlike the Caliph 'Umar, Godfried de Bouillon showed no mercy. All Muslim and Jewish inhabitants were slaughtered. The result was a backlash against Christians throughout the Islamic empire.

In Andalusia, Seville fell to the Christian Castilian armies in 1248. Non-Christian influences in Spanish society were rooted out. Thousands of Muslim and Jewish families fled to North Africa and settled in cities like Fez and Tangiers, which would continue to harbor thriving Jewish communities or *Mellahs* until the Six Day War in 1967.

The Court of the Lions in the Alhambra Palace in Grenada, where the last Muslim sultan of Al-Andalus, Muhammad XII (also known as Boabdil) surrendered the last Muslim stronghold in Spain to the Catholic monarchs Ferdinand II of Aragon and Isabella of Castille.

In Córdoba, the new Christian rulers built the Torre de la Calahorra across the city's *Puente Romano* or Roman bridge, to guard the approaches to the city. From here, they plotted the conquest of the final Muslim outpost in Andalusia, the city of Granada. From here, too, they sent forth an institution that would hold sway for three hundred years, known as the Spanish Inquisition.

And the relationship between the three faiths would never be the same.

Epilogue

Ancient Judaism believed that this God spoke to mankind through patriarchs and the prophets from Abraham to Jeremiah. Christianity accepted the Jewish tradition of prophecy, but believed that the ultimate revelation of God's will came with Jesus, the Christ. When Islam appeared, it accepted all of the foregoing prophets, but held that *its* messenger – the prophet Muhammad – received God's revelation in its purest and most unadulterated form.

Throughout the foregoing narrative, we discovered how much these faiths actually have in common. All three religions trace their origins to Abraham. All three interpret life through the prism of good and evil, in terms of obedience and disobedience to God's word and law. All three hold that men and women can communicate with God through the agency of prayer, in the belief that God will listen and intercede on their behalf in the journey through life.

And all three faiths are essentially positive in outlook. All believe that under God's guidance, mankind has advanced and will ultimately reach the End of Times, when human beings will be judged and the righteous shall be rewarded.

There are further striking similarities. As we have seen, orthodox Judaism and Islam continue to uphold the ancient ban on "graven images." To this day, Judaism and Islam continue to share many tenets of purity and diet. For both Muslims and Jews, pork is abominable. Like orthodox Jews, Muslims engage in ritual ablution, and distinguish between ritually 'clean' and 'unclean' substances, which must be washed prior to worship.

To Christianity, however, the concept of physical purity is less important. Jesus made a clear distinction between outward, physical cleanliness and true purity of a person's heart. The act of baptism is not a physical cleansing in a ritual sense, but a one-time immersion by which the faithful signal their embrace of Jesus Christ.

But Christianity and Islam have other things in common. As we have seen, Muslims hold Mary and Jesus in great esteem. The name of Mary, in fact, occurs more often in the Qur'an than in all the books of the New Testament combined. Jesus is invariably referred to as 'Jesus, son of Mary'. The Qur'an affirms the 'immaculate' virgin conception of Jesus, as described in the Gospels of Matthew and Luke. In fact, the Qur'an draws a parallel between Jesus and Adam, who was likewise born without the intervention of mortal seed. However, the purpose of the virgin birth account in the Qur'an is to demonstrate that Jesus was pure, created by the will of God – not that he was a divine being himself.

Furthermore, the Qur'an presents an account of Jesus' death that differs from the New Testament. For Muslims, it is inconceivable that a holy man like Jesus would be permitted by God to die in such a shameful manner as by crucifixion. Therefore, the Qur'an states that "they neither killed nor crucified him; it only appeared to be that way to them," for "God took him up Himself" (Q 4:157-158). Other references suggest that a *Doppelgänger* was substituted, so that another man was crucified in Jesus' stead. This is not dissimilar from beliefs that circulated in certain Gnostic communities.

It would be disingenuous not to note other, very significant differences between the three traditions. Jews believe that with the Hebrew Scriptures, God's word is complete. Judaism does not accept that God spoke to prophets or messengers beyond the Jewish orbit. Christians and Muslims, on the other hand, *do* believe that God continued to reveal himself. For Christians, Jesus is the living embodiment of God's will -- the *Logos* made incarnate. However, Christians do not generally accept that Muhammad was also God's prophet.

Islam, then, is the only faith that accepts the divine revelation of both Jews and Christians as contained in the Hebrew Bible and the New Testament. That is why mainstream Muslims still refer to Jews and Christians as 'People of the Book.'

However, Muslims also believe that the Qur'an is not only God's final word, but also his purest revelation, superior to the other two scriptures. Indeed, Muhammad is considered the 'Seal' of the long line of prophets that began with Adam.

One of the most important differences between Christianity and Islam is that Muslims do not accept the divinity of Jesus. The Qur'an maintains that Jesus himself never claimed to be the Son of God (which some biblical scholars tend to agree with), and that his presumed divinity is an erroneous interpretation by his followers. To Muslims, Jesus was divinely inspired, not God made into flesh. This issue is important to Islam, because it denotes the essential difference between monotheism and polytheism. As we have seen, Muhammad faced a widespread pagan cult in Mecca, which the city elders were prepared to defend to the death. For Muslims (as for Jews), the fact that God is One is therefore a bedrock article of faith, also enshrined in the Ten Commandments. For Jews and Muslims, there simply cannot be another divine being other than God Himself.

ULTIMATELY, ALL THREE FAITHS believe that mankind's redemptive path lies in faith in God. For Muslims, this path is defined in the Qur'an and requires absolute, total submission (*muslim*) to God. For Christians, the path is faith in the redemptive value of Jesus' sacrifice and resurrection. And for Jews, the path is a moral life in full observance the Law as described in the Torah.

Given this common ground between the three monotheistic faiths, we cannot fail to marvel at the intolerance and violence that has characterized our modern era. In many ways, the 21st century has witnessed a level of interfaith hatred, hostility and bloodshed not seen since the Middle Ages and the era of the Crusades.

The most obvious root of this hatred is a resurgent fundamentalism -- the idea that all religious practices other than one's own are false and subversive. Fundamentalism has pervaded our modern world more than ever before; not just in militant Islamic circles, but also among certain evangelical Christian sects in the United States, as well among ultra-right political parties in Israel. In this era of fierce interfaith tensions, we need to rediscover the values of tolerance and diversity that lie at the core of these ancient traditions.

Select Bibliography

- The Origins of Judaism

Baines, John and Málek, Jaromír, *Cultural Atlas of Ancient Egypt*. Abingdon: Andromeda Oxford, 2000

Bertman, Stephen, *Life in Ancient Mesopotamia*. New York: Oxford University Press, 2005

Bosworth, A.B., *Conquest and Empire: The Reign of Alexander the Great;* New York, Cambridge University Press, 1988

Breasted, James Henry, *Ancient Times: A History of the Early World*; Boston: The Athenaeum Press, 1935

Clayton, Peter A. *Chronicle of the Pharaohs;* London: Thames & Hudson, 1994

Cline, Eric: *From Eden to Exile: Unraveling Mysteries of the Bible*. Washington, D.C.: National Geographic Society, 2006

Collon, Dominique, *Ancient Near Eastern Art*. London: Trustees of the British Museum, 1995

Coogan, Michael D., Ed., *The Oxford History of the Biblical World*. New York: Oxford University Press, 2001.

Coote, R.B. and Whitelam, K.W., *The Emergence of Early Israel in Historical Perspective*. Sheffield, Almond Press, 1987.

Cotterell, Arthur, *Ancient Civilizations*; London/New York, Penguin Press, 1988

Davies, W.D. et al., *The Cambridge History of Judaism* (Vols. I-III); Cambridge: Cambridge University Press, 1999

Eynikel, E., *The Reform of King Josiah and the Composition of the Deuteronomistic History*. Leiden: E.J. Brill, 1996

Finkelstein, Israel et al (Ed), *From Nomadism to Monarchy: Archaeological and Historical Aspects of Early Israel.* Jerusalem: Israel Exploration Society, 1994.

Finkelstein, Israel and Silberman, Neil Asher, *The Bible Unearthed: Archaeology's New Vision of Ancient Israel and The Origin of its Sacred Texts.* New York NY: The Free Press, 2001.

Fritz, Volkmar et al., *The origins of the ancient Israelite states.* Sheffield: Sheffield Academic Press, 1996

Gardner-Wilkinson, J., *The Ancient Egyptians: Their Life and Customs,* Vols I-II; London: Studio Editions, 1994 (Reprint)

Hall, H.R., *The Ancient History of the Near East;* New York: The MacMillan Company, 1913

Isbouts, Jean-Pierre, *National Geographic's The Biblical World.* Washington, DC: National Geographic Society, 2007

Mare, W. Harold, *The Archaeology of the Jerusalem Area;* Grand Rapids, MI: Baker Book House, 1987

Mazar, Benjamin et al., *Views of the Biblical World;* Jerusalem: International Publishing Company; 1960

McCurley, Foster R, *Ancient Myths and Biblical Faith: Scriptural Transformations;* Princeton: Princeton University Press, 1969.

Mitchell, T.C., *The Bible in the British Museum: Interpreting the Evidence.* London, British Museum Press, 1988

Neusner, Jacob, *Judaism When Christianity Began: A Survey of Belief and Practice.* Louisville, Ky: John Knox Press, 2002

Rainey, Anson F., *Egypt, Israel, Sinai : archaeological and historical relationships in the biblical period;* Tel Aviv: Tel Aviv University, 1987

Rohl, David M., *Pharaohs and Kings: A Biblical Quest;* New York, Crown Publishers, 1995

Seton-Williams, M.V., *Egyptian Legends and Stories;* New York, Rubicon Press, 1998.

Shanks, Hershel, *Ancient Israel: from Abraham to the Roman destruction of the Temple*; Washington, D.C. : Biblical Archaeology Society, 1999

Silberman, Neil Asher et al., *The Archeology of Israel: constructing the past, interpreting the present*; Sheffield, England : Sheffield Academic Press, 1997

Steinsaltz, Adin, *Biblical Images: Men and Women of the Book;* New York: Basic Books, Inc., 1984

Woolley, C. Leonard, *Ur of the Chaldees: A Record of Seven Years of Excavation;* New York: Charles Scribner's Sons, 1930

• The Origins of Christianity

Boatwright, Mary T. et al., *The Romans From Village to Empire;* Oxford: Oxford University Press, 2004

Borg, Marcus J., Jesus: *Uncovering the Life, Teachings and Relevance of a Religious Revolutionary.* San Francisco, CA: HarperSanFrancisco, 2006

Chancey, Mark A., *The Myth of a Gentile Galilee.* Cambridge, UK: Cambridge University Press, 2002.

Chancey, Mark A., *Greco-Roman Culture and the Galilee of Jesus.* Cambridge, UK: Cambridge University Press, 2005.

Charlesworth, James H. et al, *Jesus Jewishness: Exploring the Place of Jesus in Early Judaism*; New York, Crossroad Publishing Company, 1991

Chilton, Bruce, *Rabbi Jesus.* New York: Doubleday, 2000.

Crossan, John Dominic, *Jesus: A Revolutionary Biography*; New York: HarperCollins Publishers, 1994.

Crossan, John Dominic and Reed, Jonathan L., *Excavating Jesus;* New York: HarperCollins, 2001.

Daniel-Rops, Henri, *La Vie Quotidienne en Palestine au Temps de Jesus;* Paris: Librarie Hachette, 1961

Ehrman, Bart, *Jesus: Apocalyptic Prophet of the New Millennium*; New York: Oxford University Press, 1999.

Ehrman, Bart, *Lost Christianities: The Battles for Scripture and the Faiths we never knew.* Oxford: Oxford University Press, 2003

Elsner, Jas, *Imperial Rome and Christian Triumph*; New York: Oxford University Press, 1998

Fredriksen. Paula, *Jesus of Nazareth, King of the Jews*; New York: Alfred A. Knopf, 1999.

Freke, Timothy and Gandy, Peter, *The Jesus Mysteries;* New York: Harmony Books, 1999

Freyne, Séan, Galilee from Alexander the Great to Hadrian, 323 B.C.E. to 135 C.E.: A Study of Second Temple Judaism. Wilmington, DE: Michael Glazier, 1980

Goodman, Martin, *State and Society in Roman Galilee, A.D. 132-212.* Totowa, N.J.: Rowman & Allanheld, 1983

Hezser, Catherine, *Jewish Literacy in Roman Palestine.* Tübingen: Mohr Siebeck, 2001

Horsley, Richard A, *Bandits, Prophets and Messiahs: Popular Movements in the Time of Jesus.* Harrisburg, PA: Trinity Press, 1999

Horsley, Richard A, *Galilee: History, Politics, People.* Harrisburg, PA: Trinity Press, 1995

Horsley, Richard A, *Jesus and the Spiral of Violence: Popular Jewish Resistance in Roman Palestine.* Minneapolis, MI: First Fortress Press, 1993

Isbouts, Jean-Pierre, *Young Jesus: Restoring the Lost Years of a Social Activist and Religious Dissident.* New York: Sterling, 2008

Kloppenborg Verbin, John S., *Excavating Q: The History and Setting of the Sayings Gospel.* London: T & T Clark, 2000

Mack, Burton L., *The Lost Gospel: The Book of Q and Christian Origins.* New York, N.Y.: HarperSanFrancisco, 1993

McCane, Byron R., *Roll Back the Stone: Death and Burial in the World of Jesus.* Harrisburg, PA: Trinity Press International, 2003

Meier, John P., *A Marginal Jew: Rethinking the Historical Jesus,* Vols. 1,2 and 3. New York: Doubleday, 1994

Mitchell, Stephen, *The Gospel according to Jesus*; New York: HarperCollins, 1991.

Neusner, Jacob, *The Mishnah: A New Translation.* New Haven, CT: Yale University Press, 1988.

Pagels, Elaine, *The Gnostic Gospels*; New York: Random House, 1979

Pagels, Elaine, *Beyond Belief: The Secret Gospel of Thomas*; New York: Random House, 2003

Porter, Stanley (Ed), *Paul and his Theology* (Pauline Studies Vol. 3). Leiden: Brill, 2006

Safrai, S, et al. (Ed.), *The Jewish People in the First Century,* Vol. 2. Philadelphia, PA: Fortress Press, 1976.

Sanders, E.P., *Jesus and Judaism.* Philadelphia: Fortress Press, 1985

Sanders, E.P., *The Historical Figure of Jesus.* London: Penguin Books, 1992.

Schiffman, Lawrence H., Reclaiming the Dead Sea Scrolls: The History of Judaism, the Background of Christianity, the Lost Library of Qumran; New York: Doubleday, 1995

Schwartz, Seth, *Imperialism and Jewish Society*; Princeton, N.J.: Princeton University Press, 2001

Shorto, Russell, *Gospel Truth;* New York, Riverhead Books, 1997

Sperber, Daniel, *The City in Roman Palestine.* Oxford: Oxford University Press, 1998

Stemberger, Günter, *Jewish Contemporaries of Jesus: Pharisees, Sadducees, Essenes*. Minneapolis: Fortress Press, 1995

Tenney, Merrill C., *New Testament Times*; Peabody, MA: Hendrickson Publishers, 2001

Udoh, Fabian E., *To Caesar what is Caesar's: Tribute, Taxes and Imperial Administration in Early Roman Palestine* (63 B.C.E. – 70 C.E.). Providence, RI: Brown Judaic Studies, 2005

Whiston, William, *The Works of Josephus*; Translation; Philadelphia, Kregel Publications, 1960 (Reprint)

Wilson, Ian: *Jesus: The Evidence;* London, Weidenfeld & Nicholson, 1996

Wroe, Ann, *Pilate: The Biography of an Invented Man*. London, Random House, 1999

- The Origins of Islam

Abd Al-Wahid Dhannun, D. Taha: *Muslim Conquest and Settlement of Northern Africa and Spain;* Exeter Arabic and Islamic Series, 1988

'Aishah 'Abd al-Rahman, Anthony Calderbank, "Islam and the New Woman," in: *Journal of Comparative Poetics* (19): 200 (1999)

___, *The Challenge of the Scriptures: The Bible and the Qur'an*. Muslim-Christian Research Group. Maryknoll, NY: Orbis Books, 1989.

Armstrong, Karen, *Muhammad: A Biography of the Prophet;* New York: HarperCollins, 1992

Bosworth, C.E., *The Islamic Dynasties: A Chronological and Genealogical handbook*. Edinburgh: Edinburgh University Press, 1967

Brown, Brian, *Noah's other son: bridging the gap between the Bible and the Qur'an*. New York: Continuum, 2007

Fatani, Afnan H. (2006), "Hajar", in Leaman, Oliver, *The Qur'an: an encyclopedia*. Great Britain: Routeledge, pp. 234–236

Firestone, Reuven, "Abraham's Journey to Mecca in Islamic Exegesis: A Form-Critical Study of a Tradition," in: *Studia Islamica* (76): 15–18, (1992)

Heft, James, *Beyond violence: religious sources of social transformation in Judaism, Christianity, and Islam.* New York: Fordham University Press, 2004.

Hitti, Philip K., *History of the Arabs*; New York: Palgrave MacMillan, 2002

Holt, P.M. (Ed), *Cambridge History of Islam, Vol 2B: Islamic society and civilization.* Cambridge, UK: Cambridge University Press, 1970

Hotaling, Ed, *Islam Without Illusions*; Syracuse, N.Y., Syracuse University Press, 2003

Humphreys, R. Stephen, *Islamic History: A Framework for Enquiry*: Princeton, NJ, 1991
Khalidi, Tarif: *The Muslim Jesus: Sayings and Stories in Islamic Literature;* Cambridge, MA: Harvard University Press, 2001

Kaegi, Walter: *Byzantium and the Early Islamic Conquests;* New York: Cambridge University Press, 1992

Kennedy, Hugh, *The Prophet and the age of the Caliphates : the Islamic Near East from the sixth to the eleventh century.* New York: Pearson/Longman, 2004

Khalidi, Tarif: *The Muslim Jesus: Sayings and Stories in Islamic Literature;* Cambridge, MA: Harvard University Press, 2001

Labid Ode, from "Seven Golden Odes", *Saudi Aramco World*, Vol 14, Nr 18; October 1963.

Lewis, Bernard: *The Middle East*: London: Phoenix Press, 1995

Lings, Martin: *Muhammad: His Life Based on the Earliest Sources;* Vermont: Inner Traditions Society, 1991

Mann, Vivian et al, *Convivencia: Jews, Muslims, and Christians in medieval Spain*. New York : G. Braziller in association with the Jewish Museum, 1992.

McAuliffe, Jane Dammen, *Cambridge companion to the Qur'an*. Cambridge, UK: Cambridge University Press, 2006

Menocal, Maria Rosa, *The ornament of the world: how Muslims, Jews, and Christians created a culture of tolerance in medieval Spain*. Boston : Little, Brown, 2002.

Mehler, Carl, *Atlas of the Middle East*. Washington, D.C.: National Geographic Society, 2003

Peters, Frank E., *Jerusalem: the holy city in the eyes of chroniclers, visitors, pilgrims, and prophets from the days of Abraham to the beginnings of modern times*. Princeton, N.J.: Princeton University Press, 1985.

Tottoli, Roberto, *Biblical Prophets in the Qur'an and Muslim Literature*. Richmond, UK: Curzon Press, 2002

Yazbeck, Yvonne et al, *Daughters of Abraham: feminist thought in Judaism, Christianity, and Islam*. Gainesville, Fla.: University Press of Florida, 2001.

Watt, W. Montgomery, *Muhammad: Prophet and Statesman;* Oxford: Oxford University Press, 1961

Zafrulla Khan, Muhammad, *The Qur'an;* English translation with Arabic text; Brooklyn, N.Y.: Olive Branch Press, 1997

Vasiliev, Alexander, *History of the Byzantine Empire, 324-1453;* Wisconsin: University of Wisconsin Press, 1975

Notes

Introduction

In 1945, a group of shepherds discovered a treasure trove of thirteen Gnostic codices. Copied from Greek into Coptic, the language current in Egypt at that time, the books contained forty-five Christian texts that are not included in the New Testament, including such tantalizing documents as the "Gospel of Thomas," the "Gospel of Peter" and the "Gospel of Mary."

Over the last century, many scholars have carefully perused the text of both Matthew and Luke in search of telltale signs that could identify an oral source. Using old-fashioned detective work, by rating the authenticity of a given phrase according to various criteria, they were able to piece together this source document which biblical scholarship refers to by the initial Q. This letter is derived from the German word *Quelle* or "source." The format of Q is not a Gospel narrative, but a straightforward inventory of sayings, without any attempt to place these in a theological or chronological framework. In fact, the artificially constructed document of Q bears a strong resemblance to the Gospel of Thomas discovered in 1945. Neither Thomas nor Q says anything about Jesus' Passion and death on the cross (though some scholars believe there are allusions).

Gospel of Thomas: see Pagels, Elaine, *The Gnostic Gospels.* New York: Random House, 1979.

• The Origins of Judaism

Mesopotamian Creation epic from: Pritchard, James B., *The Ancient Near East: Vol I*; pp 35-6.

The oral tradition known as "J" is so termed because it refers to God as *Yahweh,* in contrast to another narrative in Genesis which calls God *El* or *Elohim,* meaning "the Lord."

Ibn Abbas on the Muslim holy day, from: Al-Kisa'i, "Stories of the Prophets," in Jeffery, A., *A Reader on Islam*; pp. 171-172.

Adam made from matter, in: Abdul-Sâhib Al-'âmeli, *The Prophets, Their Lives and Their Stories*; p. 16

Adam descends to India, while Eve is sent to Jeddah, from: Speyer, *Erzählungen,* pp 61-73

Muhammad on paradise as reward for the faithful, from: Abdul-Sâhib Al-'âmeli, *The Prophets, Their Lives and Their Stories*; p. 28

Muhammad on suicide as an evil punishable with hell, from: *Sahih al-Bukhari,* Volume 8, Book 73, number 73 and number 126. This is reinforced in Volume 2, Book 23, Number 445 and Volume 8, Book 78, Number 647

The seventy-two virgins of paradise, from: Al-Tirmidhi, Sunan. Vol. IV: "The Features of Heaven as described by the Messenger of Allah". Chap. 21. Hadith: 2687, and also quoted by Ibn Kathir in his Tafsir (Qur'anic Commentary) of Surah Rahman (55), ayah (verse) 72.

All women restored to beauty and youth, "virgin-like", from: Shamaa-il Tirmidhi, Chapter 035, Hadith Number 006 (230)

Mortals lower than angels, from: Psalm 8:5. Some translations use "divine beings" or even "God" instead of "angels."

Biblical references involving water disputes include the conflict with the herdsmen of Lot; the argument with servants of king Abimelech, the Philistine king of Gerar, and Abraham's offer of seven ewes to seal his ownsership of a local well, accordingly named "Beer-sheba."

The identification of Ur in Sumeria with the Biblical "Ur of the Chaldeans" is not universally supported by scholarship. Some have argued that the Biblical Ur was located closer to Haran, where Terah will settle with his family.

The Eridu Genesis tablet, from: Pritchard, James B., *The Ancient Near East: Vol I*; p 30.

The interpretation of the name 'Nuh' based on the verb 'naha', from: Brinner, William M, "Noah" in *McAulliffe,* Vol. III, p. 543.

Jesus on the dimensions of the Ark, from: Leaman, Oliver, *The Qur'an*; p. 463.

Rabbinic references to people mocking Noah occur in, among others, Babylonian Talmud Sanhedrin108a-b

The reference to the Ark coming to rest on mount Lubar is found in Jub. 5:27-31 - "And the waters prevailed on the face of the earth five months, one hundred and fifty days. And the Ark went and rested on the top of LUBAR, one of the mountains of Ararat."

The Tower of Babel being built by Nimrod, from: Ibn Jarir al-Tabari, *History of the Prophets and Kings*, ca 920 CE.

"To El of the Sources of the Floods," Ugaritic tablet, from: Pritchard, James B., *The Ancient Near East, Vol 1*; Princeton: Princeton University Press, 1958; p. 93.

On the salt pillar near the Dead Sea, see: Frumkin, Amos, "How Lot's Wife became a Pillar of Salt," in: *Biblical Archaeological Review,* May/June 2009, Vol 35; pp. 38-44; 64.

According to Genesis, after Abraham and Sarah travel to Egypt, they meet Pharaoh, who is extremely smitten with Sarah. In the presence of so powerful a man, Abraham can do little more than assure Pharaoh that Sarah is merely "my sister." Thus ensues an unseemly liaison between Sarah and the King of Egypt. One day, however, Pharaoh discovers the truth -- that the object of his desire is actually a married woman. Pharaoh summons Abraham and asks, "What is this that you've done to me? Why did you not tell me that she was thy wife? Why did you tell me, she is my sister?" (Gen. 12:18-19). Abraham apologizes, and Pharaoh is mollified. Not only does he permit Abraham, Sarah and their tribe to leave Egypt unmolested; but Abraham is also allowed to keep the many gifts that the besotted Pharaoh bestowed upon him and his wife. One of those gifts is a slavewoman named Hagar.

Hagar as Abraham's legitimate spouse, rather than his concubine, in: 'Aishah 'Abd al-Rahman, Anthony Calderbank (1999). "Islam and the New Woman," in: *Journal of Comparative Poetics* (19): 200.

Hagar as a royal princess, from: Fatani, Afnan H. (2006), "Hajar", in Leaman, Oliver, The Qur'an: an encyclopedia, Great Britain: Routeledge, pp. 234–236

God orders Abraham to leave Hagar and his son in order to test him, from: Firestone, Reuven (1992), "Abraham's Journey to Mecca in Islamic Exegesis: A Form-Critical Study of a Tradition". Studia Islamica (76): 15–18.

Mount Moriah as Temple Mount, in: 2 Chronicles 3:1

Abraham's son urges him to protect his garment from the bloody strike, so as not to upset his mother, from: Firestone, Reuven, "Abraham in the Qur'an," in: *Encyclopedia of the Qur'an,* p. 10.

Moab burning his son as sacrifice, from: 2 Kings 3:27. The stratagem was effective, for the battle turned, "and great wrath came upon Israel."

Jeremiah on child sacrifice: "And they built the high places of the Ba'al, which are in the valley of Ben-hinnom, to cause their sons and their daughters to pass through the fire to Molech; which I did not command them, nor did it come into my mind that they should do this abomination, to cause Judah to sin." Jeremiah 32:35

Ishmael as the forefather of Muhammad, in: Al-Hasani Al-'amili, *The Prophets, Their Lives and Their Stories,*" p. 164

For a detailed reconstruction of the route of the Exodus as presented in the Bible, see Isbouts, Jean-Pierre, *National Geographic's The Biblical World*; pp 131-137.

"The city proper contains numerous homes of three or four roofs each." Herodotus, Histories, I:180

• The Origins of Christianity

The relationship between Herod's tax policies, the socio-economic upheaval in Lower Galilee, and the ministry of Jesus, is further explored in Isbouts, Jean-Pierre, *Young Jesus: Restoring the Lost Years of a Social Activist and Religious Dissident;* New York: Sterling, 2008.

A *dunam* is a measure used throughout the Middle East to this day. In Palestine it equals some one thousand square meters, though elsewhere in the Middle East exact sizes may vary.

"Many of the townships of Lower Galilee were no less Hellenized and urbanized than anywhere else in the Roman world." See Chancey, Mark A., *Greco-Roman Culture and the Galilee of Jesus.* Cambridge, UK: Cambridge University Press, 2005.

On Luke's census under "Quirinius, governor of Syria": Attempts by conservative scholars to place Quirinius in Syria at an earlier date (based on an inscription found in Antioch, which credits one of his military victories) are not convincing.

Mamzers as children born of an illegitimate sexual union: Mishnah Yebamot 4:13

"Sepphoris was not exclusively Greek." See, for example, Chancey, Mark A., *The Myth of a Gentile Galilee.*

The just will receive the afterlife while the wicked will be punished: "And the spirits of you who have died in righteousness will live, and your spirits will rejoice and be glad, and the memory of them will remain in front of the Great One for all the generations of eternity." As for sinners, "Know that their souls will be made to go down into Sheol, they will be wretched, and their distress will be great." The Book of Enoch, 103:4,7.

"Herod was introduced to the lovely Herodias, the wife of his half-brother Philip." Scholarship is divided over the question whether this Philip was Antipas' brother Philip, Tetrarch of the Gaulanities, or Herod Philip I

"You shall not uncover the nakedness of your brother's wife; it is your brother's nakedness:" Leviticus 18:16

King Ahab ruled from 874 to 853 B.C.E.

"The tractate *Sanhedrin* in the Mishnah specifically describes the conditions under which a "false prophet" ought to be put on trial": Mishnah Sanhedrin 1:5

"Today, in Jericho, there are still houses that are roofed in exactly this way." See: Strange, James F. and Shanks, Hershel, "Has the House Where Jesus Stayed in Capernaum Been Found," in: *Biblical Archaeological Review,* 8:06, Nov/Dec 1982.

"The Temple treasury did pay for various municipal needs, including the maintenance of Jerusalem's waterworks." See: P.T. Sheqalim IV, 48a; T.B. Ketuboth 105a-106a. See also S. Safrai, *The Jewish People in the First Century,* Vol. 2.; page 879.

On the Jerusalem aqueduct affair, see: Josephus, *Antiquities,* XVIII.3 § 2

"A great many were killed; many others were wounded." Josephus, *Antiquities,* XVIII.3 §2

"Paul was accused of taking Gentiles past the *soreg.*"Acts 21:26-30

Regarding the burial of Jesus: The Book of Deuteronomy states that "When someone is convicted of a crime punishable by death and is executed, and you hang him on a tree, his corpse must not remain all night upon the tree; you shall bury him that same day, for anyone hung on a tree is under God's curse. You must not defile the land that the Lord God gave you for possession" (Deuteronomy 21:22-23). This was affirmed in the Misnah (Mishnah Sanhedrin 6:4)

"Condemned men may not be buried in their family plots": Mishnah Sanhedrin 6:5

"For three days [after death] the soul hovers over the body": Midrash Job 14:22

As a fragrance, myrrh had a long history in ancient Judaism. Exodus refers to myrrh as one of the three compounds of "sacred anointing oil" to be used in the sanctuary (Exodus 30:23). The Psalms refer to myrrh as a perfuming agent for clothes (Psalm 45:8).

"James, the brother of Jesus known as Christ, and several others on the charge of breaking the Law": Josephus, *Antiquities,* XX: 9,1

• The Origins of Islam

Reference to the Kedar tribe: "Woe is me, that I am an alien in Meshech, that I must live among the tents of Kedar." Psalms 120:5.

Reference to the Tema tribe: "Ishmael's Line," in: Walton, John H. et al, *The IVP Bible Background Commentary.* Downers Grove, IL: InterVarsity Press, 2000.

Reference to a Quranic code unique to the historical context of the Qur'an: See Nasr Hamid Abu Zayd, *Mafhum al-nass,* 1990

The search for the source and purpose of narratives in the Qur'an gained a major impetus with the first Notre Dame Conference on "The Qur'an in its Historical Context" in 2005, attended by Muslim scholars from Western as well as Near Eastern universities, including Iran. This led to a second Notre Dame conference in April of 2009 on Quranic Origins and the study of the Qur'an as literature. While traditional Muslim scholars continue to eschew critical research of the Qur'an, these and other conferences in the West continue to encourage a rapprochement between Muslim and non-Muslim scholars in exploring the literary and historical underpinnings of the Qur'an and its narratives.

The Nestorites followed the teachings of Nestorius (386-451), who believed, among others, that Jesus was born as a man, not a God, and that therefore the Virgin Mary should be referred to as "The Mother of Christ," not "The Mother of God."

According to Mark, Jesus, too, recited the Shema, but then added another commandment, taken from Leviticus: "You shall love your neighbor as yourself," adding, "on these two commandments hang all the Law and the Prophets." See Mark 12:28-31.

The *Ashura* fast on the tenth day of the Jewish month of Tishri: Sunni Muslims still celebrate *Ashura* (literally, "the tenth") as a day of thanksgiving. For Shi'a Muslims, however, *Ashura* is a day or mourning, since it commemorates the assassination of Husayn ibn Ali, grandson of Muhammad and the third Shi'a imam, who fought against the Umayyad caliph Yazid I.

Some recent scholarship has suggested that the city of Yathrib was already known as 'Madinah' before Muhammad's arrival

Muhammad once called Abraham "his father," the first true Arab prophet: see Ibn Maja, *Sunan,* II, 1165 nr. 3525.

"Muhammad prayed for his sons as Abraham once prayed to God for his sons Ishmael and Isaac," see: Totoli, Roberto, *Biblical Prophets in the Qur'an and Muslim Literature*; p. 124
A *hanif* is usually translated as a "monotheist" (as distinct from Abraham's contemporaries, who were polytheists) and by implication, an "upright man"

Eutychius' history was continued and expanded to 1028 by Yahya ibn Sa'id, in which form it became known in Antioch and then Europe

"Among the Jews the effort was to preserve a properly written text, whereas the Muslims have been more concerned with a properly remembered text." See: Peters, Francis, *The Monotheists,* Vol II; p. 33

Other Books by the Author

Isbouts, Jean-Pierre, *National Geographic's The Biblical World*. Washington, DC: National Geographic Society, 2007

"The National Geographic Society, under the editorship of Professor Isbouts, has produced a visually stunning atlas of the Bible. The quality of the historical commentary for each period matches that of the illustrations." DONALD SENIOR, *The Bible in Review*

Isbouts, Jean-Pierre, *Young Jesus: Restoring the Lost Years of a Social Activist and Religious Dissident*. New York: Sterling, 2008

"In "Young Jesus," Jean-Pierre Isbouts reconstructs the Hellenistic Roman world of Jesus' childhood. With the help of information garnered from recent studies and archaeological discoveries at Sepphoris, he offers intriguing speculations about how those missing years may have shaped young Jesus of Nazareth." *U.S. News and World Report*

Also be sure to see the TV Special, "Young Jesus: A Historical Reconstruction of Jesus' Childhood and Adolescence," written and directed by Jean-Pierre Isbouts and broadcast on PBS Stations in Easter of 2008. Now available on DVD.

JUST RELEASED:

Isbouts, Jean-Pierre, *Angels in Flanders: A Novel of World War One*. Santa Monica, CA: Pantheon Press, 2010.

Four young women decide to set up their own medical post on the front lines in Flanders when they discover that most wounded soldiers die of shock during the long ride to field hospitals in the rear. A riveting and deeply moving saga of love, passion and bravery in the midst of some of the worst carnage the world has ever seen.

For more information about these and other titles please visit the author's website at www.jpisbouts.org

CPSIA information can be obtained
at www.ICGtesting.com
Printed in the USA
BVHW041134221222
654829BV00004B/37

9 781460 919040